THE CATHOLIC CHURCH

Belief, Practice, Life & Behaviour

GCSE RELIGIOUS STUDIES FOR EDEXCEL A

Michael Keene

Folens

Acknowledgements

BBC: 91, 93, 95, 96, 99; BBC/www.bbc.co.uk/religion/programmes/songsofpraise/: 94; Dawn Booth: 51;
Corbis: © Burstin Collection/CORBIS 116, © Philip James Corwen/CORBIS 148, © Najlah Feanny/CORBIS 82,
© Natalie Fobes/CORBIS 75, © Origlia Franco/CORBIS SYGMA 142, © Philip Gould/CORBIS 149,
© Hulton/Deutsch Collection/CORBIS 224, © images.com/CORBIS 39, © Allen T. Jules/CORBIS 104, © Teru
Kuwayama/CORBIS 12, © David Lees/CORBIS 40, 151, © Richard T. Norwitz/CORBIS 59, © Tim Pannell/
CORBIS 80, © Reuters/CORBIS 193, 202, 205, © Royalty-free/CORBIS 29, 54, 69, 149, © Michael St Maur
Sheil/CORBIS 3, © David Turnley/CORBIS 62, 107, Peter Turnley/CORBIS 200, © Josh Westrich/zefa/
CORBIS 33, Paola and Tony Dellasanta: 52; educationphotos.co.uk/Walmsley: 213; Empics/PA: 43;
Alex Keene, The Walking Camera: 6, 7, 11, 15, 16, 19, 24, 31, 35, 37, 45, 52, 61, 65, 66, 76, 79, 85, 87,
101, 103, 115, 118, 121, 122, 125, 127, 129, 134, 125, 136, 138, 141, 145 147, 152, 153, 159, 161, 163,
165, 167, 168, 170, 171, 172, 174, 176, 178, 180, 182, 183, 187, 189, 194, 197, 199, 208, 209, 210, 214,
217, 219, 221, 222; Simon Rawles/CAFOD: 111; Rex Features/Sipa: 26; St Vincent de Paul Society 109;
Worth Abbey/www.worthabbey.net 266

The New Jerusalem Bible, Darton Longman and Todd, 1985, The Reader's Edition, CCC published by Burnes
& Oates, Popular and definitive edition, published 2000.

In this book, the abbreviations BCE (Before Common Era) and CE (Common Era)
are used instead of the more familiar BC and AD. In practice, however, these mean the same.
Words in bold in the text are defined in the glossary.

© 2006 Folens Limited, on behalf of the author.

United Kingdom: Folens Publishers, Apex Business Centre, Boscombe Road, Dunstable, LU5 4RL.
Email: folens@folens.com

Ireland: Folens Publishers, Greenhills Road, Tallaght, Dublin 24.
Email: info@folens.ie

Poland: JUKA, ul. Renesansowa 38, Warsaw 01-905.

Editor: Dawn Booth

Layout artist: Jason Billin

Cover design: Jason Billin

Cover image: Alex Keene, The Walking Camera

First published 2006 by Folens Limited.

Every effort has been made to contact copyright holders of material used in this publication. If any
copyright holder has been overlooked, we should be pleased to make any necessary arrangements.

British Library Cataloguing in Publication Data. A catalogue record for this publication is available
from the British Library.

ISBN 1 84303 823 4

CONTENTS

Believing in God

In this topic you will find out about:

- the reasons that most people have for believing in God;
- the search for meaning and purpose in life together with the presence of religion in the world and a belief in God;
- the reasons that many people have for not believing in God;
- the problems thrown up by the presence of evil and suffering and the responses of the Catholic Church to it;
- the ingredients of prayer as they are explained by the Catechism;
- the different forms that prayer has taken in the Catholic tradition.

KEY WORDS

Agnosticism An uncertainty whether God exists or not.

Atheism The belief that God does not exist.

Benevolent The fact that God is kind and has the welfare of the created order at heart, as believed by many people.

Causation The scientific belief that everything in the universe has a cause, something which brought it into existence.

Conversion When a person's life changes direction after a deep religious experience.

Design The belief that all parts of the natural world show that they have been designed by their Creator.

Moral evil Actions, which are carried out by human beings, that cause suffering in others.

Miracle Something out of the ordinary, beyond scientific explanation, that seems to require belief in God.

Natural evil Natural events that cause suffering in the world but which are not caused by human behaviour, for example floods, earthquakes and so on.

Numinous The feeling that one is in the presence of someone or something greater than oneself.

Omnipotent The belief held by Christians that God is all-powerful.

Omniscient The belief that God knows everything in the past, the present and the future.

Prayer A conversation or communication with God.

1 A CATHOLIC UPBRINGING AND BELIEF IN GOD

Being brought up in a Catholic family, as in any Christian family, is likely to encourage a child to believe in God from a very young age. To begin with the child will have been baptised with both parents and godparents taking baptismal vows on his or her behalf. As the child grows older they will become more aware of those vows and the obligations that they bring with them. Children are also included in the family devotions and these introduce them to **Bible** stories as well as teaching them to pray from an early age.

A Catholic upbringing

Catholics place a very high degree of importance on family life and the value of teaching children spiritual habits that will stay with them for the rest of their lives. Almost all Catholic churches include children's Liturgies as part of the regular **Sunday Mass**. This again is an important teaching time – when children learn how God cares for them and how they must serve him as they grow up. They also learn **prayers** that they can use when they pray to God in their quiet moments. Learning to thank God for all of his blessings is an important part of being a Catholic and one that all children need to be taught by their Church and parents.

The importance of school and Church

As children grow older, so school and the Church play an increasingly important part in their spiritual growth and development.

Most Catholic parents want their children to go to a Catholic school if that is possible. This means that the children can spend the most important years of their lives studying in a school where the Christian values of hard work and caring for others is recognised. A Catholic school will also give them the opportunity of attending Mass and receiving spiritual guidance from the parish **priest**, who will be a regular visitor. At the same time, Religious Education lessons give them a deeper understanding of their own Catholic faith – which they might study up to GCSE level – as well as other world faiths. School assemblies provide another opportunity of learning about their faith, as well as worshipping with other members of the school community.

▶ *The Mass is the most important worship celebration of the Catholic Church and so it is important for Catholic children to share in it from an early age.*

The Importance of Church

The local Catholic Church plays a very important role in the life of all Catholic children as they grow up. It is the main place where they learn the meaning and importance of the main Christian festivals – especially **Advent/Christmas** and **Lent/Easter** – although this is, of course, reinforced within the family by the giving of Christmas presents, Easter eggs and so on. There are often visual symbols in church to reinforce the meaning of these festivals. Two of the most important of these – found in many churches – are the Christmas **crib** and the Easter garden.

The Church plays a very important part in the spiritual life of growing children in other ways as well. It prepares a child for his or her first Communion and later for **Confirmation**. Confirmation is the service at which young people take for themselves (confirms) the vows that their parents and godparents took for them when they were baptised.

Most Catholics find that their religious upbringing – at home, at school and in their church – is a crucial element in their belief in God that sustains them as an adult.

▶ *The Church provides visual reminders, such as this crib, of the important occasions in the Church year.*

TASKS

1. Describe how a Catholic upbringing makes it possible for a person to grow up believing in God.
2. Describe the part played by the following in the Catholic upbringing of a child:
   a. The home
   b. The school
   c. The Church

2 RELIGIOUS EXPERIENCE AND CATHOLICS

We have already seen how most people who are given a Roman Catholic upbringing grow up to believe in God, although they do not necessarily become regular church worshippers. The religious experiences that Catholics have are similar to those experienced by other Christians and followers of different religions.

The nature of religious experience

Most religious experiences can be placed in one of the following groups:

1. *A feeling of the numinous.* This refers to a feeling, or an awareness, that one has of being in the presence of something, or someone, greater than oneself. It might come to a person when he or she is in a beautiful religious building with its breathtaking architecture; when a person is at a concert and he or she is overwhelmed by the beauty of the music; or it might come when a person is at a church service and something touches him or her at a very deep level. Catholics would want to give the name 'God' to this overwhelming presence, although other people might find another way of explaining it. The great 20th-century thinker, Rudolf Otto, described numinous as recognising that people could experience it without, necessarily, believing in God.

2. *A conversion experience.* Some people, when they are trying to describe what they believe to have been an experience of God, say that they have been converted. This means that their lives were going in a certain direction and then they met God – and their lives were totally turned around. Such experiences are found in the Bible, for example **Saul** on the Damascus Road (Acts 9.1–19). Conversion experiences are typical today of **Evangelical** expressions of Christianity,

A service in the shrine at Knock – this is a place of pilgrimage and many people believe that it is a place of healing as well.

such as **Pentecostalism**, the **Baptist Church** and other churches. Some even teach that you cannot be a true believer without having undergone a religious 'conversion'. There are such experiences among Catholic believers, although the majority of them cannot remember a time when they did not believe in God.

3. *Answers to prayer.* Many people come to believe in God because they believe that their prayers have been answered. They may have prayed for someone, even themselves, to be healed from a serious illness. If their prayers are then 'answered' they are likely to believe in God. Some people visit healing services or places associated with healing, such as Lourdes.

4. *Miracles.* Most Christians believe in the possibility of miracles (an event that does not seem to have a rational explanation) although few have actually experienced one themselves. Catholics believe that miracles are possible and they put forward two reasons for this:

- There are many examples in the Bible of miracles taking place. In the life of Jesus, for instance, there were miracles in which the power of nature was tamed or healing took place. The supreme miracle was the raising of Jesus from the dead (the **Resurrection**).

- Catholics believe in a God who has absolute power (**omnipotence**) and complete knowledge (**omniscience**). There can be no question of God's ability to perform miracles. This is why Catholics are happy to accept the miracles associated with shrines at which the Virgin Mary and other saints are believed to have appeared in the past. Miracles, for example, are associated with Lourdes in France, Santiago de Compostela in Spain and Knock in Ireland.

Clearly, if a person believes that prayers are answered and that miracles take place then they will believe in God – and find that faith deepened by their experience.

TASKS

1. Explain why having a religious experience might lead a person to believe in God.
2. "There is no way that miracles can happen today." Do you agree with this comment? Give reasons for your answer, showing that you have thought about more than one point of view.

✳ DISCUSSION POINT

Do you find it easy, difficult or impossible to believe in miracles in the 21st century? What do you think about people who hold the opposite point of view to the one you hold?

3 THE APPEARANCE OF THE WORLD AND BELIEF IN GOD

Many people look at the world in which we live and find strong reasons for believing in God. In particular they look at the following.

The evidence from design in the world

Hoping to demonstrate that God must exist, some theists (believers in God) point to the order and design that they find in the natural world to prove their thinking. This is called the teleological argument for God's existence. It is an argument first suggested by Paul in the **New Testament**.

> **A** *" ... ever since the creation of the world, the invisible existence of God and his everlasting power have been clearly seen by the mind's understanding of created things. "*
>
> *(Romans 1.20)*

This argument was also put forward in the 18th century by the theologian William Paley. He suggested that the clear evidence for design in the universe was one of the strongest reasons for believing in God. His argument fell into two parts:

- **The watch**. If a person suddenly found a beautiful watch in an uninhabited place with its balancing wheels and mechanism working perfectly what would he or she think – even if he or she had never seen a watch before? That it had come into existence by accident? No! That it had always existed? No! That it had been made by a skilled watchmaker? Yes! Only a skilled watchmaker could make such a beautiful watch.

- **The universe**. The universe is a far more complicated piece of machinery than a watch. We can see this by simply looking at the animals, birds and human beings that share the earth. Something as intricate as the universe must have an eternal and infinite Creator with unlimited power.

In the 1930s, Paley's argument was taken a step further by the philosopher F.R.Tennant. He argued that God had created the earth with everything in place so that animal and human life could develop by evolution. A slight variation in any part of the equation – such as in the law of gravity – would have made the creation of life impossible. This fine balance is clearly deliberate and shows a clear sense of design. Who could that designer have been but God?

The evidence from causation

This theory has two parts:

- **Everything has a cause**. If you look at the universe in which we live you will discover that everything has a cause. Nothing exists without having been caused. Take that person with the black eye. What happened? He was in a fight and someone hit him. Result: a black eye. We all exist. Why? Two people made love and we were the end result. Try as hard as you might you will not find anything that does not have a cause.

- **The universe has a cause**. There is no exception to the rule that everything has a cause. Even the universe itself must fit the rule. It, too, must have a cause. What could have 'caused' the universe? It did not just happen. It is impossible to believe that it came into existence by accident. The only possible explanation for the universe is that God created it. Any other explanation is totally inadequate.

B 66 *The question about the origins of the world and of man has been the object of many scientific studies which have splendidly enriched our knowledge of the age and dimensions of the cosmos, the development of life-forms and the appearance of man. These discoveries invite us to an even greater admiration for the greatness of the Creator...* 99
(CCC 283)

◀ *Is this beautiful sunset a reason for believing in the existence of God – or not?*

TASKS

1. What is the argument for God's existence based on the evidence for design in the universe?

2. **a.** What is meant by causation?

   b. How might some people find this to be a persuasive argument for believing in the existence of God?

✳ **DISCUSSION POINT**

Do you find the evidence from design or the argument from causation persuasive arguments for believing in God? Give reasons for your opinion.

4 BELIEVING AND NOT BELIEVING IN GOD

We have already seen several reasons that many people have for believing in God. Here we will look at two more reasons together with the main reasons why many people do not believe.

1. The search for meaning and purpose in life

Many people instinctively believe that life must have some meaning and purpose. They feel that they have been brought into existence for a reason, just as they marry, have children and go out to work for good reasons. Some people reach the end of their life still looking for this meaning and purpose, and many find it in their religious faith. Others, however, find a purpose in life without believing in God.

2. The presence of religion the world

Some people find the presence of religion in the world to be convincing proof that God exists. More than 60% of the 6000 million people in today's world claim allegiance to one of the major world religions. They find that religion:

- provides them with an explanation of how and why life began;
- teaches them how they can establish some kind of spiritual contact with God;
- gives them a clear set of moral rules by which they can live their life day by day;
- provides them with a way of 'focusing' their life through prayer or **meditation**.

The Catechism teaches that there is plenty of evidence in the world for the existence of a spiritual dimension. You can see the evidence that the Catechism mentions in extract A.

▼ The immense damage and loss of life brought about by the Tsunami in 2004 caused many people to doubt the existence of God.

B 66*The human person: with his openness to truth and beauty, his sense of moral goodness, his freedom and the voice of his conscience, with his longings for the infinite and for happiness, man questions himself about God's existence. In all this he discerns signs of his spiritual soul. The soul ... can have its origin only in God.*99
(CCC 33)

Why People do not Believe in God

There are four main reasons why people do not believe in God:

1. Scientific explanations of the world can lead people to become **atheists** (people who do not believe that God exists) or **agnostics** (people who are not sure whether God exists). Science explains how the universe and all forms of life began on earth without mentioning God.

2. Problems with the idea of the miraculous can lead people to become atheists or agnostics. While some people believe in God because they believe Jesus performed miracles and was brought back from the dead, others do not believe because they can find no room for the miraculous in the scientific world in which we live.

3. People who do believe may lose their faith in God because their prayers go unanswered. In the **Gospels**, Jesus encouraged his followers to believe that God would answer their prayers but every Christian has many experiences of prayers going unanswered. It may be a prayer for healing from disease or illness; a prayer for peace in the world; or a prayer that the needs of so many starving people in the world will be met.

4. The evil and suffering in the world may cause many people to lose their faith in a benevolent and all-powerful God who could do something about it. Personal faith might be shattered by:

*   The frequency of natural disasters that bring suffering and death to millions, such as the Tsunami disaster in the Indian Ocean at the end of 2004.

*   A personal experience of suffering through an accident or illness.

Few people are untouched by suffering. You will read more about suffering in C.1.5 and C.1.6..

TASKS

1. Explain the main reasons why many people find it impossible to believe in God.
2. "The widespread acceptance of religion in the modern world is a good reason for believing in God." Do you agree with this comment? Give reasons for your answer, showing that you have thought about more than one point of view.

5 THE PROBLEM OF EVIL AND SUFFERING

Catholics believe that there are two kinds of evil:

- Moral evil. The evil that a person brings on themselves or others by what they do. This happens because God has given human beings free will and it is up to them how they use it.

- Natural evil. This is the evil that shows itself through natural disasters such as earthquakes, floods and droughts.

The problem of evil and suffering

There is a great deal of evil and suffering in the modern world. This causes a major problem for the person who believes in God because of what he or she believes about Him:

- All Catholics believe that God is good (benevolent) and so they believe that he must want to eliminate all suffering.

- All Catholics believe that God knows everything (is omniscient) and so he must have been aware of the drawbacks of the world that he was creating. He must also know of the real possibility of natural disasters and of the suffering of people before it happens to them – and yet does nothing about it.

- All Catholics believe that God is all-powerful (omnipotent) and so is able to do something about the suffering in the world. Why, then, is God so often inactive? This is the question that every Christian frequently asks.

Catholic responses to evil and suffering

Catholics do not believe that there is a single simple answer to the problem of evil and suffering. They do believe, however, that in the end everything will be made clear – including the reason why some people have been allowed to suffer much more than others. Among the suggested explanations are:

1. Suffering is a necessary part of life. You cannot have life as we know it without some form of suffering. The Christian writer, C.S. Lewis, lost his wife to cancer less than two years after he married her. You can read in extract A what he wrote after this very sad personal experience.

> **A** *Try to exclude the possibility of suffering which the order of nature and the existence of free-wills involve and you will find that you have excluded life itself.*
>
> (The Problem of Pain, C.S. Lewis)

2. After death all the pain and suffering will be forgotten in the joy of a new risen life. You can read what Paul had to say about this in extract B.

B **"**In my estimation, all that we suffer in the present time is nothing in comparison with the glory which is destined to be disclosed for us...**"**
(Romans 8.18)

3. Jesus Christ, the Son of God, was put to death by his enemies. This is the supreme example for all Christians of suffering. When God brought Jesus back from the dead he showed that light comes out of darkness. The resurrection of Jesus guarantees this.

4. Suffering is caused by sin. Sin is the whole attitude of heart and mind that leads us to disobey God. Much of our suffering can be directly traced to our sinful actions.

5. Evil and suffering come from **Satan** – the Adversary – whose sole purpose is to oppose the will of God.

▲ Christians believe that the crucifixion of Jesus teaches them that they must accept suffering when it comes to them as the will of God.

6. While Catholics cannot hope to understand much of the suffering in the world, they do know that it sometimes deepens a person's faith. When people do not understand the reason for their suffering, or the suffering of others, they trust in God and try to help those who are in pain. They might spend time with those who are suffering, carry out voluntary work in a hospital or **hospice**, or organise meals. Prayer is one way of helping those who suffer. Praying for others (**intercession**) is an important part of all prayer (see unit C.1.6).

TASKS

1. **a.** Describe the meaning of each of these terms when applied to God:
   i. omnipotence
   ii. omniscience
   iii. benevolence
   b. Why are each of these beliefs about God challenged by evil and suffering?
2. Describe four ways in which Catholics seek to understand the meaning of suffering.

6 CATHOLICS AND PRAYER (1)

The Catechism asks the question, "How do we obtain God's Grace?", and answers it simply:

"We must obtain God's Grace chiefly by prayer and the holy Sacraments."

In units C.1.6 and C.1.7 we will take an extended look at the Catholic practice of prayer which, like many other aspects of Catholic spirituality, has its roots in the Scriptures.

Prayer in the Scriptures

The word 'prayer' comes from the Latin word *precari* – to entreat or beg. Prayer is a conscious lifting of the heart and mind to God, an act that brings a person into contact with the divine. As such, it plays an extremely important part in the spiritual life of all Catholics. In the **Old Testament** there are two main reasons for prayer:

1. To give praise to God.

2. To meet a basic human need.

▲ *Catholics believe that it is important that children learn to pray from an early age; if they do it is then much more likely that they will continue the habit into adult life.*

Both of these ideas are carried over into the New Testament. At the beginning of the ministry of Jesus we find him praying (Luke 3.21–22) while shortly afterwards he spent forty days praying and fasting in the desert (Luke 4.1–12). A little later he withdrew from the crowds to pray (Luke 5.16). The best-known prayer of Jesus is the **Lord's Prayer**, or the '**Our Father**', which Jesus offered as a model prayer to his **disciples** (extract A). As such it remains an essential part of almost every Catholic act of worship.

> **A** **"**... you should pray like this: Our Father in heaven, may your name be held holy, your kingdom come, your will be done, on earth as it is in heaven. Give us today our daily bread. And forgive us our debts, as we have forgiven those who are in debt to us. And do not put us to the test, but save us from the Evil One. **"**
> (Matthew 6.9–13)

The different ingredients of prayer

The Catechism explains that there are five ingredients of true Christian prayer:

Blessing and adoration. This is a two-way process between God and the worshipper. The worshipper blesses God and adores him simply because of who he is. God blesses the worshipper through the grace of the **Holy Spirit**. This is where all prayer begins.

Petition. It is by this ingredient that we express an awareness of our relationship with God. We are sinners who know that we have turned away from God. By presenting our prayer of petition and seeking God's forgiveness we show that we are turning back to God.

Intercession. Both Jesus and the Holy Spirit intercede with God for all worshippers. This is the reason why we can intercede with God for others – extract B.

> **B** *"The intercession of Christians recognizes no boundaries: 'for all men, for kings and all who are in high positions', for persecutors, for the salvation of those who reject the Gospel."*
> (CCC 2636)

Thanksgiving. Once a person has appreciated who God is and what he has done for him or her, the prayer of thanksgiving inevitably follows. Worshippers have much to thank God for:

- all of the good things in life that they enjoy
- the presence of God with them in their everyday lives
- the sense of God's forgiveness that they enjoy
- the salvation that they enjoy through their faith in Christ.

One of the names for the central act of Catholic worship is the **Eucharist**, which means 'thanksgiving'.

Praise. This is the form of prayer that recognises that God is God. It praises God for his own sake and gives him glory, not just for what he has done but because of what he is. The prayer of praise unites our spirit with the Holy Spirit to bear witness that we are children of God.

TASKS

1. What can we learn from the Bible about prayer?
2. What are the five ingredients that, according to the Catechism, are at the heart of all Christian prayer?

✳ DISCUSSION POINT

Do you think that God always answers our prayers? If not, what do you think the point of praying is?

7 CATHOLICS AND PRAYER (2)

Different ways of praying

The Catholic Church teaches that prayer should be a natural and regular activity for all Catholics. It accepts that there are many different ways of praying:

- Mental praying that takes place in the mind and may or may not use words. If words are used then the prayer does not usually follow a set pattern. Both meditation and contemplation are forms of mental prayer (see below).

- Vocal praying that usually makes use of a set pattern of words, which may be spoken or sung. At times, though, it can be extempore (unplanned).

- Bodily praying that simply makes use of movement, such as dance, to express one's deepest feelings to God.

Within the worship of the Catholic Church, however, two aspects of prayer have been particularly important, as discussed below.

Meditation and contemplation

The Catholic Church has a very strong monastic tradition that goes back to the 4th century. You will find out more about this in topic J.5 Option 2. Both meditation and **contemplation** belong within this tradition although, in recent years, **monks** and **nuns** have made great efforts to share their experiences of prayer with others.

- **Meditation**. This is a form of mental prayer that involves a deep concentration on the presence and activity of God. Found in other religions as well as Christianity, meditation controls the thoughts so that a person can focus on the presence of God. The Scriptures are often used to help with meditation.

- **Contemplation**. Contemplation is a stage beyond meditation as a form of prayer. Through it a person becomes aware of the joy and beauty of God; infinity, truth and the majesty and love of God. In its most intense form, associated with some of the saints of old, contemplation leads to an ecstatic union between the worshipper and God.

The rosary

The **rosary** ('rose-garden') is a traditional Catholic aid to prayer. It is made up of five groups of ten beads, which are separated on a string from each other by larger single beads. These are easily distinguishable to the touch. Attached to each single bead is a group of three further beads, another single bead and a cross or crucifix. In using the rosary four prayers are involved:

- The prayers start at the crucifix with the **Creed**.

- The 'Our Father' is said on a single bead.

- The **'Hail Mary'** is said on each of the group of three beads (extract A).

A **"**Hail Mary, full of grace, the Lord is with thee. Blessed art thou among women and blessed is the fruit of thy womb, Jesus. Holy Mary, Mother of God, pray for us sinners, now, and at the hour of our death. Amen.**"**

- The '**Gloria**' (extract B) is said on the single bead that comes at the end of the circle.

B **"**Glory be to the Father, and to the Son, and to the Holy Spirit. As it was in the beginning, is now and ever shall be, world without end. Amen.**"**

In this way the worshipper works his or her way round the whole set of beads. While saying the rosary the person also contemplates 15 'mysteries' in the life of Jesus:

- The 'joyful' mysteries: the **Annunciation**, the birth of Jesus and so on.

- The 'sorrowful' mysteries: Gethsemane, the crown of thorns, the death and so on.

- The 'glorious' mysteries: the Resurrection, the **Ascension**, the taking up into heaven of the Virgin Mary and so on.

For many older Catholics the fingering of the beads on a rosary is automatic. This leaves them free to meditate on the most important events in the life of Jesus.

▲ Many people find that it is easier if they have an aid, such as a rosary or a crucifix, to help them with their prayers.

TASKS

1. Catholics often say the Our Father, the Hail Mary and the Gloria one after each other. What do you think the link is between the three prayers?

2. In the Hail Mary, Catholics pray to Mary 'now, and at the hour of our death'. Why do you think that Catholics feel the need to do this?

EXAM HELP

In the examination

Make sure that you know about:

REASONS FOR BELIEVING IN GOD

- The influence of a Catholic upbringing on belief in God. The importance of family life in the Catholic Church. **Infant baptism**. Baptismal vows and their influence on a person's life. The value of family devotions – learning stories from the Bible and how to pray. Children's Liturgies as part of the church's worship. Learning to thank God for all of life's blessings.

- The importance of school and Church in the life of a Catholic child. Most Catholic children attend a Catholic school if possible – they learn Christian values, go to Mass at school, come under the guidance of the parish priest, attend Religious Education lessons that confirm them in their faith, and learn to worship with other members of the Catholic community. The local Catholic church is very important to children. In it they learn the importance of the Christian festivals and worship. It prepares the children for their first Communion and later for confirmation.

- Religious experience and Catholics. Similar experiences to other Christians. The experience of the numinous – being overwhelmed by an experience of beauty or an overwhelming presence of the divine. A conversion experience – common to Evangelical Christians, although the majority of Catholics never have one. Answers to prayer – perhaps a prayer for healing – confirms religious faith. A belief in miracles – shared by most Catholics, often associated with holy places such as shrines. Many instances of miracles in the Bible. Catholic belief in the omnipotence of God makes a belief in miracles possible. The appearance of the world convinces many people that God exists. This stems from the appearance of purpose and design in the world. Argument put forward by Paul. Associated with William Paley in the 18th century – based upon the intricate machinery of a watch and the complexity of the universe. Also stems from the fact that everything has a cause – including the universe. Who could have brought the universe into existence apart from God?

- Two further arguments for God's existence – the human search for meaning and purpose in life, and the widespread acceptance of the importance of religion. The reasons why so many people believe – an explanation of how and why life began opens up the possibility of establishing spiritual contact with God, provides a clear set of moral rules and provides prayer and meditation as a way of focusing oneself.

- Reasons why people do not believe in God. Scientific explanations are sufficient. Problems with the idea of the miraculous. Unanswered prayers leading to a loss of faith. The presence of evil and suffering in the world leading people to question the existence of God.

Sample exam questions

1. What is a Catholic child likely to learn from his or her upbringing which makes it likely that he or she will believe in God?

2. Describe the importance of:
   a. the school
   b. the church in the spiritual growth of a Catholic child

3. What kind of religious experiences may persuade a person to believe in God?

4. "I believe that the presence of design in the universe is the most persuasive reason for believing in God." Do you agree? Give your reasons, showing that you have thought about more than one point of view.

5. "There are many reasons why a person today might find it very difficult, or impossible, to believe in God." Do you agree with this comment? Give your reasons, showing that you have thought about more than one point of view.

EVIL AND SUFFERING

- The difference between natural and moral evil. The dilemma that suffering presents to a Catholic – if God is good he must want to eliminate suffering, if God knows everything he must be aware of suffering before it happens, if God is all-powerful he must be able to eliminate suffering – and yet he doesn't. Catholic responses to the problem of evil and suffering – suffering is a necessary part of life, suffering is forgotten in the after-life, the example of Jesus and suffering, suffering caused by sin, suffering caused by the activity of Satan, people cannot hope to understand the reasons for suffering.

Sample exam questions

1. "The presence of evil and suffering are the most persuasive reasons for not believing in God." Do you agree with this comment? Give reasons for your answer, showing that you have thought about more than one point of view.

2. What answers does the Catholic Church provide to the problem of evil and suffering?

3. a. How strong do you think the arguments are against the existence of God?
   b. Which of the arguments do you think is the more persuasive? Give reasons for your answer showing that you have thought about more than one point of view.

EXAM HELP

CATHOLICS AND PRAYER

- The teaching on prayer from the Scriptures. The importance of prayer in the life of Jesus. The Lord's Prayer – the model prayer for all Christians and the central prayer in Catholic worship. The five ingredients of prayer and their meaning – blessing and adoration, petition, intercession, thanksgiving for all God's goodness, a sense of his presence, forgiveness and salvation, and praise.

- The different kinds of prayer encouraged in the Catholic tradition – the importance of meditation and contemplation. The meaning of these two kinds of prayer. The rosary – the meaning of the different beads – the Lord's Prayer, the Hail Mary and the Gloria. The use of the rosary as a means of meditating on the most important events in the life of Jesus.

Sample exam questions

1. What are the different elements that the Catechism encourages Christians to include in their prayers?

2. What do Catholics understand by:
   a. meditation
   b. contemplation?

3. a. Describe a rosary.
   b. How does a Catholic use a rosary?
   c. How does a rosary help a Catholic meditate on the life of Jesus?

4. Describe three prayers that Catholics use regularly in their prayers.

Matters of life and death

In this topic you will find out about:

- the beliefs that Catholics and other Christians hold about life after death;
- the funeral services held by Roman Catholics and other Christians;
- the non-religious reasons some people have for believing in life after death;
- the important Catholic belief in the 'Sanctity of Life';
- the facts about abortion;
- the facts about **contraception**;
- the different attitudes of Christians to euthanasia – the reasons for supporting and opposing it.

KEY WORDS

Abortion The legal removal of the foetus from a woman's womb, usually before it is old enough to survive on its own.

Assisted suicide A friend or relative helping someone to take his or her own life; illegal in the UK.

Euthanasia An easy and gentle death that takes place at the time of the person's choosing.

Heaven The place of paradise that all Catholics hope to reach after a time spent in **purgatory**.

Hell The place of torment and punishment reserved for those who have rejected Jesus.

Immortality of the soul The Catholic belief that the soul never dies and lives on after the body has died.

Non-voluntary euthanasia When someone is unable to ask for euthanasia themselves and someone else, usually a relative, makes the decision for him or her.

Paranormal Unexplained events that are believed to have some kind of spiritual explanation, for example ghosts, spirits and so on.

Purgatory Catholics believe that the souls of most believers go to a place between earth and heaven, where their souls are purified and made ready for heaven.

Resurrection The Catholic belief that after death the body remains in the grave until it is brought back to life; Jesus was brought back to life by God.

Sanctity of life The Catholic belief that the whole of life is sacred and belongs to God.

Voluntary euthanasia The situation when someone asks for his or her life to be ended; illegal in the UK.

8 CHRISTIAN BELIEFS ABOUT LIFE AFTER DEATH

Although the beliefs of Catholics and other Christians about life after death are similar there are also important differences between them:

The beliefs of Catholics about life after death

The beliefs of Roman Catholics about life after death can be summarised as follows:

1. Roman Catholics believe that when people die the souls of very good believers are rewarded by being taken directly to heaven. These are believers who have been purified already and so do not need any further cleansing.

2. Catholics who die in God's grace but with sins that are unforgiven are sent to purgatory; this is the vast majority of believers. Purgatory is a place of cleansing, located between earth and heaven. The Catholic Church teaches that those left on earth can pray for those in purgatory to shorten the time that they spend there. Intercessions (prayers) can be made through indulgences and **penance**. In the Liturgical Year, November is set aside to pray for those in purgatory.

3. Those who have rejected God's grace during their lifetime and have refused to believe in him will go to hell.

4. At some time Jesus will return to earth – an event known to Christians as the **Second Coming**. When this happens, all those who have died will be brought back to life. Souls and bodies will be reunited and people will take on their 'spiritual bodies'.

5. God has appointed Christ to judge everyone. This judgement will determine whether a person spends eternity in heaven or hell. This will be in a 'new heaven and a new earth'. The inhabitants of this 'new' place will be made up of those who went directly to heaven when they died and those who have passed through the purifying fires of purgatory.

6. The Catechism also holds out hope for those who belonged to other religions (extract A).

> ▶ Christians believe strongly that death is not the end but is the beginning of everlasting life.

> **A** *"Those who, through no fault of their own, do not know the Gospel of Christ or His Church, but who nevertheless seek God with a sincere heart … may achieve eternal salvation."*
> (CCC 847)

The beliefs of other Christians about life after death

While some non-Catholics believe in purgatory the vast majority do not. Most of them believe in the Second Coming of Christ and the coming judgement of all human beings. They disagree with Catholics, however, over what happens between death and heaven:

1. Some believe that the soul remains in the grave after death until the judgement of Christ. When Jesus returns, the dead are brought back to life and stand with those who are still alive before the judgement seat of Christ. Everyone will then be judged on the basis of the life that they have lived – whether they have responded to the claims of Christ or not. If they have trusted in Christ for their salvation and had their sins forgiven they will go to heaven. If they have not they will be judged and sent to hell.

2. Some believe that the soul returns to God in heaven immediately a person dies. The body is then resurrected when Jesus returns and the two are reunited. The majority of this group of Christians do not believe in hell as a literal place of torment and punishment.

These two groups of Christians are spread across the different Christian denominations.

TASKS

1. Describe four beliefs that Roman Catholics hold about life after death.
2. Describe four beliefs about life after death that Roman Catholics share with other Christians.
3. What do Catholics believe happens after death to members of other religions?

✳ DISCUSSION POINT

What do you think happens to people after they die?

9 CHRISTIAN FUNERALS

Christianity strongly teaches, as we have seen, that death is not the end and that the soul lives on for ever (called the Immortality of the soul). Christians also believe that, at the end of time, the body of each believer will be brought back to life to share in Christ's own victory over death. This belief is at the heart of every Christian funeral service.

The Catholic funeral service

Catholics hope that they can be prepared for death by celebrating the **sacraments** of **Anointing the Sick** and Penance. They hope that they can avoid hell and the purification of purgatory by these Sacraments.

▲ *The Catholic Requiem Mass sums up all that the Catholic Church believes about life after death.*

There are several parts to the Catholic **Requiem Mass**:

1. The priest greets the cortege (the coffin followed by the chief mourners) at the door of the church. He sprinkles holy water over the coffin. The cortege is then led into church and the coffin is placed in the **sanctuary**. The Antiphon is sung:

   ❝*Eternal rest grant to them, O Lord, and let light perpetual shine on them.***❞**

2. The priest delivers his **homily**. This is a tribute to the dead person saying something about his or her life and faith in God. The homily also speaks of the hope that every Christian believer has that death is not the end – there is a life beyond the grave: eternal life.

3. The Eucharistic Prayer (extract A) states the Christian belief that Jesus banishes all sadness at the death of the loved one. Life beyond the grave may be different to life on earth but death is not the end – it is the beginning of everlasting life.

> **A** ❝*In him, who rose from the dead, our hope of resurrection dawned. The sadness of death gives way to the bright promise of immortality. Lord, for your faithful people life is changed, not ended. When the body of our earthly dwelling lies in death we gain an everlasting dwelling place in heaven.*❞
> (*Eucharistic Prayer*)

Burial or cremation then follows.

Other Christian funeral services

An Orthodox Funeral

At a funeral in an **Orthodox church**:

- As soon as a person has died his or her body is washed, dressed in new clothes and placed in an open coffin at the front of the church. The coffin remains open until the end of the service to remind everyone that death is God's punishment for sin.

- The tragedy of death is accompanied by the hope of resurrection. This hope is symbolised by the candles that are burning throughout the service and the incense that is sprayed over the coffin.

- Readings from the Bible emphasise the resurrection of the dead and the hope that is shared by all believers in God, that death is not the end.

> **B** 	*Give rest, O Christ, to all thy servants with thy saints. Where sorrow and pain are no more, neither sighing but life everlasting. Thou only art immortal, the creator and maker of man. And we are mortal born of earth and unto earth will we return, all we go down to the dust.*
>
> *(Kontakion, an Orthodox funeral prayer)*

A Nonconformist Funeral

Services that are held in Baptist, Methodist and United Reformed churches have much in common and include:

- Hymns, prayers, Bible readings and a short eulogy (hymn of praise) to the dead person.

- A short service held in church and probably followed by another service, called the 'committal', held in the crematorium or at the graveside. In this the body of the dead person is either committed to the ground or to the flames of the fire – in either case, to God's safe keeping.

TASKS

1. Explain how a Catholic Requiem Mass reflects the beliefs of the Catholic Church about life after death.

2. "Once you have died that is all there is to it. A belief in life after death is no more than wishful thinking." Do you agree with this comment? Give some reasons for your answer, showing that you have thought about more than one point of view.

✴ DISCUSSION POINT

What kind of funeral service, if any, would you like to have after you die? What reasons lie behind your answer?

10 NON-RELIGIOUS REASONS FOR BELIEVING IN LIFE AFTER DEATH

Most religious people believe in a life after death. It is part of the belief system to which they belong; whether they are Christians, Jews, Muslims or Hindus.
A person does not have to be religious, however, to believe in some form of survival after death. People who do not depend on their religious beliefs to inform them about life after death usually put forward three reasons for believing in some form of survival after death.

Reason 1: The evidence of ghosts and spirits

Many people believe that there are ghosts or spirits in the world of dead people who have not been able to reach either heaven or hell. These are spirit apparitions through which the souls of dead people are able to show themselves. Some people believe that houses can be haunted, when paranormal events happen, and exorcists are called in to remove them.

Reason 2: Visitations from dead relatives

Thousands of people claim that they have been visited by dead relatives or friends, or to have felt their presence in some way. Cases have been reported of people being warned of some coming event or disaster through one of these visits. Many people visit Spiritualist Churches so that a medium, a go-between between the spirit and the physical world, can relay a 'message' to someone who wants to be able to communicate with a dead relative or close friend. It should be noted that although many of these Churches call themselves 'Christian Spiritualists' the established Churches do not accept them as orthodox in their Christian beliefs.

Reason 3: 'Near-death' experiences

Some patients who have come around after major surgery have reported experiences, while they were unconscious, when they seemed to have left their bodies. Some claim to have seen a searing light or to have looked down on their body from above. Others say that they have drifted along a tunnel towards a bright light, experiencing considerable peace and joy on the way. They may have recognised figures from their past or people connected with their religious experiences. It seems that near-death experiences are common in people who belong to many different religions – and to no religion.

In addition, some people believe in life after death because it does not seem possible to them that life should simply end. Many people, for example, believe in reincarnation with its many rebirths because they occasionally feel that they have met someone or visited a place before.

Not believing in life after death

Surveys suggest that about 25% of the population do not believe in any form of survival after death. Many people are sceptical about the three reasons given above for believing. They point out that all of these so-called 'experiences' could easily have other explanations. There could, for instance, be a mechanism in the brain that triggers off feelings of euphoria as death draws near; a lack of oxygen to the brain is known to do this. Very few, if any, encounters with ghosts or spirits have stood up to close examination. Light is known to play tricks and most of us have some image of an afterlife which this could trigger off. So-called 'ghostly' experiences always seem to take place in the dark! Non-believers would simply say that there is no evidence for any kind of existence beyond the grave. The Talmud, an ancient Jewish holy book, warns that as 'no eye has seen it' any comments about life after death are pure speculation – and to be avoided. Others, more constructively, would suggest that all of us live on, in some way, in our children and that this is a form of immortality.

▲ All parents live on in their children and this is a form of immortality.

TASKS

1. What evidence for some form of survival after death do non-religious people give?
2. What is meant by a 'near-death' experience?

✳ DISCUSSION POINT

Why do you think that a belief in some form of life after death is very important to many people who do not believe in God?

11 THE SANCTITY OF LIFE

> **A** **"**Human life is sacred because from its beginning it involves the creative action of God and it remains forever in a special relationship with the Creator, who is its sole end. God alone is the Lord of life from its beginning until its end: no one can, under any circumstances, claim for himself the right directly to destroy an innocent human being.**"**
> (CCC 2258)

The sanctity of human life

It is the teaching of the Catholic Church, expressed in the Catechism (extract A) that all life is a gift from God and so is sacred (holy). Everyone must treat it as holy by preserving and valuing it in all their actions. The supreme example that life itself is holy is the **Incarnation** – the birth of God in Jesus. Jesus experienced the complete range of human feelings and emotions. He was fully human showing that God valued human life very highly.

There are many references in the Bible that underline this belief in the sanctity of life:

- **GENESIS 1**. The story of creation. According to this story, God created the whole of nature: the heaven and the earth (day 1); the dry land and the seas (day 2); all kinds of vegetation (day 3); the sun, moon and stars (day 4); all living creatures that lived in the air, in the seas and on the land (day 5) and ending with the first human beings (day 6). God was absolutely delighted with his handiwork; after each day of creation God saw that it was 'good'. This is the foundation for believing in the sanctity of all life; each part of the creation by God was perfect.

- **EXODUS 20.13**. The **Ten Commandments** are part of a much larger list of laws that God gave to the Jews before they reached the Promised Land. When they reached their destination, the Jews passed from being a nomadic to a settled people with a home of their own – and these laws were designed to help them settle down. The Jews were to have a huge respect for all life – and were not to commit murder.

- **ROMANS 14.8**. Paul is giving a general principle here to his readers. He tells them that they are to live their lives in such a way that great credit is brought to God – whether they are eating or drinking or observing holy days. You can find the principle stated clearly in extract B.

> **B** **"**... while we are alive, we are living for the Lord, and when we die, we die for the Lord: and so, alive or dead, we belong to the Lord.**"**
> (Romans 14.8)

To do this we must treat everyone as if they are particularly important to God: holy.

- **1 CORINTHIANS 6.19**. Here Paul is making a point about sexual immorality, although the principle has wider application. He is telling the Corinthian Christians that they must be careful what happens to their bodies because they are a dwelling-place, a **temple**, for God's Holy Spirit (extract C). It follows, then, that no one owns themselves. God has bought them and paid an enormous price for them – the death of Jesus. This should make them extremely careful about how they treat themselves; how they allow others to treat them and how they treat everyone else.

C **"Do you not realise that your body is the temple of the Holy Spirit, who is in you and whom you received from God? You are not your own property, then; you have been bought at a price. So use your body for the glory of God."**

(1 Corinthians 6.19–20)

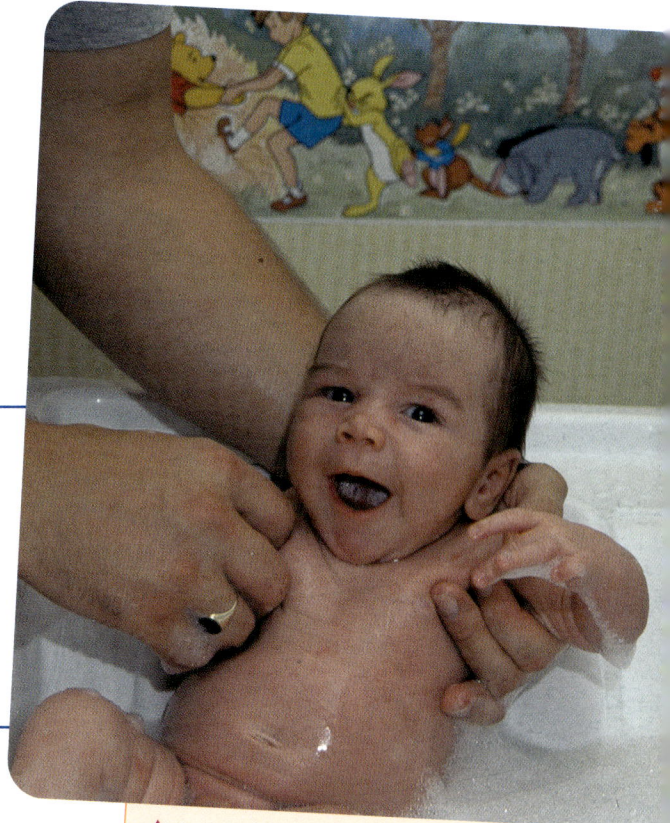

▲ *Most people would say that this is the supreme example of the sanctity of life.*

TASKS

1. **a.** Catholics speak a great deal of the 'sanctity of life'. What do they mean when they use this phrase?
    b. Describe two social issues in which the sanctity of life is likely to be an important part of the discussion.

✴ DISCUSSION POINT

At the same time as remembering the sanctity of life, do you think it is also important to keep 'the quality of life' in mind? Talk about two social issues in which both of these things might play an important part in any discussion.

12 ABORTION – THE FACTS

The word '**abortion**' can be used in two very different ways. It can refer to:

- the deliberate killing of an unborn baby by using a surgical procedure. This is called an induced abortion;

- a 'spontaneous abortion', which is otherwise known as a miscarriage. This is the expulsion of the foetus from the womb by the body's own activity. It is thought that about 30% of all pregnancies end in miscarriage – often so early in the pregnancy that the mother does not know it is happening.

Induced abortion has been condemned in every age of the Church by **Popes**, Councils and **bishops**. They have taught that abortion is indefensible since the unborn child is innocent of any offence and incapable of defending itself.

> **A** **❝***The child, by reason of its physical and mental immaturity, needs special safeguards and care, including appropriate legal protection before as well as after birth.*❞
>
> *(United Nations Declaration on Human Rights)*

Abortion legalised in Britain

Before 1967, abortion was illegal in Britain. Instead, about 200 000 illegal, 'back-street', abortions were carried out each year and these often had disastrous consequences. They frequently led to serious injury or even the death of the woman. About 60 women died in the country each year as a direct result. In 1967, the Abortion Act made abortion legal in Britain if certain criteria are met, although the Abortion Act of 1990 denies legal abortion after the 24th week of pregnancy.

CHECK IT OUT

...her life is at risk should the pregnancy continue.

...two doctors agree that an abortion is legal under the Act.

A WOMAN CAN HAVE A LEGAL ABORTION IN BRITAIN AS LONG AS...

...there is a substantial risk that the baby might be born with a physical or mental disability.

...there is a risk of injury to the woman's physical or mental health.

...there is a risk that an additional child in the family would threaten the physical or mental health of existing family members.

Abortion on demand?

Opponents of abortion argue that the Abortion Act virtually created 'abortion on demand', meaning abortion without any real restrictions. Those who support abortion say that the Act confronted the realities of the situation in dealing with thousands of dangerous illegal abortions. Certainly the number of women having an abortion in Britain is much higher than it was thirty years ago:

1968	1971	1990	1991	1993	1999
157 000	104 000	173 900	190 000	180 000	177 000

About 20% of all abortions in Britain are carried out on women from outside the country, especially from Spain and Eire where abortion is illegal. About 18% of all pregnancies, one in every six, now end in an abortion. The largest increase in the number of abortions over the years has been in women in the 16–19 age group. One in every forty women in this group now has an abortion each year.

▼ *The question of just when life begins is the most important that has to be answered in any discussion about abortion.*

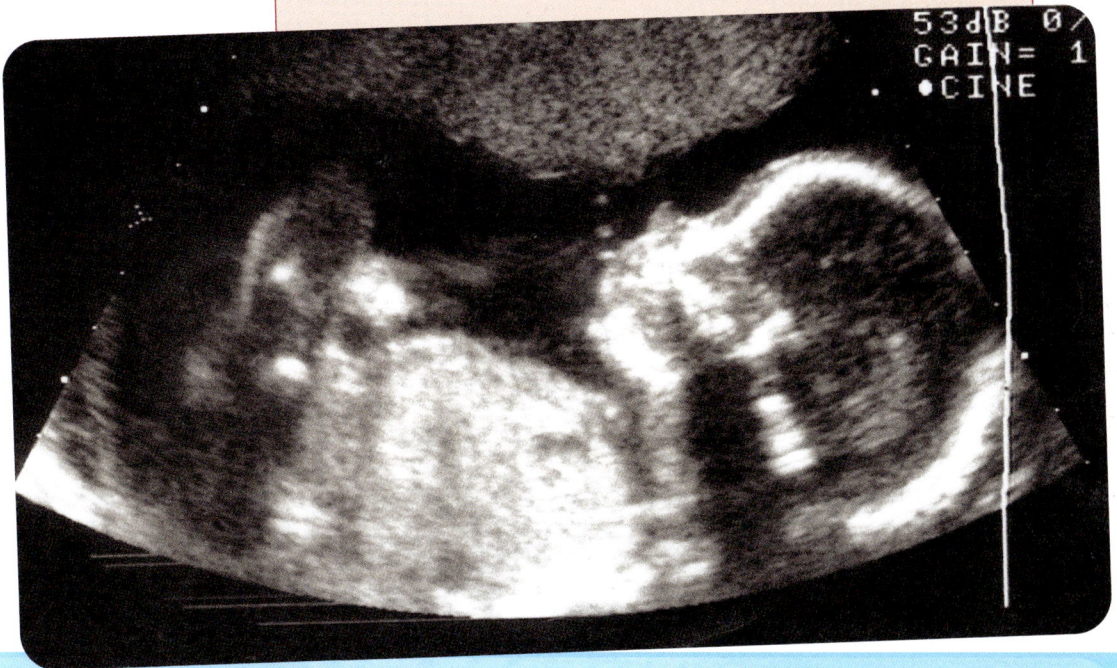

TASKS

1. What is an induced abortion?
2. On what grounds can a woman obtain an abortion in Britain?

✳ DISCUSSION POINT

Do you think that Catholics who have an abortion or Catholic medical workers who help women to have an abortion should be punished by the Church?

13 ABORTION – ARGUMENTS FOR AND AGAINST

Abortion probably raises stronger emotions than any other moral issue. In the USA, for instance, opponents of abortion have, from time to time, burned down clinics and murdered doctors held responsible for carrying out the operations.

To understand such intensity of feeling, we must examine the arguments used to justify and oppose abortion.

Arguments used to justify abortion (pro-choice)

Pro-choice groups believe that abortion is acceptable because:

- every woman has the right to choose what she does with her own body. The foetus is part of that body until it can exist independently;

- every child has the right to be born into a loving family which is able to provide for its basic needs – shelter, food and clothing. If this basic care cannot be provided, then an abortion is justified. There are too many unwanted babies already in the world – why add to that number?

- other members of a pregnant woman's family also have their rights. This includes the woman's partner and other children. If the woman discovers that her baby is going to be born disabled, then she has the right to decide whether she, and her family, can cope;

- a woman who becomes pregnant after a rape should not be compelled to carry her rapist's child. The child will be a constant reminder to her of the violence that she has suffered;

- no one has the right to impose their own moral views on other people;

- if abortion was illegal, then we would go back to the old situation with back-street abortions and surely no one would want that to happen.

Arguments against abortion (pro-life)

Catholics and pro-life groups believe that abortion is wrong because:

- every child is a precious, and unique, gift from God. No one has the right to destroy that gift. This rule is absolute and even covers the case where a woman has been raped;

- every baby is defenceless and needs protection. The right of the unborn child to life certainly equals that of the mother;

- Catholics believe an embryo is a human being from the moment it is conceived, since it has the potential to grow into a full human being. This is as true of someone who will be disabled as it is of the able-bodied;

- abortion places an intolerable burden on doctors and nurses, many of whom may have serious moral and religious objections to it. In any case, the Hippocratic Oath, which all doctors sign, commits them to save life – not destroy it.

When does life begin?

This crucial question goes to the heart of the debate about abortion.
There are three possible answers:

- **Answer 1.** Life begins at conception. The Roman Catholic Church and pro-life groups teach that life begins the moment when the sperm and egg fuse and embed themselves in the woman's uterus.

- **Answer 2.** Life begins at some definite point in the pregnancy but no one is quite sure when. Some believe that life begins when the baby starts to move in the womb. Others believe that life begins when God implants the soul in the body – and the person becomes a whole being.

- **Answer 3.** Life begins when a baby can survive on its own outside the womb. Until this time, the baby remains dependent on its mother for its survival.

There is no clear answer to the question 'When does life begin?' and this makes any discussion about the rights and wrongs of abortion very difficult.

▲ *This baby is wanted and its parents are looking forward to its birth with great excitement, but the birth of a baby is fraught with difficulties for some people.*

A **❝**Human life must be respected and protected absolutely from the moment of conception. From the first moment of his existence, a human being must be recognized as having the rights of a person – among which is the inviolable right of every innocent being to life…abortion and infanticide are abominable crimes.**❞**
(CCC 2270–71)

TASKS

1. What are the arguments that could be put forward for maintaining that abortion should be available?
2. What are the main arguments for opposing abortion?

14 PROTESTANT CHURCHES AND ABORTION

Within **Protestant** Churches there are two clear viewpoints on abortion.

1. Abortion is always wrong

Many **Protestant** Christians, largely from Evangelical Churches, agree with the Roman Catholic Church that abortion is always wrong in all circumstances. **Evangelicals** depend heavily on the teaching of the Bible for their social opinions and they point out that the Bible teaches that all people are made 'in the image of God'. The Bible also says that God has a plan for everyone's life (extract A).

> **A** *"Before I formed you in the womb I knew you; before you came to birth I consecrated you; I appointed you as a prophet to the nations."*
> *(Jeremiah 1.5)*

Many Christians, from different denominations, are against abortion because they believe that, even before a pregnancy is completed and a baby is born, God has a plan for that life.

2. Abortion is acceptable in certain situations

The **Church of England** and the **Methodist Church** combine strong opposition to abortion (extract B) with recognition that there are a limited number of conditions under which an abortion is morally acceptable. It is acceptable if:

- The mother is very young and would clearly be incapable of looking after a baby. The legal age for sexual intercourse in the UK is 16 and anyone under this age who is pregnant would fall into this category.

- If the mother is pregnant as a result of being raped. All Christian Churches, apart from the Catholic Church, agree that a woman in this situation should not be punished by having to give birth to, and bring up, her rapist's child.

- If the mother's life would be put at risk if the abortion was allowed to continue. This is usually known early in the pregnancy and so the operation can be carried out well before the limit of twenty-four weeks.

- If the foetus is so damaged that the baby's quality of life would be severely limited if it was born.

> **B** *"All human life, including life developing in the womb, is created in God's own image and is therefore to be nurtured, supported and protected."*
> *(General Synod of the Church of England)*

Some Christians would go further and argue that the social conditions of the woman should be taken into account when an abortion is being considered. All would agree, however, that the final decision must be left to the woman without any outside pressure being placed on her.

Catholics believe that the conception and birth of a baby are the result of collaboration between a husband, a wife – and God.

Many Christians believe this because:

1. They do not agree with the Roman Catholic Church that life begins at conception.

2. They do not agree with the Roman Catholic Church that there are 'absolute moral laws' – such laws often have to be judged against the circumstances of the time. The sanctity of life is a general guide to life but is not an absolute law that applies in every situation.

3. The teaching of Jesus suggests that love is the most important thing – and the loving thing to do in an extreme situation may be to have an abortion.

4. Modern technology, such as the amniocentesis test, makes it possible for a woman to know if the foetus she is carrying is damaged in some way – and to have an abortion if she wishes.

TASKS

1. How might a Christian who is not a Roman Catholic argue that abortion is always wrong?

2. "There are some situations in which an abortion is the most loving thing to do." What kind of situations might this speaker have in mind? Do you agree with his/her comment? Give reasons for your answer, showing that you have thought about more than one point of view.

15 CONTRACEPTION – THE FACTS

Contraception (contra-conception), or birth control, is the attempt to prevent conception as a result of sexual intercourse. The Roman Catholic Church teaches that contraception by artificial means is always wrong but it does encourage the use of natural means of birth control. You will discover the reasons for this teaching in unit 16.

The teaching of the Churches

- The Lambeth Conference of the Anglican Church, held after the First World War, stated that contraception was morally and spiritually indefensible. By the next Lambeth Conference, held in 1930, however, the Anglican Church had changed its mind. Soon afterwards, the Methodist and the Orthodox Churches expressed their support for contraception within marriage. Today, all Protestant Churches support the use of contraception for married couples.

- During his short papacy, Pope John XXIII set up a commission to look at birth control and family planning. It presented two reports after Pope Paul VI had succeeded Pope John XXIII. The majority report recommended a change in the Church's attitude of opposition, while the minority report said it should continue. Pope Paul VI supported the minority view and published his encyclical, *Humanae Vitae*, and insisted that every act of sexual intercourse should remain open 'to the transmission of life'. This remains the teaching of the Roman Catholic Church today.

Artificial family planning

Among the artificial methods of contraception condemned by the Catholic Church are:

- *The pill.* Over three million women in the UK and 50 million worldwide use this method. It offers almost 100% reliability, although some women experience side effects from using it.

- *The 'morning-after' pill.* This is a pill that can be taken after sexual intercourse has taken place to prevent conception. It acts as an 'abortifacient', making it impossible for the fertilised egg to embed itself in the wall of the uterus. It is opposed by the Catholic Church because of the way that it works – it brings about an abortion.

- *The IUD or coil.* Inserted into a woman's uterus by a doctor and left in place, the IUD brings about a 'spontaneous abortion' (miscarriage) if the fertilised egg embeds itself in the wall of the uterus. This makes it an 'abortifacient', meaning a device designed to secure an abortion.

- *The cap or diaphragm.* This is a rubber device that a woman fits over the neck of her cervix before she has sex. This prevents the sperm from reaching the fallopian tubes and uterus.

- *The condom or sheath.* This is a sheath of thin latex that a man fits over his erect penis before any sexual contact. Apart from being a contraceptive, the condom offers protection against sexually transmitted diseases, including HIV.
- *Sterilisation.* In the man, the tube that carries the sperm from the testicles is cut and in the woman, the fallopian tubes are cauterised. This is particularly unacceptable to the Catholic Church as it makes the man or the woman infertile and so rules out the possibility of any further children.

Natural family planning

Natural family planning involves monitoring a woman's menstrual cycle to determine when she is and isn't fertile. This is acceptable to the Roman Catholic Church because it does not involve any interference with the act of sexual intercourse or the natural process of conception. This is called the 'rhythm' method because it uses the natural rhythms of a woman's body to limit conception.

> **A** *"…excluded is any action, which either before, or at the moment of, or after sexual intercourse is specifically intended to prevent procreation … it is never lawful, even for the gravest of reasons, to do evil, that good may come of it."*
> (Humanae Vitae)

▶ *The Roman Catholic Church teaches that Catholics can only use contraceptives that work in harmony with the woman's body.*

1. In 1984, the Pope said, "Only natural forms of birth control do not offend the moral law established by God."
   a. What is a natural form of birth control?
   b. Name three 'unnatural' forms of birth control.
   c. Why do you think that unnatural forms of birth control might offend 'the moral law established by God'?
2. What is your own attitude to contraception? Explain your answer.
3. Describe the 'natural' form of birth control that Catholics are encouraged to use.

TASKS

16 THE CHRISTIAN CHURCHES AND CONTRACEPTION

Christians disagree about whether it is right or wrong for them to use contraception. Some think that artificial contraceptives are wrong because God might want to give them a baby. At least, they should always be open to that possibility. Others, however, believe that using contraceptives is a responsible thing for them to do if they do not want to have a baby.

The teaching of the Catholic Church about contraception

The opposition of the Roman Catholic Church to artificial contraceptives goes back centuries. During his short papacy, Pope John XXIII set up a Commission to look at the whole issue of birth control and family planning. It presented two reports after Pope Paul VI had succeeded Pope John XXIII. The majority report recommended a change in the Church's attitude, while a minority report said that the traditional opposition to contraception should continue.

▲ It was Pope Paul VI who decided that the use of contraception would be forbidden to Roman Catholics.

Pope Paul VI supported the minority report and published his encyclical *Humanae Vitae* in 1968. Condemning such artificial contraceptives as the condom and the pill, the Pope insisted that every act of sexual intercourse should be 'open to the transmission of life'. This remains the teaching of the Catholic Church today and is maintained in the Catechism of the Catholic Church (extract A) on the following grounds:

1. A willingness to use artificial methods of contraception can lead to sexual promiscuity, **adultery**, sexually transmitted diseases and broken marriages ending in **divorce**.

2. It is against the will of God. God provided sex so that human beings could procreate and have children. Every sexual act should be open to the possibility of new life being created. For the same reason, the Catholic Church condemns masturbation.

3. Forms of contraception such as the pill, the condom and the diaphragm are unnatural. Only the rhythm method is natural, working with natural events in the body.

4. Most of the problems in the modern family are created because people can use contraceptives without responsibility. If the Catholic path is followed, then many marriages would be saved and millions of people would not suffer the consequences of sexually transmitted diseases.

It is a fact, however, that many Roman Catholics do not accept the teachings of their Church on this issue. They use contraceptives and deal with any guilt that this gives them in their own way.

The teaching of the Protestant churches about contraception

For a long time, the Catholic and the Protestant Churches agreed that contraception was undesirable from a Christian point of view. The view was taken that sexual intercourse within marriage was intended by God so that couples should be blessed with the gift of children. The situation was radically changed by the Great Depression of the 1920s and 1930s, when the link between large families and poverty became obvious. The Lambeth Conference of 1930 marked a departure from previous comments by stating that there was nothing unchristian in using contraception. Used properly it would improve the health of the mother and the standard of living of most families.

Both the Church of England and the Methodist Church teach that contraception is an acceptable, and necessary, way of preventing unwanted pregnancies. Both of these Churches encourage people to make 'responsible choices', emphasising that the availability of several effective methods of contraception allows them to do this. These two Churches believe that every couple should be free to decide for themselves which method of contraception to use, as long as the method chosen is acceptable to both the husband and the wife.

The advice given by the Protestant Churches marked a shift away from the teaching that sex was primarily, or solely, concerned with procreation. It was created by God for the enjoyment of two people and is an important way of strengthening their relationship.

> **A** **❝***The Methodist Church believes that responsible contraception is a welcome means towards fulfilment in marriage, the spacing of children and the need to avoid pregnancy altogether, for example for medical reasons.*❞
> (Statement by Methodist Church in *What the Churches Say, Third Edition, 2000*)

TASKS

1. Describe and explain the different Christian attitudes towards contraception.

2. "A married couple should be prepared to have as many children as God wants to give them." Do you agree? Give reasons to support your answer and show that you have thought about different points of view. You must refer to Christianity in your answer.

✳ DISCUSSION POINT

Many Catholics follow their conscience rather than the teaching of their Church on contraception. They use contraception to limit the size of their families. Do you think they are right?

17 EUTHANASIA – THE FACTS

What is euthanasia?

Euthanasia is often called 'mercy-killing'. The word itself means 'an easy death' and it refers to killing someone painlessly to relieve their suffering, especially from a terminal (incurable) illness. There are four forms that euthanasia can take:

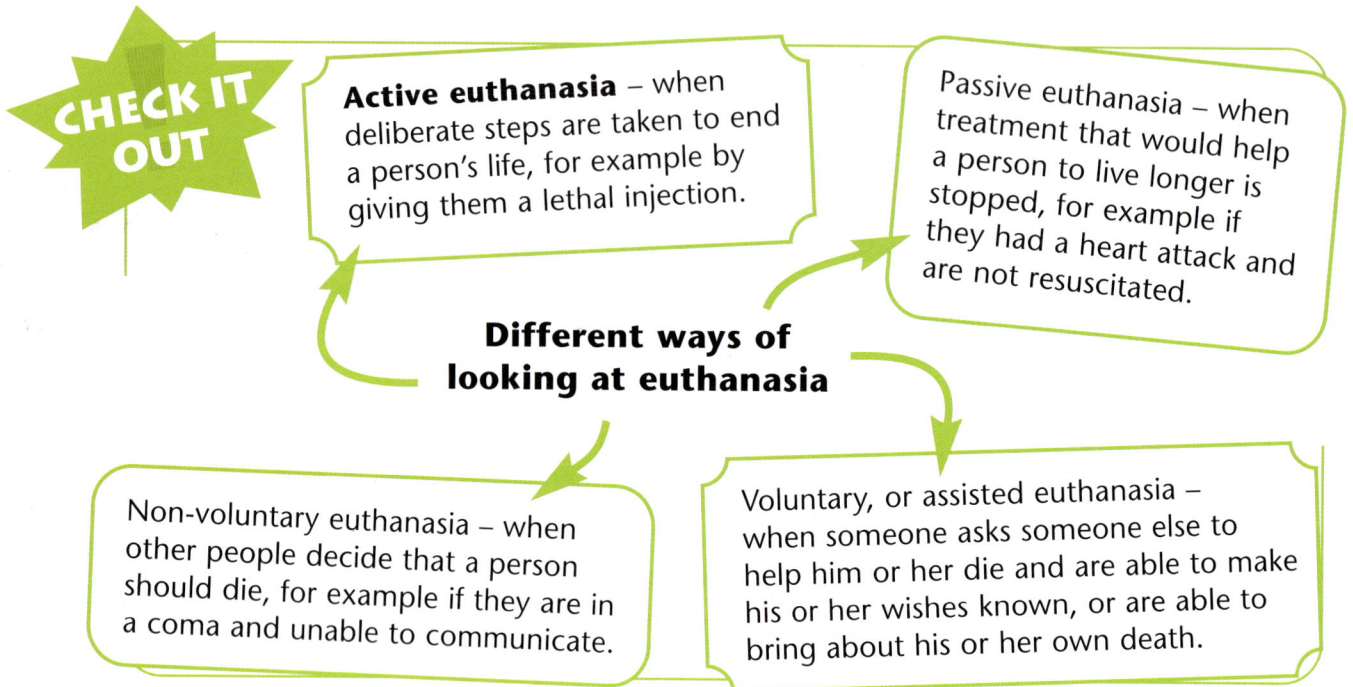

CHECK IT OUT

Active euthanasia – when deliberate steps are taken to end a person's life, for example by giving them a lethal injection.

Passive euthanasia – when treatment that would help a person to live longer is stopped, for example if they had a heart attack and are not resuscitated.

Different ways of looking at euthanasia

Non-voluntary euthanasia – when other people decide that a person should die, for example if they are in a coma and unable to communicate.

Voluntary, or assisted euthanasia – when someone asks someone else to help him or her die and are able to make his or her wishes known, or are able to bring about his or her own death.

Suicide

When someone commits suicide they take their own life – often because of depression or illness. An 'attempted suicide' is when someone unsuccessfully tries to kill themselves. Until recently this was illegal in the UK, until it was realised that someone who tries to take his or her own life needs professional help and not time spent in prison. An assisted suicide is one in which a person enlists the help of someone else to end his or her life. This is illegal in this country although a partner or close friend who provides help to someone to end his or her life is usually treated leniently by the Courts.

Euthanasia and the law

In the Netherlands and some parts of Australia, euthanasia is allowed in certain circumstances, as long as two doctors agree that the person requesting it understands what they are doing. In the UK, however, it remains illegal. There are many people who would like to see this situation changed and recent surveys suggest that they have the support of more than 60% of the general population. The Voluntary Euthanasia Society (now called EXIT) argues that many people would welcome the opportunity to have a 'happy death' if they became terminally ill.

People who want to see the law changed argue that:

1. It is a basic human right that a person should be able to decide exactly when his or her life will end. It is no longer illegal to take, or attempt to take, one's own life. It should be legal to seek the help of a partner or a friend to make this possible.

2. The quality as well as the length of a person's life should be taken into account. Medical advances mean that we can keep people technically alive without necessarily offering them a good quality of life.

3. It has legally been established that doctors can withhold treatment from a patient and also switch off life-support machines if recovery is extremely unlikely. This is really euthanasia by another name.

4. It does not make any sense to block a life-saving machine for months or years when it could profitably be used to save someone else's life.

It does seem likely that the law will be changed in the foreseeable future, to allow at least a limited form of euthanasia. Before this happens, however, considerable opposition from the Christian Churches, especially the Roman Catholic Church, will need to be overcome.

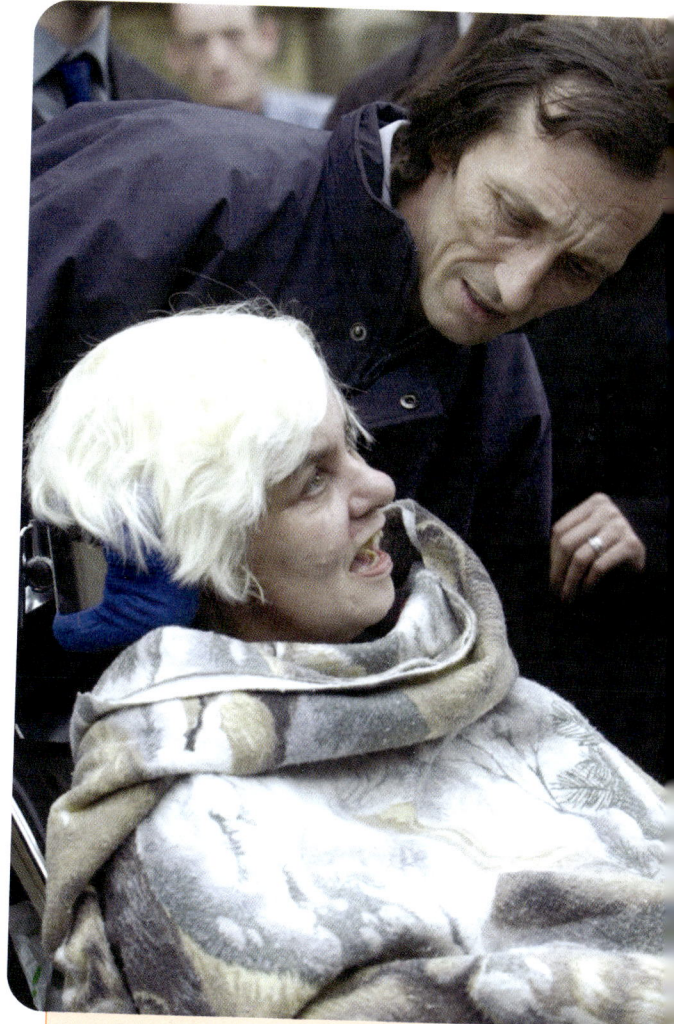

▲ *Dianne Pretty fought in the courts for the right to end her own life.*

TASKS

1. How do you think that you might respond to a close relative or friend with a terminal illness who expressed a wish to you that he or she wanted to end his or her life?

2. "Euthanasia is totally wrong. Only God has the right to decide when a person's life should end." Do you agree with this comment? Give reasons for your answer, showing that you have thought about more than one point of view.

18 CHRISTIANS AND EUTHANASIA

All of the main Christian Churches are opposed to euthanasia with two reservations:

1. The Roman Catholic Church only accepts euthanasia if the dose of painkillers that is necessary to ease the suffering is also strong enough to kill the patient. This is called 'the law of double-effect' and is accepted by all of the Churches. It is only acceptable, however, if the intention is to stop the suffering and not to kill the patient.

2. All the Churches accept that it is not necessary to go to extraordinary lengths to keep someone alive if there is no hope of recovery. There comes a time, for example, when the attempt to restart the heart after a heart-attack by applying electric shocks can stop if they are unsuccessful.

Despite the unanimous teaching of the Churches, there is widespread disagreement among Christians over euthanasia. The following are the arguments they put forward.

1. To support euthanasia

1. In some situations, to end a person's pain is the most humane thing to do. The Golden Rule of Christianity is to treat others just as you would wish to be treated by them. If you would prefer to end your own life at the time of your own choosing then you should allow the same privilege to others.

2. In the modern world we can change the direction that an illness takes, through drugs and medical equipment. This places us in more control of our lives than God. We have shown that we can act responsibly and so we should be given control over our own death or that of those close to us.

3. The religious argument that suffering is 'spiritually beneficial' is open to considerable doubt. Most people would want to end their lives at peace and not racked by pain.

2. To oppose euthanasia

1. Many Christians are opposed to euthanasia because they believe strongly in the sanctity of life. This is particularly the view of the Roman Catholic Church which opposes abortion for the same reason. It believes that God gives life in the first place and takes it away at the end. It is God's right to choose the moment that a person dies.

2. Many Christians believe that suffering has a purpose – it brings them closer to God. Suffering helps people to realise that they are mortal and that life does not go on for ever. It also helps them to appreciate the suffering that Jesus went through to achieve their salvation.

3. If euthanasia was legalised then it would be open to abuse. Relatives might put pressure on aged relatives to end their lives – to avoid the cost of continual care or to inherit some money.

4. Hospices provide the opportunity for people to end their life with dignity. The careful use of drugs to remove pain is called 'palliative care' and this is a growing branch of medicine. The problem is that there are comparatively few hospices and few people can stay in them for any length of time. Organisations such as the Macmillan Nurses, however, try to offer the same kind of care in the homes of the patients.

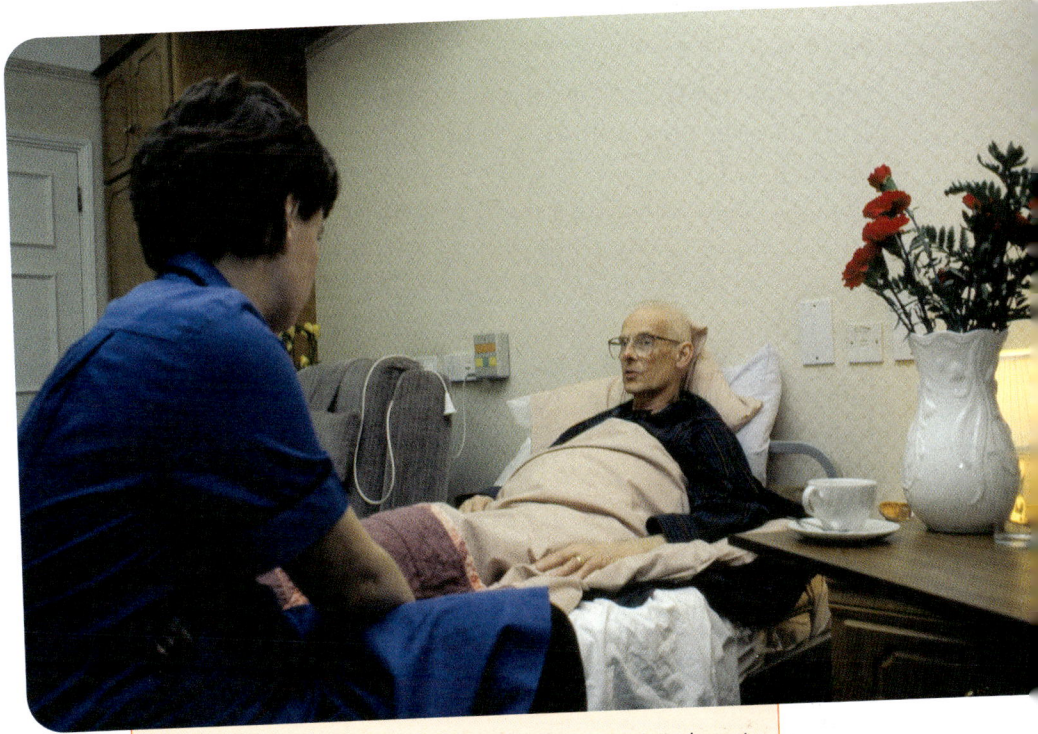

▲ *Many hospices have links with local churches and most of them do have a Christian foundation. However, they welcome patients of all beliefs or none.*

TASKS

1. What are the main arguments against legalising euthanasia?
2. What are the main arguments in favour of legalising euthanasia?
3. "All life is worth preserving, even a life that is filled with pain." Do you agree? Give reasons to support your answer and show that you have thought about different points of view. You must refer to Christianity in your answer.

�֍ DISCUSSION POINT

If euthanasia was to be legalised would you be afraid that it might be abused or would you welcome it?

EXAM HELP

In the examination

Make sure that you know about:

LIFE AFTER DEATH

- The beliefs of Catholics about life after death. They believe in the immortality of the soul: that the soul never dies. The souls of very good people go directly to heaven. The majority of souls are sent to purgatory – a place of cleansing before entry into heaven. The wicked – those who have refused to believe in God and obey his laws – shall all go to hell. Catholics disagree on whether this is a place of eternal punishment or not. The Second Coming of Jesus – his return to earth followed by judgement. The eternal destiny of all souls.

- The beliefs of other Christians about life after death. Few Protestants believe in purgatory. Difference of opinion – does the soul remain in the grave until the final judgement or does the soul return to God in heaven immediately after death? Many do not believe in hell as a literal place of punishment.

- Christian funerals. The Roman Catholic Requiem Mass. The Eucharistic Prayer expressing Christian belief that there is everlasting life. Orthodox funerals – the open coffin. The tragedy of death and the hope of resurrection. Nonconformist funerals – short service in church and committal in crematorium or at graveside. Almost all Christians believe in survival after death.

- Non-Christian reasons for believing in life after death. The evidence of ghosts and spirits. Visitations from dead relatives. Near-death experiences. The reasons many people have for not believing in life after death.

Sample exam questions

1. Explain what is meant by:
   a. purgatory
   b. heaven
   c. hell
   d. the immortality of the soul.

2. a. Sum up what Catholics believe about life after death.
   b. How do the views of Catholics about life after death differ from those held by other Christians?

3. a. Explain how certain beliefs in life after death are expressed in the Requiem Mass.
   b. Explain how the beliefs of Orthodox Christians and Protestant Christians are expressed in their funeral services.

ABORTION AND CONTRACEPTION

- The sanctity of life. The important teaching of the Catholic Church. The important texts in the Bible on which the belief is based. The importance of the Incarnation – God becoming fully human in Jesus. Note that this belief applies to the discussion on both abortion and euthanasia.

- The facts about abortion. The two different meanings of the word 'abortion'. The legal basis on which an abortion can be carried out. These are very important and need to be learned. Do we now have abortion on demand? What does this mean? The arguments for (pro-choice) and against (pro-life) abortion. The important question of when life begins – at conception, at some point during pregnancy or when the baby has independent existence? The teaching of the Protestant Churches on abortion – those who believe it is acceptable in certain situations and those who believe that it is always wrong.

- The facts about contraception – natural and unnatural methods. The teaching of the Catholic Church and the Protestant Churches about contraception. What are the 'unnatural' forms of contraception?

Sample exam questions

1. Write down three reasons why Catholics believe that all life is sacred or holy.
2. Give three reasons why the Catholic Church is totally opposed to abortion.
3. Give three reasons why many people believe that abortion is necessary.
4. "No Christian should ever use unnatural methods of contraception." Do you agree with this comment? Give reasons for your answer, showing that you have thought about more than one point of view.
5. Explain why the Catholic Church is opposed to artificial methods of contraception.
6. **a.** What does the Catholic Church mean when it speaks of 'natural' methods of contraception?

   b. Why does it find these natural methods acceptable?
7. Explain why the Catholic Church is opposed to abortion.
8. "No Catholic should ever consider having an abortion." Do you agree with this comment? Give reasons for your answer, showing that you have thought about more than one point of view.

EXAM HELP

EUTHANASIA

- The facts about euthanasia. What is euthanasia? – the difference between active euthanasia, passive euthanasia, involuntary euthanasia and voluntary euthanasia. Euthanasia and the law. Arguments for allowing euthanasia. The debate among Christians about euthanasia. The distinctive arguments of the Catholic and Protestant Churches on euthanasia. The reasons why all Churches and most Christians oppose euthanasia.

Sample exam questions

1. Explain the differences between suicide, and voluntary and involuntary euthanasia.

2. **a.** Why are many Christians against euthanasia?

   b. Do you support or oppose euthanasia? Give some reasons for the opinion that you hold.

3. "If the quality of my life was extremely low I would want steps to be taken to end it." Do you agree with this comment? Give reasons for your answer, showing that you have thought about more than one point of view. Do you think that your answer would be different depending on whether you were a Roman Catholic or a Protestant?

4. Why do many people argue that the law banning euthanasia should be changed to allow at least a limited form?

5. Do you think that the arguments in favour of euthanasia or those against euthanasia are strongest? Give as many reasons as you can for your answer.

Marriage and the family

In this topic you will find out about:

- the facts about marriage and divorce;
- the Christian attitude to sex outside marriage;
- the Catholic teachings about marriage;
- the Catholic marriage service;
- the attitude of Christians to divorce;
- family life;
- the facts about homosexuality;
- the teaching of the Catholic Church and other Christian Churches on homosexuality.

KEY WORDS

Annulment A declaration by the Catholic Church that a marriage never lawfully took place.

Cohabitation A couple who live together without being married.

Extended Family More than three generations of a family living together or very close to each other.

Faithfulness Two people living up to their marriage vows and only having sexual intercourse with each other.

Homosexuality Men or women who are sexually attracted to members of their own, rather than the opposite, sex.

Marriage A legal agreement or contract between two people to live together for the remainder of their lives.

Nuclear family Two or three generations in a family, made up of father, mother and any children.

Pre-marital sex Having sexual intercourse before one is married.

Promiscuity Having sex with more than one, probably several, partners.

Re-constituted family Takes place when one or both people in a marriage have been married before and they bring their own children into the new relationship.

Remarriage A person, or two people, marrying again after they have been married to someone else.

19 MARRIAGE AND DIVORCE – THE FACTS

In 1995 a very significant change was made in the law in the UK. In that year it became legal for a marriage to take place in any building that had been authorised for the purpose – including hotels and places of historical interest. Before this, 50% all weddings were carried out in places of worship with the remainder being performed in Registry Offices. Now only 35% of all weddings are performed in a religious building.

Marriages that are not performed in places of worship do not have any religious element. Instead the couple is asked to make two important declarations in front of everyone:

1. To confirm that there is no legal reason why either should not marry, in other words that one of them is not already married.

2. To promise each other that they will stay faithful until death separates them.

Modern marriage

The number of couples marrying in the UK each year has declined considerably in the last 50 years. In 1971, for instance, 405 000 couples married – a figure that dropped to 292 000 in 1995 and 268 999 in 2000. There are two main reasons for this change – many couples are choosing to cohabit (live together) rather than marry, or to cohabit for a time before marrying. The result is that couples are much older now when they marry than they were in the early 1970s. The average age for a woman at marriage is now 32 while the average man is 35.

Despite the strain and stress of many modern marriages, all the evidence suggests that marriage is good for us:

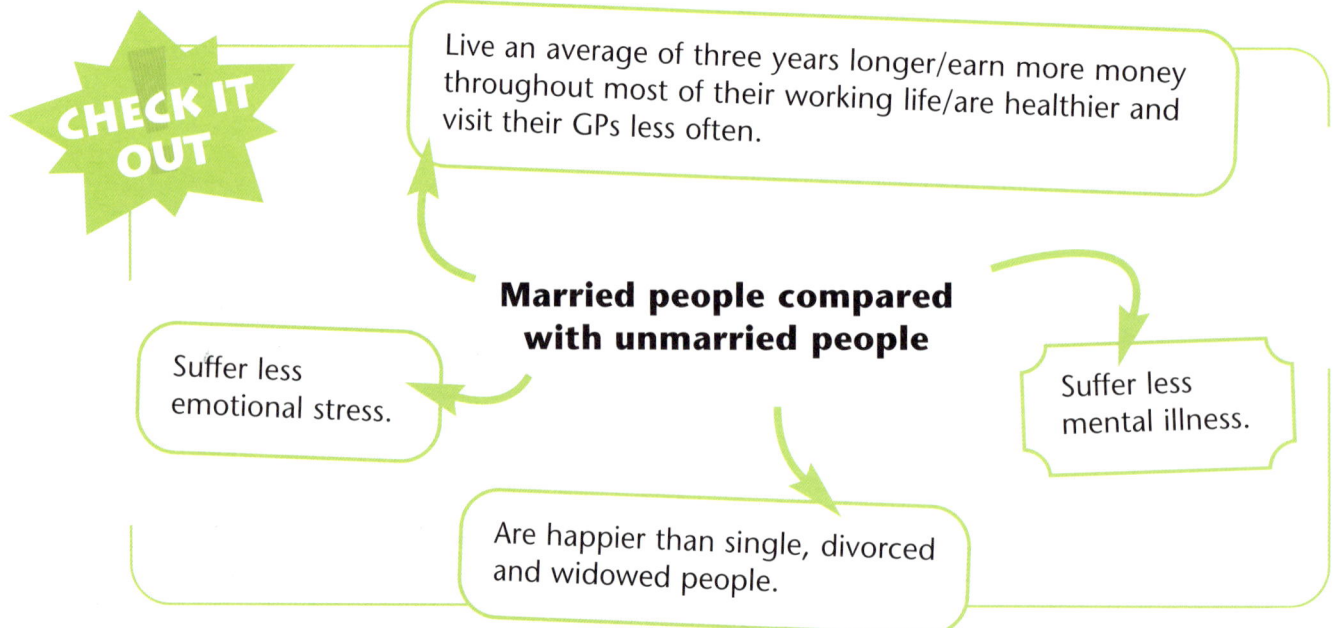

CHECK IT OUT

Live an average of three years longer/earn more money throughout most of their working life/are healthier and visit their GPs less often.

Married people compared with unmarried people

Suffer less emotional stress.

Suffer less mental illness.

Are happier than single, divorced and widowed people.

Divorce

An increasing number of marriages do not live up to the expectations of one, or both, partners. This amounts to about 160 000 divorces each year in the UK. The Divorce Reform Act (1967) allowed people to divorce if their marriage 'had irretrievably broken down'. There are five ways to prove that this has happened:

1. One or both partners had committed adultery.

2. The behaviour of one spouse was intolerable.

3. The couple had lived together for two years or more and both wanted a divorce.

4. The couple had lived apart for five years or more and only one wanted a divorce.

5. One spouse had deserted the other for more than two years.

Since then the law has changed further and a couple can now divorce after one year.

The number of divorces has increased from about 25 000 in 1961 to the present figure. In 1999 there were 143 000 children under the age of 16 involved in the divorce of their parents. Of all divorces, 75% have one or more children under this age. There are now over 1 200 000 single-parent families in this country. The Roman Catholic Church does not recognise divorce. Instead, some couples are granted an annulment which is just as if the marriage never took place.

▶ *The most recent divorce figures suggest that the number of couples going through the divorce courts is declining for the first time since 1967.*

TASKS

1. How has the pattern of marriage changed in this country since the early 1970s? Do you think the changes are good or do they have some (hidden) dangers for the future?

2. What is the law about divorce in this country?

3. "There are far too many people divorcing their partners without thinking through the implications of doing so." Do you agree with this comment? Give reasons for your answer, showing that you have thought about more than one point of view.

20 SEX OUTSIDE MARRIAGE

The Roman Catholic Church teaches that all forms of sexual activity outside marriage are wrong. These include adultery, **fornication** and homosexual intercourse. The Catechism underlines traditional Catholic moral values and argues strongly for chastity.

Chastity

Chastity, abstaining from sexual activity and intercourse, can take various forms. It includes:

- Chastity in marriage. This involves two people being completely faithful to each other – what the Catechism calls 'conjugal chastity'. This faithfulness should be the norm for every Catholic marriage.

- Chastity for widows. For those who have lost a partner, chastity means abstaining from sexual relationships until they remarry. Looking after the welfare of widows was a top priority in early Christian communities.

- Chastity for virgins. Chastity does not come easily to human beings. Human sexual feelings are very strong and, when aroused, almost overwhelming. This is why a deliberate attempt needs to be made to control them – or they will control us. The feelings are most difficult to control through adolescence and the early 20s. By controlling them, a Catholic is being faithful to his or her baptismal vows.

▲ *Many couples find the teachings of the Catholic Church hard to accept in the 21st century.*

Sex outside marriage

Fornication is an old-fashioned word, going back to the Bible, which covers any heterosexual intercourse between people who are not married. From the time of Jesus and Paul onwards, it has always been seen as a serious moral sin. This is because the only proper place for sexual relationships is within marriage.

There are four reasons for this:

1. The teaching from Genesis, underlined by Jesus, is of two people 'becoming one flesh', which is taken to mean united in sexual intercourse in marriage. Such unity of body, mind and spirit cannot take place outside of marriage.

2. Sex outside marriage risks creating unwanted babies. Cutting this risk down by using unnatural contraceptives is unacceptable to Roman Catholics.

3. Sex outside marriage cheapens and trivialises one of God's greatest gifts to the human race. It is God who has decreed that sex should be confined to marriage. This is the only relationship in which two people promise to be faithful to each other forever.

4. Sex outside of marriage excludes the sacrament that was intended by Christ to protect and make marriage, and sexual intercourse, holy.

Adultery

READ: John 8.1–11. Adultery is sexual intercourse between a married person and someone who is not his or her spouse. Under the law given to Moses by God in the Old Testament, adultery was punishable by death. Jesus adopted a much more humane and understanding attitude when he was confronted by a woman accused of adultery, although he still condemned adultery (Mark 10.19). The Roman Catholic Church teaches that adultery is contrary to the seventh commandment – 'You shall not commit adultery' – and breaks the trust which must exist between a husband and wife in a marriage that has been blessed by God.

TASKS

1. Explain the meaning of each of the following:

   a. chastity   **b.** virginity   **c.** extra-marital sex   **d.** adultery

2. Explain why the Catholic Church is opposed to sex before marriage.

3. On what basis does the Church argue that marriage is still the only proper place for sex to take place?

❋ DISCUSSION POINT

Do you think it is realistic to encourage young people to wait for sex until they are married in the 21st century?

21 THE CATHOLIC TEACHING ON MARRIAGE

When a couple marry in a Catholic Church their union is blessed and sealed by God. God establishes their 'marriage bond' in such a way that the relationship between two baptised Catholics is permanent. The married love ('conjugal love') that grows between them involves a total commitment in which bodies, feelings, minds and spirits are united. For the marriage to be successful three characteristics must be present:

1. Indissolubility

The Catholic Church, following the teaching of the New Testament and 2000 years of its own tradition, believes that a marriage can never be dissolved. The couple share a relationship that is designed by God to grow throughout their lives together. The Church, through its common faith and its celebration of the Eucharist, provides the necessary means for this to happen.

This unity of purpose between husband and wife can only grow in a marriage where both are truly equal. This is why **monogamy** is the only kind of relationship that the Church can support.

▲ The Catholic Church believes that a marriage should always be open to the possibility of new life.

2. Faithfulness (fidelity)

By its very nature, conjugal love requires that a couple must be absolutely faithful to each other. This is a direct consequence of the vows that they make to each other when they marry. You will find out more about this in unit 22. The happiness of the couple and the welfare of their children depend on this faithfulness.

This requirement is not surprising. The closest parallel to the relationship between Christ and his Church is that between a husband and wife. Just as Christ expects total faithfulness from each member of the Church, so both husband and wife should be able to expect it from each other. If a couple find this very difficult they must rely on God's love to help them.

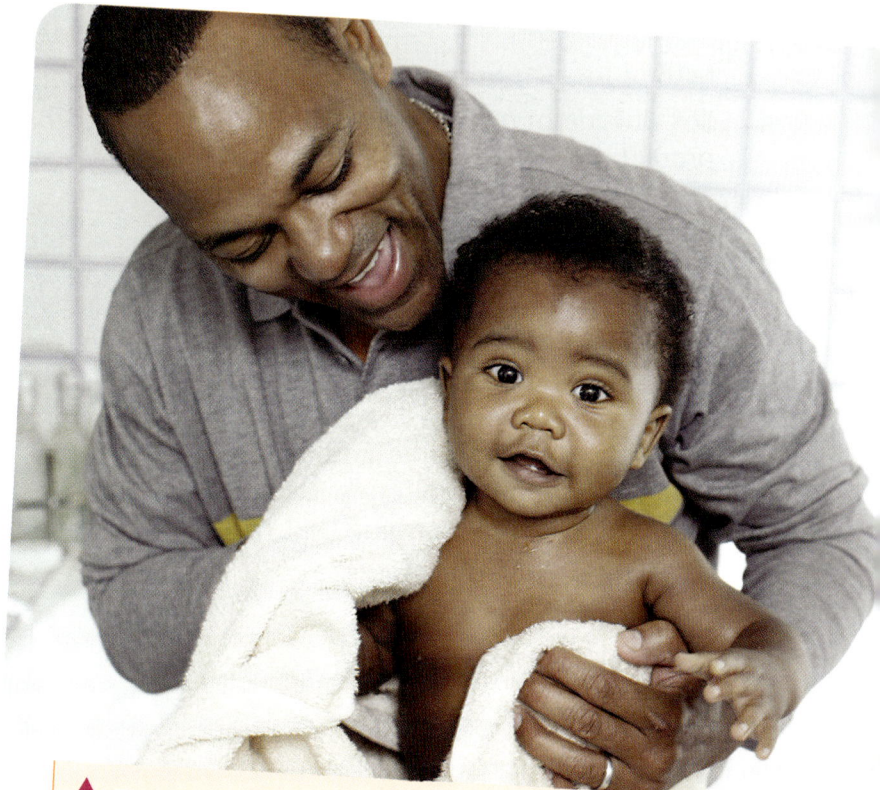

All of the other Christian Churches would agree with the teaching of the Catholic Church so far, although they have all now come to terms with divorce. They agree that almost all couples set out thinking, and believing, that their marriage will last. Sadly, though, this does not happen in many cases and the Church has a part to play helping those who are battered and bruised by the experience.

3. An openness to fertility

This can be a problem in a 'mixed marriage', when a Catholic marries someone from another Christian tradition. As we saw in unit 16, the Catholic Church is totally opposed to all artificial methods of contraception while the other Christian Churches do not share this belief. By always keeping their marriage open to the possibility of new life, Catholics believe that a couple are sharing in God's work of creation.

Children are God's supreme gift to a marriage. They bring much happiness to a husband and wife. This happiness increases considerably if a couple sees their children grow up to be believing Catholics. Even if only one partner in a marriage is a Catholic, the Church teaches that all children should be brought up in the faith.

There are, of course, many couples who are not blessed with children because either the man or the woman is infertile. You can see how the Catechism deals with this problem in extract A:

> **A** *" …[they can] have a conjugal life full of meaning, in both human and Christian terms. Their marriage can radiate a fruitfulness of charity, of hospitality and of sacrifice. "*
> *(CCC 1654)*

TASKS

1. What do Catholics believe to be the purpose of marriage?
2. "A Catholic wedding service gives the best possible start to a couple setting out on their married lives together." Do you agree with this comment? Give your reasons for your answer, showing that you have thought about more than one point of view.

✳ DISCUSSION POINT

Do you think it better if one Catholic marries another?

22 THE CATHOLIC MARRIAGE CEREMONY

> **A** **"**The love of man and woman is made holy in the sacrament of marriage, and becomes the mirror of your everlasting love.**"**
> *(The Preface of the Wedding Mass)*

The quotation in extract A summarises what marriage is for Catholics and what the sacrament of marriage is for. Marriage is a solemn contract between a man and a woman who love each other. The contract is made holy in the sacrament. The ceremony of marriage is basically very simple and will, ideally, take place with a celebration of the Mass.

The Catholic marriage service

The priest welcomes the bride and the groom before the ceremony begins. This is to show the couple that the whole congregation shares in their joy on this happy occasion. After the Mass begins, the priest invites the whole congregation to join in the celebrations.

There is a homily at a **Wedding Mass**. The priest talks to the couple about the meaning of Christian marriage. He explains how a married couple can grow closer to God through their shared love for each other. He also talks about the responsibilities of marriage. The priest then directs three questions at the couple to make sure that they understand what they are doing:

> **"**Have you come to give yourself to each other, freely and without reservation? Will you love and honour each other for life?
> Will you accept children lovingly from God?**"**

The Roman Catholic Church teaches that if a couple deliberately set out to make their marriage childless, then it is not valid in the sight of God.

The vows and the ring

As the couple make their vows to each other, the service becomes a sacrament. Each says in turn:

> **B** **"**I [name] do take thee [name] to be my lawful wedded wife/husband, to have and to hold from this day forward, for better, for worse, for richer, for poorer, in sickness and in health, to love and to cherish, till death us do part.**"**

The rings are blessed and the bridegroom places one on the woman's finger, offering it as a sign of his love and faithfulness to her in the name of the Father, the Son and the Holy Spirit. The couple have promised to give themselves to each other faithfully and exclusively. The ring is now a token of that promise.

The marriage (nuptial) blessing

The ideas in the blessing bring out two important themes in Catholic marriage:

1. A husband's human love for his wife is a model of the love that Christ has for his people – the Church.
2. Marriage is a relationship based on a faithfulness that is there for all to see.

It is a civil requirement that the Marriage Register has to be signed by the couple and a witness. A marriage certificate is given. The priest may be the authorised registrar. If not, a registrar has to be present.

TASKS

1. Describe the role performed by a priest at the wedding ceremony.
2. Why are the rings important in the wedding ceremony and what do they symbolise?
3. What are the wedding vows?
4. In his homily, a priest explains the nature and the responsibilities of a Christian marriage. Suggest two points that you think a priest might make in his homily.

▼ *Catholics believe that marriage is a sacrament that will be a constant source of blessing to them throughout their married lives together.*

23 CHRISTIANS AND DIVORCE

There is a sharp disagreement between the Catholic Church and the other Christian Churches over divorce. While the Catholic Church does not allow divorce, it is reluctantly accepted by the other Christian Churches. Among these Churches, however, there are disagreements over the remarriage of divorced people in church.

The Catholic Church and divorce

According to the Catechism there are two 'offences' against the dignity of marriage:

1. **Adultery**. Adultery is a serious sin against God and is condemned in both the Old and New Testaments:

- The prophets in the Old Testament put adultery on the same level as idolatry – and there was no greater sin than that.

- Christ went even further and condemned not only adultery but also lustful thoughts as 'adultery of the heart'.

2. **Divorce**. The Roman Catholic Church does not recognise divorce because:

- Christ taught that God's original intention was that the marriage contract should be unbreakable. Extract A shows the clear attitude of the Catechism to divorce.

> **A** *...the marriage bond has been established by God himself in such a way that a marriage concluded and consummated between baptised persons can never be dissolved.*
> (CCC 1640)

- Divorce is a grave offence against natural law. It breaks a totally binding contract entered into by two people 'in the sight of God'.

- Divorce is immoral because it harms the spouse who is deserted by his or her partner; children suffer greatly from the separation of their parents and society suffers because divorce spreads like a plague encouraging others to take the same route.

Although the Catholic Church does not grant divorces it does, in exceptional circumstances, grant an annulment. The effect of this is to say that the marriage never officially existed. This can be granted if it can be shown that:

- One of the partners did not agree to the marriage in the first place.

- One spouse did not understand the full implications of marrying.

- The marriage was never consummated – sexual intercourse did not take place.

- One partner did not intend to keep the marriage vows or was not baptised at the time.

- One partner withheld important information at the time of marriage.

Other Christian Churches and divorce

Most non-Catholic Churches allow divorced people to remarry in church although this is up to the local priest or **minister**. If they have a strong moral objection to divorce they can refuse to remarry someone in their church. The couple, however, are then free to find someone who will marry them. Many Churches offer a church blessing to a couple where one has been divorced after they marry in a civil wedding.

Many non-Catholic Christians do object to divorce. They cannot see how the life-long vows of faithfulness to someone else can be made more than once in a person's lifetime. Others, though, are prepared to support someone who has been divorced and now wishes to remarry on two main grounds:

1. They believe in a God who forgives. They know the great trauma that the break-up of a marriage brings and will support anyone who is trying to find happiness.

2. The teaching of the New Testament is not as clear on divorce as some people claim. Although on one occasion Jesus appeared to rule out divorce entirely, on another he appeared to allow it if fornication (adultery) had taken place (Matthew 19.9).

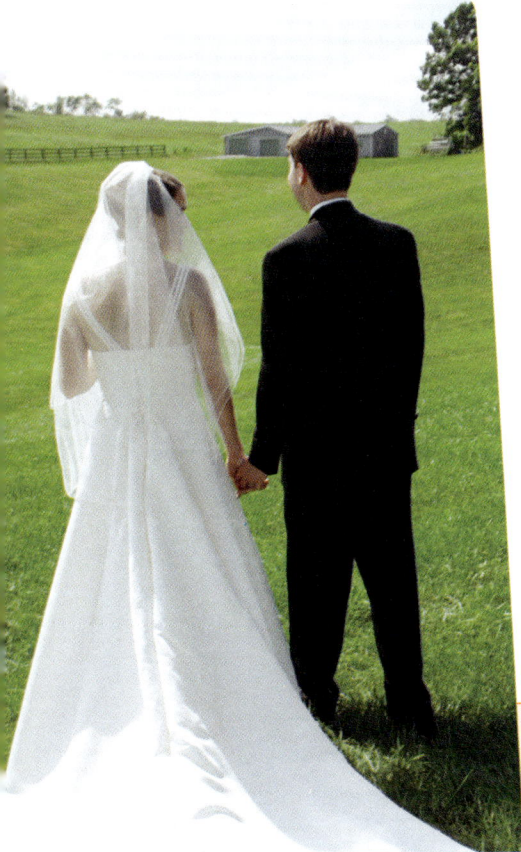

◄ *The Christian Church deplores the number of failing marriages that we have in the 21st century.*

TASKS

1. What is the clear attitude of the Catholic Church to divorce – and why?
2. Why do some Christians believe that while divorce is always regrettable it has to be accepted?
3. "The Catholic Church teaches that divorce is always wrong and unacceptable." Do you agree with this comment? Give some reasons for your answer, showing that you have thought about more than one point of view,

✳ DISCUSSION POINT

**The Catholic Church takes a very strong line against divorce.
Do you agree with it?**

24 FAMILY LIFE – THE FACTS

In our society, as in almost every other, family life is the basic building block on which everything is built. The form it takes may vary, but the family is found everywhere because it meets the basic needs of people better than anything else.

Four definitions

When you are talking about the family there are four important definitions that you must know:

1. The nuclear family. This is the most common family arrangement in this country and other Western countries. It consists of a mother, a father and their biological children. In the nuclear family only two generations live together under the same roof, although grandparents may sometimes share family life as well. When the children grow up, they move away to live and eventually start a nuclear family of their own.

2. The extended family. This is the family reflected in the Bible and still to be found in much of the world, particularly Africa and India, today. This means a family that includes several generations of relatives, such as grandparents, aunts and uncles all living under the same roof or nearby.

3. The re-constituted family. This describes the situation where one or both adults in a family have been married before and sometimes bring children of their own into the new relationship.

4. The dysfunctional family. This is a family where relationships between members have broken down and none of the roles are clear.

Family arrangements

About 50% of people in this country are part of a nuclear family. The remainder live in a variety of different family arrangements including:

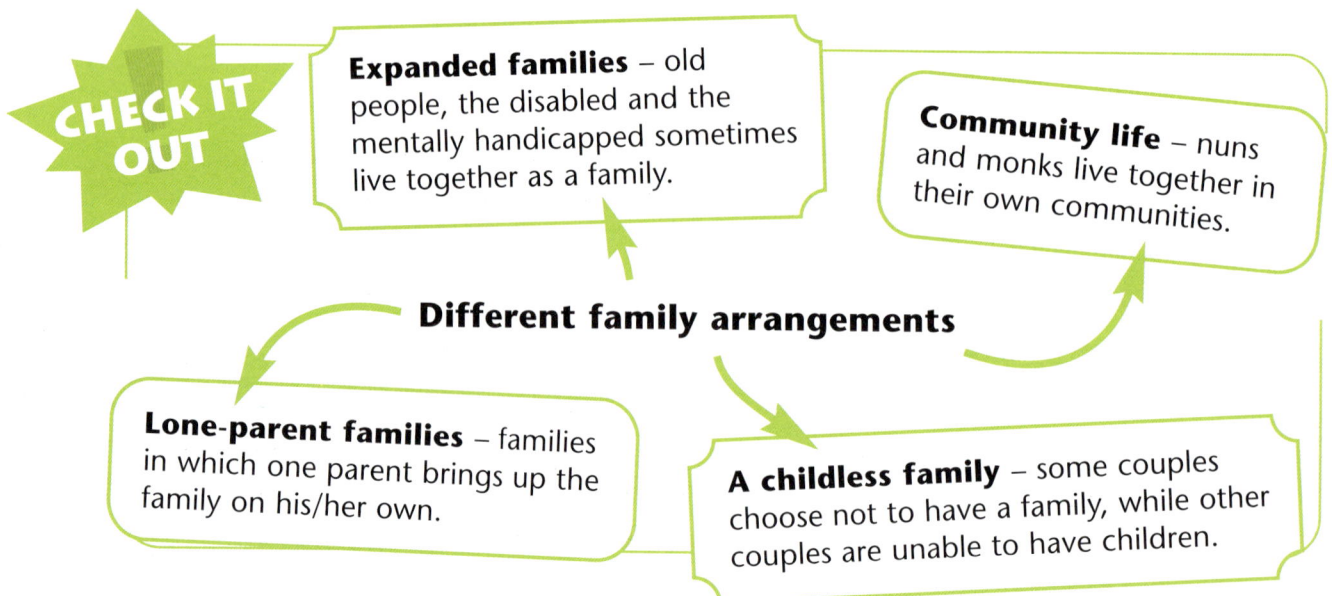

CHECK IT OUT

Expanded families – old people, the disabled and the mentally handicapped sometimes live together as a family.

Community life – nuns and monks live together in their own communities.

Different family arrangements

Lone-parent families – families in which one parent brings up the family on his/her own.

A childless family – some couples choose not to have a family, while other couples are unable to have children.

Christians believe that family life is the best way of looking after the most vulnerable people in society.

The importance of family life

Most people, including Christians, feel that family life is very important for everyone. There are five main reasons for this:

1. We gain our sense of identity from our family – our physical characteristics, name, values and so on. If a child is adopted he or she will not, of course, inherit the genetic characteristics of his or her parents.

2. It teaches us what behaviour is and is not acceptable – a process called 'socialisation'. This prepares us for the roles that we will play as we grow up – including those of being mothers and fathers. It is from our parents that we learn what is right and wrong.

3. It provides us with our first experiences of 'bonding' – with our parents, brothers, sisters and other relatives. We learn how to give and receive love as well as discover how to deal with our strongest emotions – especially those of anger and excitement.

4. Family life is the way that society looks after its most vulnerable members – especially the very young and the very old.

5. Living in a family is the way that those with strong religious beliefs try to pass them on to their children. The Catholic Church stresses that this is a very important reason for family life.

TASKS

1. **a.** What are the main functions of a family?

   b. What are the differences between a nuclear and an extended family?

2. "A family has a much better chance of staying together if it worships together." Do you agree with this comment? Give reasons for your answer, showing that you have thought about more than one point of view.

25 CATHOLICS AND FAMILY LIFE

The first people that we relate to in life are our parents, while our brothers and sisters are our first friends. This means that our most important early experiences take place within the family. This is why the Catechism refers to the family as 'the domestic church' since it is within the family that Catholics have their first experience of belonging to a Christian community. Jesus learned this from Mary and Joseph, his parents, as part of the Holy Family.

Catholics and family life

Catholics believe that both parents and children have clear responsibilities to each other within family life. Both the New Testament and the Catholic Church teach what those responsibilities are. So:

Parents should:

▲ *Churches of all denominations know that their future health depends on keeping the support of their children and young people when they become adults.*

- Undertake responsibility for meeting the physical needs of their children. In particular they will feed, clothe and provide shelter for them.

- Meet the spiritual needs of their children by being 'the first heralds of faith' and 'ministers of faith' to them. They do this most effectively by living out the Christian life in front of them; setting a good example at all times; taking their children to church regularly and encouraging them to be confirmed when the time is right.

- Help their children to grow in virtue and holiness – a task that is helped immeasurably if they attend 'a truly Christian school'. In a 'mixed marriage' (one between a Catholic and a non-Catholic) the couple are encouraged to agree that the child should be brought up in the Catholic faith. This helps a child to make three of the most important decisions in his or her life:
  - which profession or occupation to follow
  - who to marry and when
  - whether to seriously consider responding to a religious **vocation** – either a calling to the priesthood or a religious order.

Children should:

- Obey and respect their parents as the Bible, particularly the Ten Commandments and the **Apostle** Paul, commands them. Only in this way can children hope to grow in true wisdom and understanding of life. Through respecting their parents, children will also learn to respect others – especially their teachers, employers, older relatives and those who run local and national government.

- Look after their parents when they are no longer able to look after themselves – see extract A. Children must work out just what this should mean in practice – whether they should have them living with them or make an alternative arrangement.

> **A** 66*The fourth commandment reminds grown children of their responsibilities toward their parents. As much as they can, they must give them material and moral support in old age and in times of illness, loneliness or distress.*99
> *(CCC 2218)*

The Church and the upbringing of children

The Church is involved in the task of bringing up children in several ways:

1. By welcoming children at all of its services – especially in the celebration of Mass.

2. By running Catholic schools. It does this in partnership with the State and provides an education that combines all educational needs with a spiritual emphasis.

3. The Church provides training preceding the child's first communion and confirmation.

4. In some churches there are special groups and services to help children understand more about their faith.

5. In most churches there are special youth activities combining sporting, social and spiritual activities.

TASKS

1. What responsibilities does the Catholic Church believe that parents have towards their children?
2. What responsibilities do children have towards their parents?
3. How does the Catholic Church try to support family life?

26 HOMOSEXUALITY – THE FACTS

The facts about homosexuality

The word homosexual comes from two Latin words meaning 'same' and 'sex'. A homosexual is a man or a woman who is sexually attracted to members of his or her own rather than the opposite sex. Although known homosexual activity stretches back at least as far as the Ancient Greeks, the word itself did not enter the English language until 1869. The word 'lesbian' was coined about the same time to describe female homosexuals. This word was taken from the Greek island of Lesbos where, in the 7th century BCE, Sappho expressed her love and adoration of other women through her poetry. In recent years many male homosexuals have preferred to call themselves 'gay' to counter the popular misapprehension that all homosexuals are sad people.

No one knows how many homosexuals there are in the UK. The common estimate is that about one in every 15 people is gay, which would make a total of about four million. Of these, 60% are men and 40% women. Of this number only about 15% are openly gay – having 'come out' – with the vast majority preferring to keep their sexual orientation private, many of whom are married. There is still a great deal of prejudice against homosexuals and many people are homophobic in their attitude towards them.

Homosexuality and the law

Until 1967 it was illegal to engage in male homosexual activity, although no law has ever existed in the UK making female homosexual activity illegal. This possibility was once raised in front of Queen Victoria in the late 19th century and she refused to believe that any member of her sex would do such a thing!

In 1967, homosexual activity among men became legal as long as two conditions were met:

1. All such activity took place in private.
2. Those involved were consenting adults over the age of 21.

The age of consent was further reduced to 18 in 1994. It now stands at 16 – the same age for legal heterosexual activity. This is symbolically important because it means that the law now treats heterosexual and homosexual sex in exactly the same way. From December 2005, homosexuals have been able to enter into a civil partnership that gives them certain legal rights, although the partnership falls far short of being a 'marriage'.

Why are some people homosexual?

It is important to note the following:

1. In the 19th and early 20th centuries, homosexuality was considered to be a disease and was defined in this way in many medical textbooks. This viewpoint is no longer seriously put forward. Doctors now widely agree that people do not choose the homosexual lifestyle – it chooses them. People are born homosexual due to their genetic makeup.

2. When people choose to form homosexual relationships and friendships they are acting in the way that their nature is leading them. An earlier explanation that homosexuals are boys who had strong links with their mothers and weak links with their fathers has now been widely rejected.

3. The reason why so many people keep their homosexuality secret is that many people in society are still homophobic – meaning that they have a deep fear of homosexuality. The most extreme example of homophobia in recent years was the policy of the Nazis who set out to eliminate all homosexuals, along with Jews and gypsies, managing to eliminate more than one million of them.

> ▶ *In almost every church congregation there will be homosexuals but most of them prefer to keep their sexual orientation secret.*

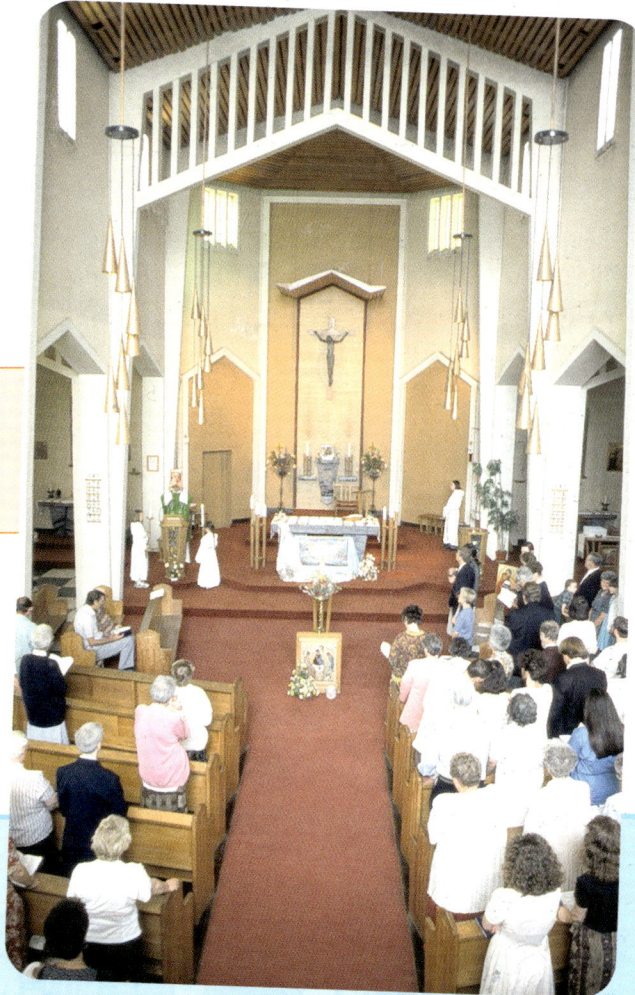

TASKS

1. Write a sentence or two to explain the meaning of:
 a. homosexual
 b. lesbian
 c. gay

2. Describe how male homosexuality became legal in the UK and what the current law says.

✳ DISCUSSION POINT

Do you think the time will come when society treats heterosexuals and homosexuals in exactly the same way?

27 THE CATHOLIC CHURCH AND HOMOSEXUALITY

Although they may not agree in many other areas, the Roman Catholic Church and many Evangelical Protestant groups find themselves agreeing about homosexuality. They both believe that the teaching of the Bible is very clear on the subject:

The teaching of the Bible

The Old Testament

The Old Testament condemns homosexual acts in two places:

- *"You will not have intercourse with a man as you would with a woman. This is a hateful thing [to God]."* (Leviticus 18.22)

- *"The man who has intercourse with a man in the same way as with a woman: they have done a hateful thing together; they will be put to death; their blood will be on their own heads."* (Leviticus 20.13)

As you can see, the penalty for homosexual activity was death.

The New Testament

Jesus made no comment directly about homosexuality, simply saying that the coming together of a man and a woman until they are 'one flesh' is God's ideal for everyone. St Paul, however, roundly condemned sexual relationships between men (extract A). He also condemned homosexuals strongly in 1 Corinthians 6.9–10 at the same time as attacking adulterers, thieves, drunkards, slanderers and swindlers.

> **A** *"That is why God abandoned them to degrading passions: why their women have exchanged natural intercourse for unnatural practices; and the men, in a similar fashion, too, giving up normal relations with women, are consumed with passion for each other, men doing shameful things with men..."*
>
> (Romans 1.26–27)

▶ *Taking part in the celebration of the Mass is one way that Catholics can learn to control their sexual feelings – including homosexual ones.*

These condemnations from the Bible have influenced people's opinions and behaviour throughout the centuries. They have also affected the laws passed relating to homosexual activity in many Western countries, including the UK.

> **B** *"Tradition has always declared that 'homosexual acts are intrinsically disordered'...They close the sexual act to the gift of life... Under no circumstances can they be approved."*
> (CCC 2357)

The teaching of the Catholic Church

As extract B makes very clear, the Catholic Church is totally opposed to homosexual sex between either men or women. This does not mean, however, that it is opposed to homosexuals or that it expects them to change the way that they behave. It accepts that the tendency of a person towards homosexual rather than heterosexual affection is not a sin and so the Church does not condemn it.

Homosexuals are expected to live a life of chastity. This means that they abstain from all homosexual activity. To do this they must control their sexual feelings by using the spiritual activities that the Church offers to give them inner strength:

- by 'disinterested' friendship: friendships that have no sexual overtones;
- by the Sacraments, especially the Eucharist;
- by prayer.

Through using these spiritual gifts, every believer, including homosexuals, can approach the desired state of perfection.

There is also, both within the Catholic Church and outside agencies, counselling help for those people who wish to keep their homosexual feelings under control. The Catholic Church tries to treat individual homosexuals non-judgementally and with great sensitivity.

TASKS

1. Write two paragraphs summing up what the Catholic Church teaches about homosexuality and how it should be dealt with.
2. "I believe that homosexuality is a normal activity and should be accepted as such by the Christian Churches." Do you agree with this comment? Give the reasons for your answer, showing that you have thought about more than one point of view.

❋ DISCUSSION POINT

Are you happy with the view of many Churches, including the Catholic Church, that homosexual orientation is acceptable while homosexual activity is not?

28 OTHER CHRISTIAN CHURCHES AND HOMOSEXUALITY

As we saw in unit 27, there are some Protestant groups who agree with the Roman Catholic Church's position that all homosexual relationships are sinful because they are condemned in the Bible. People who believe this will be found in all the Christian denominations. There are, however, many Protestants who believe that this is a too simplistic view of the Bible and of human sexual behaviour.

1. The Church of England and homosexuality

The question of homosexuality is one that threatens to split the **Anglican Church** wide open. On one side are African Christians who regard homosexuality as one of the most serious moral sins that a believer in God can commit. On the other side are Christians from Western churches who are much more tolerant of homosexuality, yet accept that it falls below God's ideal – that of a committed relationship between a man and a woman. At the moment this issue is unresolved and it is difficult to see what the way forward can be.

In the Western Anglican Churches there is a compromise in place. At the end of a debate in the General Synod of the Church of England in 1987, the conclusion was that a Christian who was a homosexual can accept their sexual orientation if they do not take part in any homosexual activity. This ruling was applied to homosexual priests but not to ordinary members of the congregation. Surveys suggest that as many as one in four priests in the Church of England are gay.

> **A** "We do not reject those who believe that they have more hope of growing in love for God and neighbour with the help of a loving and faithful homophile relationship."
>
> (Church of England Report on Homosexuality)

2. The Methodist Church and homosexuality

The Methodist Church is more positive in its acceptance of homosexual relationships. As you can see in extract B, it describes loving and permanent relationships between homosexual men and between homosexual women as 'appropriate'. It goes on to say that these relationships are 'the Christian way of expressing their sexuality' for homosexuals. There is no suggestion here that a line can be drawn between the sexual orientation of a person and the expression of that preference through sexual behaviour. In other words, if someone is a homosexual they are going to want to have homosexual sex and that is natural.

> **B** 	**"For homosexual men and women permanent relationships characterised by love can be appropriate and the Christian way of expressing their sexuality."**
> *(Methodist Church Report 1979)*

3. Reasons for a liberal approach

The views of the Catholic Church and some Protestant groups against homosexuality can be described as 'conservative'. The views of those who find homosexual behaviour acceptable could be described as 'liberal'. The liberal approach is based on the following arguments:

1. The teaching of the Bible was written for a very different time. Paul, for example, assumed that homosexuals were really heterosexuals who were looking for variety in their sex lives. We now know very differently. In any case, a handful of obscure references in the Bible hardly makes a convincing case. There are many other practices condemned in the Old Testament, such as having sex with a menstruating woman, but no one follows that guidance today.

2. Strong same-sex friendships are referred to in the Bible, such as that between David and Jonathan in the Old Testament, and this is not questioned.

3. Christians believe that the Church should be a community in which people are loved and accepted 'for what they are'. This 'all-inclusive' body, called the Church, must include homosexuals.

4. Too often the Christian Church has been accused, with justification, of being 'homophobic'. Some of its statements and documents over the centuries would support this accusation. This is an attitude that should not be allowed to go unchallenged.

▲ *There are many homosexuals within, and outside, the Church who are far from happy with the way that the Christian Church treats them.*

TASKS

1. a. What divisions are there in the Anglican Church over homosexuality?

 b. Why do you think that this particular issue causes such deep divisions?

2. "Being a Christian and being a homosexual cannot be reconciled. You can be one or the other but not both." Do you agree with this comment? Give reasons for your point of view, showing that you have thought about more than one point of view.

EXAM HELP

In the examination

Make sure that you know about:

MARRIAGE AND DIVORCE

- Changes in modern marriage patterns. Marriages can now take place in any registered building with no religious element. Reduction in the number of people marrying in religious buildings – especially churches. Number of people marrying is in marked decline – couples choosing to cohabit either instead of or before marriage. Considerable increase in the average age for marriage in both men and women. The physical and mental benefits of marriage.

- The grounds for divorce under Divorce Reform Act (1967). The importance of the phrase 'the irretrievable breakdown of a marriage' as the only ground for a divorce. The four ways of proving that a marriage has irretrievably broken down – adultery, intolerable behaviour, separation with both wanting a divorce (two years), separation with one person wanting a divorce (five years); desertion. Single-parent families. The number of children involved in parents' divorce.

- Catholic opposition to all forms of sexual activity outside marriage. The importance of chastity both inside marriage (fidelity) and outside marriage (no fornication or promiscuity). Reasons why marriage is the only place for sexual activity for Catholics – the teaching of the Bible, the risks, cheapens sex and excludes the sacrament of marriage.

- Make sure you know the meaning of marriage, cohabitation, pre-marital sex, promiscuity, adultery.

Sample exam questions

1. **a.** What is cohabitation?

   b. What effect is cohabitation having on the number of couples who are marrying?

2. What are the different ways in which a marriage can be shown to have 'irretrievably' broken down?

3. What is the Catholic teaching about sex outside marriage?

4. What is adultery and what is the attitude of the Catholic Church to it?

5. What does the Catholic Church mean by annulment and why is it important?

MARRIAGE, DIVORCE AND FAMILY LIFE

- The teaching of the Catholic Church on marriage. Conjugal love. The importance of indissolubility in all Catholic marriages rules out the possibility of divorce. The importance of the Church's Sacraments in providing the spiritual strength for a marriage. The importance of faithfulness between the husband and wife and to the vows that are taken. The parallel between marriage and the relationship between Christ and the Church. Acceptance of divorce within other Christian Churches. Openess to fertility is an important mark of a Catholic marriage – total rejection by the Church of artificial methods of contraception. Children are the supreme gift of God. The importance of children being brought up in the faith. The problems of mixed marriages – marriages between Catholics and non-Catholics.

- The Catholic marriage service. Marriage is a sacrament in the Catholic Church. The three questions asked of the bride and groom. The importance of the vows. The ring as a symbol of everlasting love. The nuptial blessing – human love as a token of Christ's love for the Church. The importance of faithfulness.

- The Catholic Church and divorce. The two offences against the dignity of marriage – adultery and divorce. Reasons why the Catholic Church is totally opposed to divorce. Annulment – the meaning of and the grounds on which it can be granted. The teaching of the other Christian Churches and divorce. The two opinions held by non-Catholic Christians. The problem caused by remarriage in non-Catholic churches.

- The four definitions of the family – nuclear, extended, reconstructed and dysfunctional families and the meaning of each. The different family arrangements – expanded community, lone-parent and childless. The importance of family life – our sense of identity, morals, our first experience of bonding and inheriting religious beliefs from parents. The parents' responsibilities in family life – meeting the physical, emotional and spiritual needs of their children. The children's responsibilities in family life – obedience, respect and caring for parents in later life. The Church and the upbringing of children.

Sample exam questions

1. What do Catholics believe the purpose of marriage to be and what is the Church's teaching on it?

2. "Going through a Catholic wedding service makes an important contribution to making that marriage work." Do you agree with this comment? Give reasons for your answer, showing that you have thought about two different points of view.

3. "It is impossible for a Catholic to think of divorcing his or her partner even if that marriage is not working." Do you agree with this comment? Give reasons for your answer, showing that you have thought about more than one point of view.

EXAM HELP

HOMOSEXUALITY

- The facts about homosexuality and the meaning of the words 'homosexual' and 'lesbian'. Examples of homosexuality in the community. Homosexuality and the law – changes that have taken place. The reason why some people are homosexual. The teaching of the Bible on homosexuality. The teaching of the Catholic Church on homosexuality. The Church of England and homosexuality. The Methodists and homosexuality. The reasons for a liberal approach to homosexuality.

Sample exam questions

1. What does the law allow in the UK as far as homosexual behaviour is concerned and when was the law changed?
2. Why are some people homosexual?
3. What is the teaching of the Old and New Testaments about homosexuality?
4. Sum up the teaching of the Catholic Church on homosexuality.
5. What is the teaching of Christian Churches, other than the Catholic Church, on homosexuality?
6. Do you agree that it is impossible for a person to be a Christian and a practising homosexual? Give reasons for your answer showing that you have thought about more than one point of view.

Social harmony

In this topic you will find out about:

- the growth towards equal rights for men and women – the areas where inequality remains;
- the teaching of the Bible about the rights of men and women;
- the treatment of the sexes in the Christian Church;
- the development of Britain as a multi-ethnic society;
- the Catholic Church and racial harmony;
- the growth of Britain as a multi-faith community;
- the relationship between Christianity and other religions.

KEY WORDS

Discrimination Prejudice in action, acting as if some people are inferior to others because of their sex, colour or class.

Equality Everyone being equal and given equal opportunities whatever their race, sex or class.

Multi-ethnic society A society that contains people from different races and countries living together.

Multi-faith society A society in which there are people who belong to many different religions.

Prejudice Considering some people to be inferior because of their sex, race or class.

Racism Treating a person or group of people as inferior because of their country of origin or skin colour.

Religious freedom A society in which people are free to practise their religion without any hindrance.

Religious pluralism A society that accepts there are many religions and that all should have the freedom to worship.

Sexism Discrimination directed against someone because of their sex, whether male or female.

29 EQUAL RIGHTS FOR MEN AND WOMEN?

Of every 100 babies born in the UK, 52 will be male and forty-eight female. At the moment of birth both sexes are treated equally, but from that moment onwards the situation changes. The expectations that we have of boys and girls are frequently different and this can be seen in the words that we often use to describe them. While boys may be described as strong, tough or 'little rascals', girls are described as pretty, sweet or 'angelic'. These descriptions reveal our expectations.

As children grow up, the same basic expectations remain. Females are expected to be more caring and to demonstrate this in the way they behave. Males are expected to be forceful and successful at whatever career they follow. As they grow up they will discover that they have come into a very unequal world. 'Equality' means that the two sexes are treated equally and given equal opportunities in life.

Sexual equality today

There are important inequalities between men and women in the UK today. Here are some of them:

- Women are likely to do more of the housework – even if they work full-time. They are much more likely to give up full-time work to look after any children that are born.

- Women are more likely to be the victims of domestic violence.

- After a divorce, women are much more likely than men to be granted full custody of the children, so affecting their chances of returning to work.

- Educationally, girls are likely to outperform boys at GCSE.

- The salary levels of women are significantly lower than those of men. On average, women earn 75% of what men earn. Nine out of every ten part-time workers are women. Women are much more likely to be in the lower-paid occupations.

- Women are more likely than men to experience poverty. One of the poorest groups in society is 'single mothers' and there are about 1 200 000 of these in the UK.

- Nearly all of Britain's six million 'carers' are female. This form of work is known as 'invisible' as it is generally unpaid, although some state benefits are now paid to carers. Many of these women would like to return to work but there is no one to look after the people for whom they are caring.

- In politics there are far fewer women than men in Parliament making the laws.

> **A** 66*Times have changed. Today women no longer expect to be just a mother and a housewife – they have aspirations. They can see just what they would like to achieve. Although they can see where they would like to go, however, they rarely get there. Women today face a glass ceiling – they can see the top jobs but they cannot get there.*99
> (The Guardian, October 1998)

The law and inequality

'Sexism' means that a person is discriminated against because of his or her sex – whether male or female. 'Prejudice' refers to the attitudes that people have towards those who are different from them and 'discrimination' occurs when that prejudice is put into practice. Until 1882, women in the UK could not own property in their own name and it was only in 1892 that they were allowed to vote in local elections and stand as councillors. In 1918, women over the age of thirty were allowed to vote in parliamentary elections and ten years later this age was reduced to twenty-one – the same age as men at the time. At the same time women were allowed to stand as MPs.

In 1970, for the first time, it was made illegal for women to be paid less than men for doing the same job of work (the Equal Pay Act). In 1975 it was made illegal to discriminate against women in the workplace because of their sex (the Sex Discrimination Act). At the same time it became illegal to discriminate against a woman because she was married or pregnant. However, while most people now accept this principle, in practice it remains very difficult to bring about true equality. How do you prove that a woman lost a job because she is a woman?

▶ *Is this an example of genuine equality in action?*

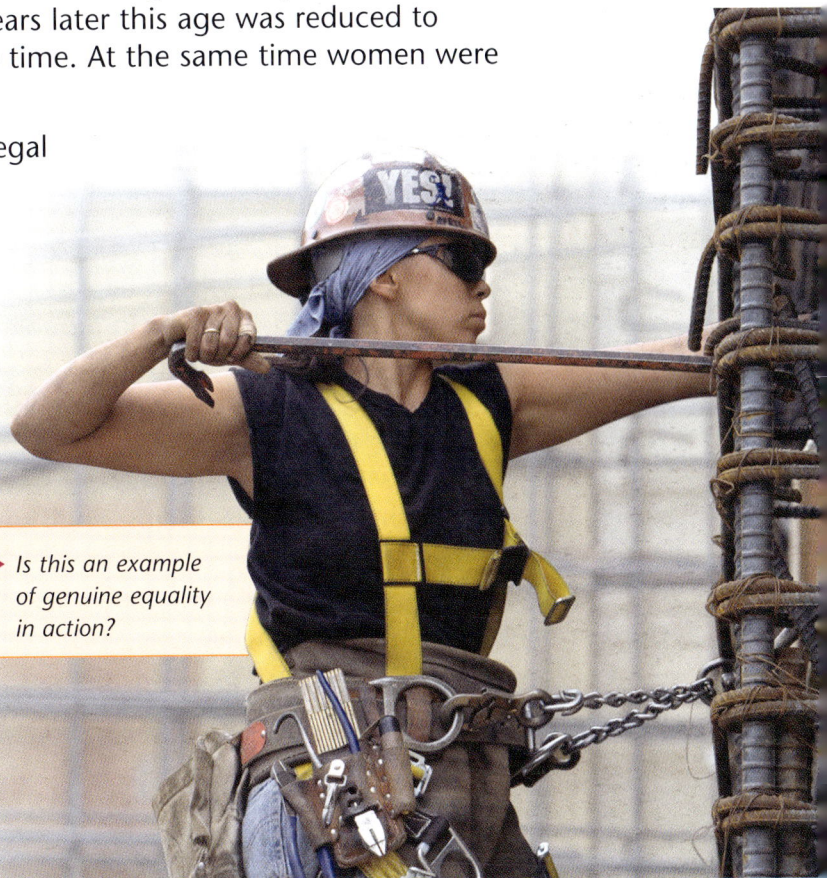

TASKS

1. Write down five pieces of evidence to support the argument that woman have gained many rights since the beginning of the 20th century.

2. Write down eight pieces of evidence that indicate that men and women are still treated differently and given different opportunities.

✳ DISCUSSION POINTS

a. Are there areas of life where you think that boys and girls – men and women – have a genuine equality with each other?

b. Are there areas of life in which you think that men and women are still treated unequally – and what do you think should be done about it?

30 MEN AND WOMEN IN THE BIBLE

It is very important to realise that the Bible was written at a very different time, and in very different social circumstances to those that exist today. It is true to point out, however, that there are two very different lines of teaching found in the Bible about the role of women in society.

Men and women are equal

There is a strong element of teaching in the Bible that suggests that men and women are equal. There are several examples to show that Jesus treated men and women equally:

- He surprised his disciples by speaking openly to a Samaritan woman in public. A Jewish man would not be expected to speak to a strange woman in a public place (John 4).

- Many women were among his followers, although none of them were among the twelve disciples. It was these women who stayed with Jesus during the last few hours of his life on the cross after all of his disciples had deserted him (Matthew 27.55).

- Jesus spent time teaching in the Court of the Women in the Temple in **Jerusalem** (Matthew 21.23–22.14).

- Jesus appeared to women first of all after he had risen from the dead (Matthew 28.1–8), although the women were not initially believed when they passed the message on to his disciples. In fact the witness of women was not generally believed and they were not allowed to give evidence in a court of law.

- Speaking of the Christian community, Paul insisted that everyone was equal in it – Jew and Greek, slave and freeman, male and female "for you are all one in Christ Jesus" (Galatians 3.28).

- Speaking to the Christians in Philippi, Paul clearly counted many women among his co-workers. At the same time he was very concerned that two of them, Euodia and Syntyche, had fallen out with each other (Philippians 4.2).

▲ *Paul held Eve responsible for bringing sin into the world.*

Men and women are unequal and different

There is a strong element in the Bible's teaching to suggest that men and women are not equal:

- In the story of creation in Genesis it is the man (Adam) who is created first before the woman (Eve) is created out of his rib. It is the woman who commits the first sin and who then suggests that the man should do the same thing. This is the source of the belief in **original sin** and it was the woman who was to blame. The woman is punished by having to bear children, with all its pain, for the rest of her life.

- Paul expected women to be subservient to their husbands in every married relationship. He compared the relationship between a husband and wife to that between Christ and the Church – one is very clearly expected to be subservient to the other (extract A).

> **A** *"Wives should be subject to their husbands as to the Lord, since, as Christ is head of the Church and saves the whole body, so is a husband the head of his wife..."*
>
> *(Ephesians 5.22–23).*

- Timothy was the young leader of a church who asked the older Paul for advice. He wrote two letters to Timothy. In one of them he taught that no woman should be allowed to have authority in the Church or even to speak in public. The reason that he gave was that Adam was created first and led astray in the Garden of Eden through his wife's weakness – and not the other way around (extract B). This showed how weak women were and that they should not be allowed to have any authority over men in the Church or to teach them.

> **B** *"...women are to wear suitable clothes and be dressed quietly and modestly... During instruction, a woman should be quiet and respectful. I give no permission for a woman to teach or to have authority over a man. A woman ought to be quiet..."*
>
> *(1 Timothy 2.9–12)*

TASKS

1. What teachings are there in the Bible to suggest that men and women are equal?
2. What teachings are there in the Bible to suggest that men and women should not be treated as equal?

✳ DISCUSSION POINT

Can you think of any reasons for the teaching of St Paul that women should not have any authority over them or teach?

31 MEN, WOMEN AND THE CHRISTIAN CHURCHES

The Roman Catholic Church and women

The Catholic Church teaches that men and women have been created by God to be absolutely equal but also to be different with other roles to perform. 'Being man' and 'being woman' are states that have been willed by God and both carry the dignity that this brings. Man and woman are born with one and the same dignity 'in the image of God'. By being male and female they reflect the Creator's wisdom and goodness. This equality between male and female is reflected in the marriage service as extract A shows:

> **A** **"**May her husband put his trust in her and recognise that she is his equal and the heir with him in the life of grace.**"**
> (Catholic Marriage Service)

The Catechism takes us back to God's original intention for man and women when he created them. He created them together and willed each for the other. It quotes the book of Genesis – "It is not good that the man should be alone. I will make a helper fit for him" – to show that God never intended that men or women should live alone. Man and woman 'were made for each other'.

> **B** **"**...he created them to be a communion of persons, in which each can be a 'helpmate' to the other, for they are equal as persons ('bone of my bones...') and complementary as masculine and feminine.**"**
> (CCC 372)

It is very important, therefore, that both men and women should feel equally valued by the Church. They should be given equal opportunities for service although it must be recognised that women might feel more at home in some avenues of service than others. Working among children in the parish, helping and visiting the sick and poor, and comforting those who are grieving the loss of a loved one are some of the areas for which women are particularly suited.

The Protestant Churches and women

There are many Protestant Churches, especially those of an Evangelical persuasion, that teach that the Bible lays down unchangeable principles for the way that women should behave in church. The Brethren movement, for instance, insists that women have their heads covered in church and that they remain silent at all times. It goes a stage further in that family relationships are affected, as church members accept that the wife must always bow to the authority of her husband. This is based on the Bible:

- The teaching in Genesis 2 that Adam was created before Eve and that she was made out of his rib.

- The choice of Jesus that only men could be included among his disciples.

- The teaching of Paul that women must accept the authority of their husband within the home and must remain silent in church.

Most Protestant Churches, however, accept that men and women are equal in all respects. They do not teach that the husband has authority over his wife in the home or that women are unable to have a teaching role in the Church. All major Protestant Churches allow women to be priests or ministers and so to have a leadership role within the Church. They believe that their approach is equally faithful to the teaching of the Bible:

- The basic teaching in the creation story is that God created the first man and woman to be equal with each other.

- The teaching found in St Paul, that in Christ there is neither male nor female as "all are one in Christ Jesus".

- The attitude of Jesus towards women in the Gospels.

▼ *Women are admitted to positions of leadership in all Protestant Churches.*

TASKS

1. How does the Catholic Church see the role of women in the Church in the modern world?

2. What is the attitude of the different Protestant Churches towards the role of women in the modern world?

3. "There should not be any role closed to women in the modern Church." Do you agree? Give reasons for your answer, showing that you have thought about more than one point of view.

32 BRITAIN AS A MULTI-ETHNIC SOCIETY

A ❝If a stranger lives with you in your land, do not molest him. You must count him as one of your own countrymen and love him as yourself...❞
(Leviticus 19.33–34)

Immigration into Britain

People have been coming from other countries to settle in Britain for centuries. Roman, Viking and Norman invaders all intermingled with local inhabitants, most of whom were invaders themselves. These 'incomers' have left their mark on Britain's language, culture and way of life. Over the centuries, there have been two main reasons why many people have settled in Britain:

- *Reason 1.* To find work. During the early 19th century, immigrants, mainly from Ireland, moved to Britain to find work – usually building houses, roads and railways. They settled permanently in towns such as Liverpool and Glasgow.
  Then, in the 1950s and 1960s, different Governments encouraged people from the Caribbean, India and Pakistan to immigrate to Britain. They came because the Second World War had robbed the country of a large section of its labour force.

- *Reason 2.* To escape persecution. It was for this reason that many Jews and Poles fled to Britain before, during and after the Second World War. Boat people from Vietnam and Kurds from Turkey also arrived during the 1970s and the 1980s for the same reason.

Many immigrants found it difficult to find accommodation so they settled in the poorer parts of cities such as London, Manchester and Birmingham. Today, there are about 4.6 million non-white people in Britain, some 7.9% of the total population. Tough laws were passed in the 1970s and 1980s to reduce the number of immigrants but in recent years this has become a bitter issue again.

People from different ethnic groups are protected by the law against discrimination in the workplace but there is evidence for believing that it still occurs.

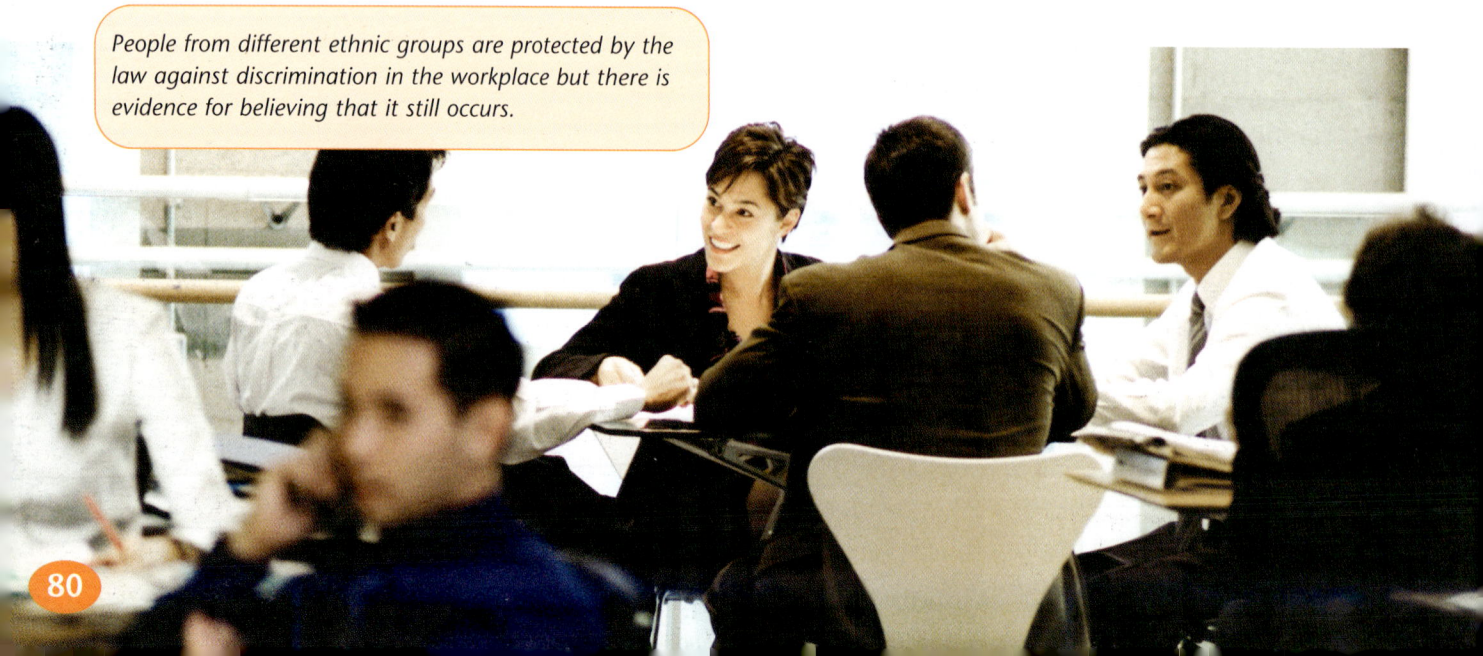

> **B** **"***The Church reproves, as foreign to the mind of Christ, any discrimination against men... on the basis of their race, colour, condition in life or religion.***"**
> *(Second Vatican Council)*

The law and race relations

Ever since immigration began in earnest at the end of the Second World War, immigrants, especially black immigrants, have faced harassment, abuse and violence. The Race Relations Act (1976) was a major step forward to protect black people in Britain. It seems to have made little difference, however, to the attitudes of people. The British Social Attitudes Survey of 1998 found that:

- 35% of people interviewed described themselves as being 'racially prejudiced';
- 66% of people from ethnic minorities who were interviewed were convinced that they had been denied a job or a place to live because of their skin colour.

Christians and race

Later, in unit 33, we will look at the example of Jesus and the teaching of the Bible about racial prejudice and discrimination. This will include a study of the most well-known parable told by Jesus – that of the Good Samaritan. This story has a powerful point to make about discrimination. Here, we make the observation that when large numbers of immigrants came to live in Britain in the 1950s and the 1960s, the largely all-white churches did not give them a warm welcome. Instead, black people set up their own churches, which have flourished, while many other churches have declined.

TASKS

1. Describe two reasons why immigrants have arrived in the UK in the past.
2. **a.** Why was the Race Relations Act of 1976 necessary?
   b. What did the Race Relations Act of 1976 set out to do?

✳ DISCUSSION POINT

Do you think from your experience that there is much racial intolerance among young people?

33 THE CATHOLIC CHURCH AND RACIAL HARMONY

Catholics believe that God created all human beings to be equal – whether young or old, male or female, black or white. God does not treat any human being as more important than any other. Prejudice, the belief that one group is inferior to another, is totally alien to the teaching of the Bible and to the teaching of the Catholic Church.

> **A** *"Created in the image of the one God and equally endowed with rational souls, all men have the same nature and the same origin… Every form of social or cultural discrimination in fundamental personal rights on the grounds of sex, race, colour, social conditions, language or religion, must be curbed and eradicated as incompatible with God's design."*
> (CCC 1934–35)

The teaching of the Bible and prejudice

During his lifetime Jesus did many things to show that he had no sympathy with prejudice in any shape or form. The same message is found throughout the New Testament:

1. The parable of the Good Samaritan (Luke 10.29–37). Jesus had already explained to a questioner that there were two basic commandments – that people should love God with all their heart, soul and mind and that they should love their neighbour as themselves. The questioner then wondered just who their neighbours were and Jesus told the parable of the Good Samaritan in reply.

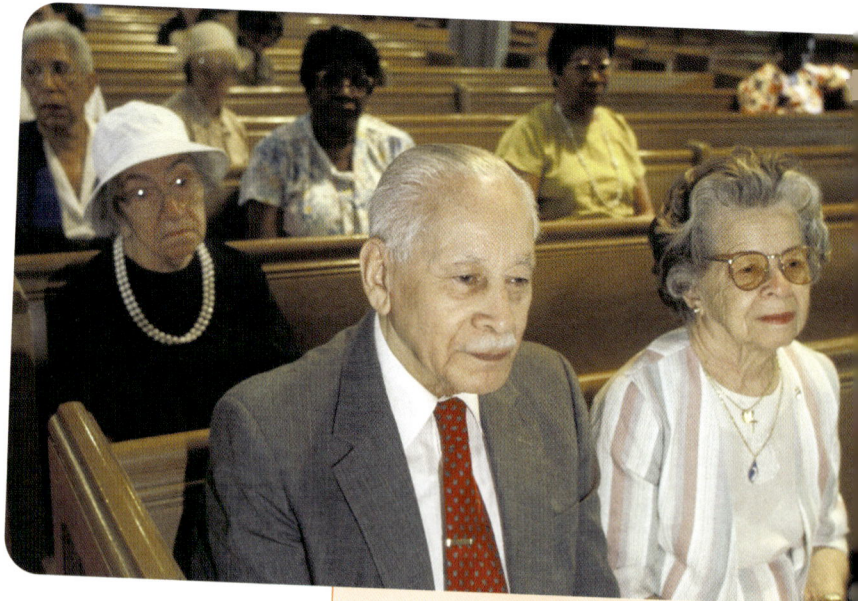

▲ *There is no room in Catholic worship for any form of prejudice or discrimination.*

The background to the parable was the intense hatred between Jews and Samaritans that had gone on for centuries. Yet, when a Jew was set upon by thieves on a desolate road, it was a Samaritan and not another Jew who came to his help. His listeners would have understood the point that Jesus was making: our neighbour is anyone who needs our help, irrespective of his or her age, sex, colour, religion or nationality.

2. Several incidents in the life of Jesus showed that he treated all people as equal. He spoke in public to a Samaritan woman, although this was something that men never did (John 4). He healed the servant of a Roman officer and commented very favourably on the officer's faith (Luke 7). A black man from North Africa, Simon from Cyrene, was compelled to carry the cross of Jesus to his place of execution when he was too weak to do so himself (Luke 23.26).

3. Jesus seemed to imply at the beginning of his ministry that he had only been sent by God to help Jews to enter his kingdom. Soon, however, non-Jews (**Gentiles**) were being welcomed as well but the early apostles, after the ascension of Jesus into heaven, found this difficult to accept. **Peter**, the leader of the early Church, was one of them until he had a vision in which a sheet had been let down from heaven (Acts 10.9–23). In the sheet were all kinds of animals that Jews were forbidden to eat. A voice from heaven told Peter to kill and eat. When Peter replied that nothing impure had ever crossed his lips the voice of God reminded him that nothing created by God could ever be described as 'impure'. It is totally unacceptable to God that any animal, or group of people, should be treated as less acceptable. God created all forms of life and they are all equally important to him. In the kingdom of God, that Jesus came to build, there is no room for any prejudice or discrimination.

> **B** 66 '*I now really understand*', he [Peter] said, '*that God has no favourites, but that anybody of any nationality who fears him and does what is right is acceptable to him.*' 99
> (Acts 10.34–35)

4. There were many divisions in society at the time of Paul – political, racial, religious and sexual. In Galatians 3.26–29 he states clearly that Jesus, by his death on the cross, overcame all of these divisions, making everyone 'one in Christ Jesus'.

In following the teaching of the Bible, the Catholic Church has set itself firmly against any form of discrimination. It has issued documents and statements making sure that its teaching has been firmly understood. For a long time it has been Church policy to only appoint cardinals from among the bishops in different countries.

TASKS

1. **a.** Describe, in your own words, the parable of the Good Samaritan.
   b. Explain what Jesus was teaching his listeners through this parable.
2. Why was the vision of Peter particularly important for the young Church's understanding of the Christian **Gospel** and the Church?

34 BRITAIN AS A MULTI-FAITH SOCIETY

The UK has a very strong spiritual heritage based on the Christian religion and this remains the case today. At the same time the UK is more of a multi-faith society than any other in the European Union.

From single-faith to multi-faith

Prior to the Second World War there were comparatively few people belonging to a non-Christian religion in the UK. The first wave of immigrants, after 1945, was mainly West Indian and Christian, and they soon began to form their own churches. Then in the 1960s and 1970s there was a large influx of people from India, Pakistan, Bangladesh and Hong Kong followed later by people from Tanzania, Uganda and Kenya. This led to the growth of significant communities of Hindus, Muslims and Sikhs in the UK. There were already many Jewish communities which were well established.

To begin with, most immigrants concerned themselves with the task of finding somewhere to live, a job and sending money back home to support their families. Then attention was given to making arrangements for their families to join them. This led to a growth of religious communities and places of worship. Mandirs, gurdwaras and mosques sprang up and these became increasingly important in local communities. Although some purpose-built places of worship were built, the majority were either converted houses or redundant churches.

Concentration

Some religions have their members scattered throughout the UK. It is more usual, however, for them to be concentrated in certain urban areas:

1. The most concentrated Jewish population is in the Greater London area, while there are also large Jewish populations in Glasgow, Leeds and Manchester. There are also sizeable populations in Birmingham, Bournemouth, Brighton, Southend and Liverpool. The oldest **synagogue** in the country, Bevis Marks in London, was opened in 1701 and is still in use today.

2. Most Muslims are found in Lancashire, Greater London, the West Midlands, West Yorkshire and parts of Scotland. The first mosque was opened in Cardiff as early as 1860.

3. The largest Hindu communities are to be found in Greater London, Birmingham and Leicester.

4. The most substantial Sikh communities are found in Greater London (especially Southall), Cardiff, Birmingham, Bradford, Coventry, Wolverhampton, Glasgow, Leeds and Leicester. The first Sikh gurdwara in the UK opened in Putney, South London, in 1911.

The size of the communities

There are no totally reliable figures for the size of the different religious communities in the UK. These figures, however, can act as a reliable guide:

CHECK IT OUT

Islam: 1 400 000 with about 670 mosques.

Hinduism: 500 000 with about 180 mandirs.

THE NUMBER OF PEOPLE BELONGING TO DIFFERENT RELIGIONS IN THE UK

Sikhism: 600 000 with about 130 gurdwaras.

Judaism: 300 000 with about 400 synagogues.

Christianity: 38 000 000 with about 49 000 churches.

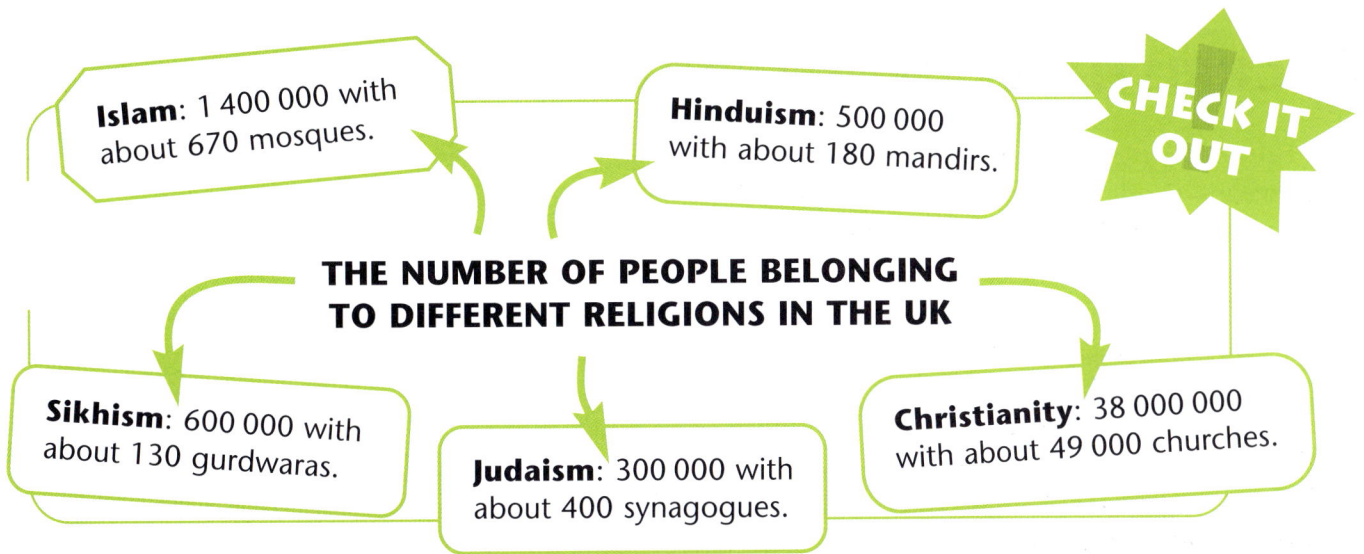

These are people who claim allegiance to the different religions. The number of people regularly attending places of worship is much lower; not much higher than 1 000 000 each Sunday for the main Christian denominations – the Church of England and the Roman Catholic Church.

▶ *This gurdwara, a converted home, has become the spiritual home and the centre of the social life of Sikhs in the area.*

TASKS

1. How did the UK move from being a largely single-faith country to become a multi-faith community?
2. What led to the formation of different religious communities in the UK and the growth of the number of places of worship?

✳ DISCUSSION POINT

Imagine that you are an immigrant, in the 1950s, who has just moved to this country. Make a list of your first five priorities as you settle into your new home.

35 CHRISTIANITY AND OTHER RELIGIONS

Christians are committed to religious freedom for all religions. They believe that everyone should have the freedom to express their religious beliefs in any way that they choose. It is Christian teaching that people should not suffer any form of religious discrimination against them. Within this framework, however, there are three approaches in the Christian community towards other world religions:

1. The exclusive approach. This expresses the belief held by many Christians, including most Roman Catholics, that there is only one approach to God – through Jesus Christ. These Christians often use the text in which Jesus is recorded as saying "I am the Way; I am the Truth and Life" (John 14.6). During the 19th and 20th centuries missionaries were sent out to preach the Christian Gospel to those who belonged to other faiths to 'convert' them, and this still happens today. The Catechism teaches that people who belong to other religions are searching for God and have some part of the truth but have not found the whole truth – which is to be found in Jesus, the Son of God, alone. The only real answer is for these people to become Christians and the Christian Church has the responsibility of taking 'the full light of the Gospel' to them.

> **A**   **"**All nations form but one community. This is so because all stem from the one stock which God created to people the entire earth, and also because all share a common destiny, namely God... The Catholic Church recognizes in other religions that search for the God who is unknown yet near since he gives life and breath and all things, and wants all men to be saved.**"**
>
> (CCC 842--43)

2. The inclusive approach. Christians who follow this approach often refer to the incident in the New Testament when Paul is visiting Athens. He recognises that in their search for the Unknown God, to whom they have built an **altar**, the Athenians are following a genuine spiritual search. Christians who follow this approach recognise that people can reach God by following different spiritual paths but only Christianity has the full truth. Those who genuinely believe in their own path are 'anonymous Christians' who will be saved in the end.

3. The pluralist approach. This approach says that all religions concentrate on reality. By following their own religious path people become more reality-centred and less self-centred. All religions, including Christianity, have produced both good and bad people. All religions are equal to each other and, in their best forms, produce better people. The Bible is one of several 'Words of God'. People are free to choose whichever religion suits them best to reach God.

Islam is one of the religions that Christianity has had much difficulty in understanding and coming to terms with.

Religions working together

The World Council of Churches was set up in 1910 to work for the eventual unity of the different Christian Churches. This has not happened, although different Churches do meet together to discuss matters of common interest. A Week of Prayer for Christian Unity is held in January each year, at which Christians from different Churches come together to talk, worship and pray. The Council of Christians and Jews seeks to promote a better understanding between two religions that have so much in common. These two religions also have a common history that has been full of bitterness and persecution, and so anything that helps to promote a better understanding in the future is to be welcomed.

Since the series of bomb explosions in London, in 2005, there have been tentative moves to establish closer links between Islam and Christianity. The Inter-Faith Network for the United Kingdom is an umbrella organisation that brings Christians, Jains, Buddhists, Jews, Hindus, Muslims and Sikhs together. It believes that greater tolerance comes from a greater understanding of those faiths to which one does not belong. It is a fact that all of the major world religions have a great deal that they share with each other – and that should be a cause for celebration rather than concentrating on the things that divide and separate. In October 2005, the student societies for Jewish and Muslim societies at Bristol University announced that they would be holding a series of joint meetings so that the two groups could begin to understand each other better.

TASKS

1. What are the three different approaches that Christians adopt towards other religions?

2. "We are living in a multi-religious society. In such a society it is totally inappropriate that any religion should set out to convert people who belong to other religions to its own faith." Do you agree with this comment? Give some reasons for your answer, showing that you have thought about more than one point of view.

EXAM HELP

In the examination

Make sure that you know about:

THE ROLE OF WOMEN IN THE MODERN WORLD

- The growth of equal rights for women. The inequalities that still exist in the UK – women do most of the housework, are more likely to suffer from domestic violence, are likely to be granted full custody of any children after a divorce, outperform boys at GCSE, are usually paid a lower salary, more likely to experience poverty or be 'carers'. The law and inequality. The early inequalities suffered by women in this country. The Equal Pay Act (equal pay with men for equal work) and the Sex Discrimination Act (discrimination against women in the workplace). Sexism. Prejudice. Discrimination.

- Men and women in the Bible. The teaching that men and women are equal – the example of Jesus (the Samaritan woman, female followers, appearance in the Court of Women, appeared first to women after the resurrection). Equality of women in early Christian community. Women as co-workers with Paul. The teaching that men and women are not equal – the responsibility of Eve for the first sin (original sin) in the story of creation, women subservient to men in the Church and at home to their husbands, in the teaching of Paul, women not allowed to speak in church in Paul's letter to Timothy based on the weakness sown by Eve in the Garden of Eden.

- Men, women and the Christian Church. The Catholic Church and women – the two sexes equal in God's sight, the dignity belonging to both sexes, that they are created for each other, they should be equally valued by the Church, some roles within Church more suited for one sex than the other. Women are equal but different in their roles. The Protestant Churches and women – some Evangelicals are opposed to women playing any role in church life, based on the teaching in Genesis, the choice of Jesus of male disciples only and Paul's teaching about male supremacy. Most Protestants believe that women are equal inside and outside church, with women priests and ministers universally accepted, based on the Bible teaching showing the attitude of Jesus towards women and the teaching of Paul that all are one in Christ.

Sample exam questions

1. If you were asked to show that women gained equality with men in the 20th century in the UK what evidence would you bring forward?

2. "It appears that women have gained equality with men in the UK but this can be misleading." Do you agree with this comment? Give reasons for your answer, showing that you have thought about more than one point of view.

3. What are the two different points of view in the Bible about the different roles of men and women?

4. Explain the attitudes of **a.** the Catholic Church and **b.** the Protestant Churches towards women.

RACIAL HARMONY AND IMMIGRATION IN BRITAIN

- The pattern of immigration into Britain. Immigration into Britain in the distant past – the impact of groups on British society, culture, way of life and so on. The reasons why people have migrated to Britain in the past – to find work and escape persecution. Historical examples of both. The problem of finding suitable accomodation. The law and race relations – racism is opposed by all major political parties. The Race Relations Act (1976) outlawed discrimination in areas of housing, education, employment, training and the provision of services as well as any use of threatening language and the publication of unacceptable material. The attitudes of some remain very difficult to change. The Social Attitudes Survey. Cool welcome to immigrants given by Christian Church.

- The Catholic Church and racial harmony. Catholics believe in the total harmony of all human beings – prejudice is totally unacceptable to the Church. Jesus showed that he had no sympathy with prejudice – the parable of the Good Samaritan, the Samaritan woman, the Roman officer, Simon from Cyrene. The welcoming of Gentiles (non-Jews) into God's kingdom. The vision of Peter with the different animals and the lesson he learned. The overcoming of social and religious divisions by Jesus, an important feature of the early Church. Division in society at the time of Paul – broken down by the death of Jesus.

BRITAIN AS A MULTI-FAITH SOCIETY

- Britain as a multi-faith community. The movement from single-faith to multi-faith. The movement of people from the Caribbean in the 1950s. The movement of Hindus, Sikhs and Muslims from other countries in the 1960s and 1970s. The importance of places of worship in the local communities. The concentration of Hindus, Muslims and Sikhs in certain areas. The long-established Jewish community. The size of the communities of the different religions.

- The attitude of Christianity to the other religions. The 'exclusive' approach that believes Christianity is the only way to God. The 'inclusive' approach. Paul's visit to Athens. People can reach God by pursuing different paths. Anonymous Christians. The pluralist approach. It does not matter what path people take to God because religion makes them better people.

EXAM HELP

Sample exam questions

1. **a.** Explain how Britain has always been a multi-ethnic society.

   b. Explain how the make-up of British society changed from the 1950s onward.

   c. Explain why so many immigrants came to Britain to live from the 1950s onward.

2. Describe how the law in Britain has tried to remove racial prejudice and discrimination.

3. How did Jesus show in his ministry that he had no sympathy for prejudice?

4. Explain how Britain became a multi-faith society.

5. **a.** What are the three different approaches that Christians pursue in their attitude to other religions?

   b. Which of these attitudes do you think is the right one? Give reasons for your answer, showing that you have thought about more than one point of view.

6. Explain how:

   a. Christians try to work together.

   b. Members of other religions and Christians are working towards a deeper understanding of each other.

OPTION 1: Religion and the media

In this topic you will find out about:

- the growing importance of television in the lives of people in the UK and the early religious programmes, reflecting the assumption that almost all people were Christian;

- the movement towards a multi-faith society from the early 1970s and the problem that this presented for religious television;

- examination of *Songs of Praise*, the most popular religious programme ever on television;

- religious documentaries;

- moral and religious issues dealt with in 'soaps'.

As this is an optional choice in the specification there are no key words to cover.

36 RELIGIOUS BROADCASTING

The religious output of BBC radio goes back to the 1920s when the BBC first started broadcasting and its first Director General, Lord Reith, said that the aim of the BBC should be to be 'the nation's church'. Lord Reith had very strong religious beliefs and believed that the BBC and the Church should work together to deepen the religious faith of the nation. The daily *Morning Service* began on the Home Service (Radio 4) in 1927 and is still being broadcast each weekday morning today – the longest continually running radio programme.

The advent of television

Television was born in the years before the Second World War, although the television service was closed down between 1939 and 1945 as it was thought inappropriate that people should watch television while the nation was at war. In any case, the number of television sets owned in the nation was tiny and people seriously doubted whether television would ever really catch on. It was the radio that mattered to people and during the Second World War it had great importance as the only real source of immediate news.

After the war ended, however, television became increasingly important in the lives of the people of this country, as the number of people owning sets gradually increased. Television ownership was given a great boost during the Coronation in 1953. During the 1950s, about 50% of the population went to church fairly regularly and the religious output of both radio and television reflected this. Little attention was paid to other religions since there were few followers of them in this country.

Towards a multi-faith society

During the late 1960s and early 1970s major changes took place in the make-up of British society. As Britain became a multi-ethnic society so it also became multi-faith. Although most of the early immigrants from the Caribbean came from a Christian background many others were Muslim, Hindu and Sikh. This meant that broadcasters could no longer assume that those interested in religion were Christian.

This created a major problem for broadcasters; most of the immigrants did not worship in English so it was not possible to broadcast religious services – at the time the staple diet of religious broadcasts. So broadcasters tended to concentrate on special programmes explaining the reasons behind the main religious festivals – such as **Passover**, Ramadan, Diwali, the Jewish New Year and so on – and the ways in which they were celebrated.

At the same time it was recognised that only a limited amount of time could be given to the minority religions in the UK at a time when all of the major TV channels were chasing the ratings. Until recently there was a 'God slot' – a time set aside each Sunday for religious programming. This has now been abolished by ITV who, always conscious of the need to attract advertisers, does not broadcast any regular religious programmes in the early Sunday evening. The BBC, however, has the multi-faith *Heaven and Earth Show* on Sunday morning and the very long-running *Songs of Praise* in the evening.

The **Heaven and Earth Show** *reflects the current popular interest in a 'mix and match' approach to religion.*

Religious 'inserts' continue on Radio 2 and Radio 4 under the general title 'Thought for the Day'. Although these remain largely Christian there are now also speakers from other major faiths as well. The National Secular Society strongly argues that non-religious speakers should also be included but so far this has not happened.

The Churches have not found it easy to come to terms with the downgrading of religion on television. Arguments were presented to the Board of Governors of the BBC, on 13 May 2005, to discuss the future of religious broadcasting. At the time of writing it remains to be seen whether this will lead to any real changes.

TASKS

1. Describe the changes that have taken place in religious broadcasting since the 1960s and the reasons for them.
2. Describe the range of religious broadcasting that is available on radio and television.

✳ DISCUSSION POINT

A recent survey by Ofcom (the independent regulator and competition authority for the UK communications industries) into viewing habits found that only about 10% of viewers placed any value on religious programmes. What do you think is the value of religious programmes, if any?

37 ONE RELIGIOUS PROGRAMME – *SONGS OF PRAISE*

Without any doubt, the most popular religious programme on any television channel in recent years has been *Songs of Praise* – a programme that has been broadcast on BBC 1 on Sunday afternoons for more than forty years. The programme often reaches up to 5 million viewers with an average weekly viewing total of 2.5 million. It began in the mid 1960s and is still to be found on our television screens for most of the year.

Its website provides us with the following information about the programme:

- The programme was originally going to be called *Sing His Praises.*

- *Songs of Praise* has had 182 different presenters over the years – including, recently, Aled Jones, Jonathan Edwards, Diane Louise Jordan, Sally Magnusson, Eamonn Holmes and Pam Rhodes.

- *Songs of Praise* has visited over 1800 different churches, chapels and cathedrals during the time that it has been broadcasting.

- Four *Songs of Praise* producers have become bishops.

- The largest number of viewers watching a single *Songs of Praise* programme was 11.4 million (Christmas 1988). The biggest single congregation was the 60 000 people who were at the Millennium Stadium, Cardiff on 2 January 2000.

- *Songs of Praise* is regularly shown in the Netherlands, Australia, Canada and South Africa.

- In the last ten years *Songs of Praise* has visited twenty different countries – Australia, Austria, Barbados, Brazil, Bulgaria, Eire, France, Germany, the Holy Land, Hong Kong, Israel, Majorca, the Netherlands, Norway, Poland, Romania, South Africa, Spain, USA and Zimbabwe.

- In the forty years since *Songs of Praise* started over 12 500 hymns have been sung. The most popular hymn according to surveys is 'How Great Thou Art'.

- *Songs of Praise* viewers have reported seeing 'miracles' on the show – people have called in to recount seeing the Virgin Mary in a stained glass window bowing her head while others have seen statues of apostles and prophets raising their hands.

Over the years the character of the programme has changed somewhat while still being essentially based on a Christian talk and hymn format. To begin, visits were made to local churches in towns and villages. Members of the congregation who had a suitable story to tell were interviewed and asked to choose a hymn for the congregation to sing. The target audience was those people who could not attend church for one reason or another – elderly people who were housebound, young mothers with children and so on.

In recent years, however, there have been many more large gatherings in such places as the Royal Albert Hall in London and the Millennium Stadium in Cardiff. Large choirs drawn from all over the area have led the singing at these gatherings with a full orchestra accompanying.

Star names are often featured. The target audience has changed, with the 25–35 age group now firmly in mind. Interviews are conducted with people who claim that God has, in some way, touched their lives.

▶ *It takes almost a week to record one* Songs of Praise *programme with the singing, interviews and outdoor shots that make up the programme.*

TASKS

1. Make a point of watching *Songs of Praise* either live or on video/DVD. Do this before answering the following questions:

   a. Who do you think the programme you watched was aimed at?

   b. How would you describe the format of the programme?

   c. Given that the programme has been very successful for a long period of time, what do you think the secret of its success is? To answer this put yourself in the position of a regular viewer.

2. If you had the opportunity to make a series of six programmes for religious television what would you include and what kind of programmes would you produce?

✳ DISCUSSION POINT

Do you think that *Songs of Praise* takes into account the fact that fewer and fewer people are going to church and showing an interest in organised religion?

38 RELIGIOUS DOCUMENTARIES

Apart from worship-style programmes, documentaries have made up the bulk of religious broadcasting in recent years. These have covered a wide range of subjects and provide the opportunity for television to cover religions other than Christianity.

What is a documentary?

A documentary is a factual film or programme about a serious subject. It may have a strong historical element or be based on the life of someone interesting or important. In recent years, for example, documentaries have covered the life stories of people like Archbishop Desmond Tutu of South Africa in the context of his opposition to the policy of apartheid in his country. Acted conversations may be included in the documentary but these are conversations that are known to have taken place.

The aim of a documentary is to inform the viewer. This makes it very different to worship or magazine-style programmes. Obviously such programmes could be biased, so the viewer must always decide for themselves whether the picture being presented is accurate or not. In September 2005, for instance, *Panorama* presented a programme on Islam that claimed Muslim organisations were not distancing themselves from some radical preachers. The Muslim Council of Great Britain, one of the organisations criticised, protested that the programme was biased, but the protest was rejected by the producers of the programme.

▲ *Over the years the documentary series Everyman has introduced millions of viewers to serious religious and moral issues.*

Documentaries galore

As we have seen, many programmes do include investigations into religious themes in their regular schedules. There is reason to believe that people have become more interested in religious topics in recent years without wishing to become members of a religion themselves. A new six-part series on ITV began in October 2005 called *The Mosque*, offering an insight into Muslim Britain during the month of Ramadan, the season of fasting, plus a look at the impact that the London bombings have had on the Muslim community and on relationships with non-Muslims.

For a long time the BBC had a regular series called *Everyman*, which sought to cover important aspects of religion and religious beliefs, including:

- the so-called supernatural happenings in Hindu temples in London and elsewhere, when statues of the gods and goddesses were believed to drink milk;

- the attempt to launch Qibla Cola – a Muslim version of Coca-Cola;

- different aspects of Christianity, including the Roman Catholic opposition to artificial methods of birth control and the struggle in the Anglican Church over women priests. The Church's attitude to homosexuality was also covered;

- the work of mediums in the Spiritualist community. This was an in-depth study, over three programmes, called 'Talking to the Dead'. It centred on the work of Gordon Smith, the 'psychic barber', and followed his attempt to help two bereaved parents grieving the loss of their son. It asked whether mediums spread false hopes, exploited the vulnerable or simply told people what they needed to hear in troubled times.

Watching religious documentaries

Documentaries, both religious and non-religious, attract a larger audience than you might expect. All the available research suggests that:

1. There are many people who would not claim to be 'religious' or to belong to any religious group – yet are interested in religious issues.

2. Viewers look to religious documentaries to deal with the subject matter in an open, unbiased, yet critical way.

3. Viewers expect programmes to present all the relevant facts – and then leave them to make up their own minds.

4. Viewers do not like it if the programme makes an assumption about their own religious beliefs.

1. Try to watch a religious documentary on video or DVD two or three times. Note the different aspects of the subject that are shown. Do you think that the documentary gives a fair and unbiased view of the subject?

2. Would you have handled the subject differently if you had been producing the documentary?

TASKS

39 SOAPS – SERIOUS RELIGIOUS AND MORAL ISSUES

What is a 'soap'?

1. Soap operas, or 'soaps' as they are commonly known, began in the USA. Originally it was thought that they would only appeal to female viewers and so were sponsored by the manufacturers of soap powders.

2. A soap is an ongoing serial that is based on a real-life community – such as an East End pub/street/market (*EastEnders*) or a northern pub/street (*Coronation Street*). The story-line is ongoing and only ends when the programme is taken off air. Usually a soap is broadcast several times a week with different story-lines being interwoven with each other. This allows viewers to identify with the different characters and involve themselves in what is going on.

3. In a soap there is a regular set of characters who form the backbone of the story and who live in a small, enclosed geographical area. Many of them are either related to each other (based on an extended family set-up) or have known each other for a long time. The script involves the characters in real-life situations and this is where a soap gains its real interest for viewers. For the soap to be successful, viewers must really care about what happens to the characters.

4. Among the clearly defined soap operas on television are *EastEnders*, *Coronation Street*, *Emmerdale* and *Hollyoaks*. *Brookside* ran for many years on Channel 4 before being axed. *Casualty* and *Holby City* bear similarities to a soap although they are probably better described as TV dramas.

Soaps and controversial issues

Soaps are extremely popular and can attract regular audiences of around 9 million viewers. Religious and moral issues are often part of the story-line of soaps:

- A religious issue is connected to what religious people believe and do. It may, for instance, be about life after death, suffering or whether Roman Catholic priests should be allowed to marry.

- A moral issue is to do with right and wrong. This could be about euthanasia, abortion or any other social issue.

Religious and moral issues are often, of course, connected because all religions have moral teachings. Among the religious and moral issues raised in recent years in the soaps have been:

Coronation Street

- Deidre was imprisoned unjustly and there was a campaign to gain her freedom. A question was even asked in the House of Commons.

- Richard Hillman tried to murder his own family.

EastEnders

The following issues have been tackled:

- Abortion.
- Domestic violence.
- The issue of euthanasia was spread out over many episodes. Dot and Ethel were very old friends. Ethel was very old and clearly dying. She brought great emotional pressure on Dot to help her to take her own life when the time came.
- An affair between an Anglican vicar and a married woman.
- The story of Janine pushing her husband Barry to his death on their honeymoon and the murder of Den.

Brookside

- One of the most controversial issues ever tackled in the soaps was that of lesbianism, which was handled through the relationship between Beth and Margaret. The story-line included television's first lesbian kiss, which was shown in June 1994.

Hollyoaks

- The story-line of two twins dating, although they did not know that they were related.

▲ *Millions of people were drawn into Dot's dilemma in* EastEnders.

1. What are soaps and why do you think they are so popular?
2. Describe five different moral and religious issues that have been raised in recent years in soaps.
3. "One of the best things about soaps is that they get people talking about issues that they would not normally think about." Do you agree with this comment? Give reasons for your point of view, showing that you have thought about more than one opinion.

TASKS

EXAM HELP

In the examination

Make sure that you know about:

RELIGIOUS BROADCASTS

- The growth in the popularity of radio and television. Early religious broadcasts. The importance of services. The growth of a multi-faith society and the coverage given to minority faiths. The 'God slot' on television. The popular religious programmes, including *Songs of Praise.* Religious inserts in radio programmes.

- *Songs of Praise* – most popular religious television programme. Interesting information about the programme. The changing of the programme over time.

- Religious documentaries. The nature of documentaries – to inform, free of bias, to stimulate and sometimes to annoy. Documentaries with religious themes. *Everyman* documentaries – examples of subjects covered. The people who watch religious documentaries.

- What a soap is. Controversial issues dealt with in soaps. Be able to give examples of these – use up-to-date examples of your own if you can.

Sample exam questions

1. What are the different kinds of religious programmes on radio and television?

2. How do you think television programmes have shifted their focus from the 'religiously committed' to those who are 'vaguely interested' in religion?

3. In the 1930s and 1940s most people thought that the future lay with radio rather than television. How did this situation change?

4. Why do you think that *Songs of Praise* has turned out to be the most popular religious television programme of all time?

5. **a.** What is a religious documentary?

    b. Describe some of the issues tackled by religious documentaries in recent years.

6. **a.** What is a soap?

    b. Describe some recent moral and religious issues tackled by soaps on television.

    c. Why do you think that soaps are particularly suited to the tackling of such issues?

OPTION 2: Wealth and poverty

In this topic you will find out about:

- the Catholic teachings on wealth and poverty;
- further Catholic teachings on wealth and poverty;
- wealth, almsgiving, stewardship, charity, compassion and justice;
- the need for world development;
- the work of relieving poverty in the UK and in the world.

As this is an optional choice in the specification there are no key words to cover.

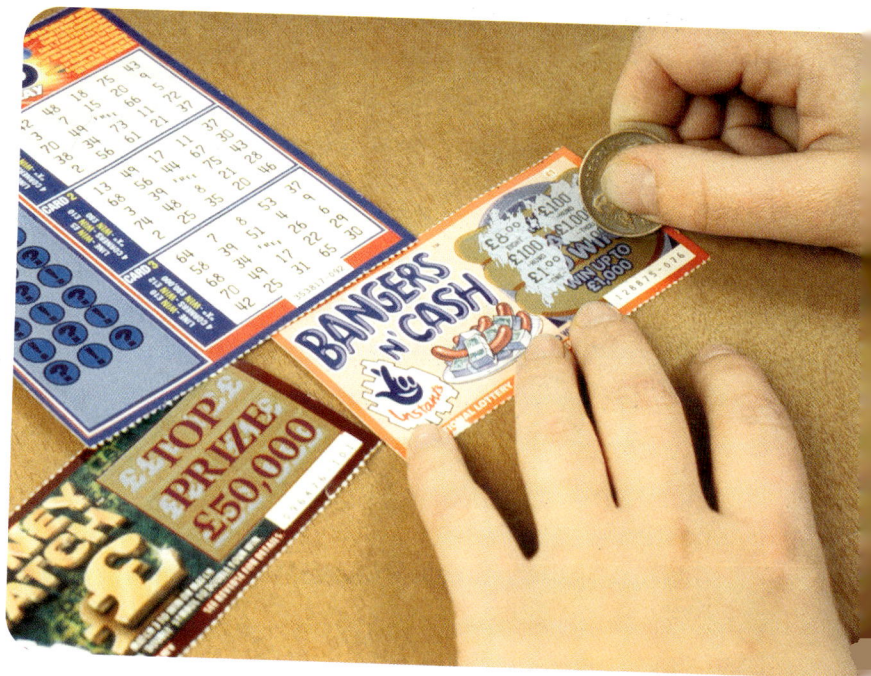

40 CATHOLIC TEACHINGS ON WEALTH AND POVERTY (1)

The teaching of the Bible on wealth and poverty is very clear:

- Wealth is a gift from God and must be used in a way that is pleasing to God. A person should use his or her wealth to meet the needs of those dearest to him or her first of all – and then the needs of others.

- Jesus taught that the possession of wealth can be a hindrance to those who would serve God and enter his kingdom. It distracts people when they should be placing God first in their life.

Two incidents in the life of Jesus

The following are two incidents in the life of Jesus in which he underlined the spiritual dangers of possessing wealth:

- The rich young man (Mark 10.17–31). A young man approached Jesus with the question – "Good teacher, what must I do to inherit eternal life?" Jesus ran through some of the Ten Commandments with him and he claimed to have kept them all since he was a child. Jesus told him that he lacked just one thing. He must sell all that he had, give the proceeds to the poor and then he would have 'treasure in heaven'. The man went away very sad because, we are told, he had great wealth. When his disciples questioned Jesus about his answer his reply greatly surprised them (extract A).

> **A** ❝'My children'… 'how hard it is to enter the kingdom of God! It is easier for a camel to pass through the eye of a needle than for someone rich to enter the kingdom of God.'❞
>
> (Mark 10.24–25)

- The widow's mite (Mark 12.41–43). Towards the end of his life, Jesus sat down with his disciples opposite the treasury of the Temple and watched people putting in their offerings. He saw a poor widow who placed small coins, the equivalent of a penny, into the treasury. He told his disciples that the woman had given more in spiritual terms that anyone else – "… for they have put in money they could spare, but she in her poverty has put in everything she possessed, all she had to live on" (Mark 12.44). Jesus was saying that it is not the size of the gift that impresses God but the sacrifice that is involved in making the gift.

The message behind these two incidents is very clear. If we have been given riches and wealth then we are obliged to use them for the good of the poor and needy. It was never God's intention that some should have far more than they need while others have barely enough to keep them alive (extract B).

> **B** **"**God blesses those who come to the aid of the poor and rebukes those who turn away from them… Love for the poor is incompatible with immoderate love of riches or their selfish use.**"**
>
> (CCC 2443, 2445)

The danger of loving money

Paul reinforced the message of Jesus about the dangers of letting wealth and riches rule one's life. He warned the young Church leader Timothy against longing to be rich – a yearning that leads to all kinds of foolishness and harmful ambitions. These will plunge people into ruin and destruction because "The love of money is the root of all evil" (1 Timothy 6.10). Notice it is not money itself but a love of it that is so dangerous. This was a message with which Jesus would have completely agreed.

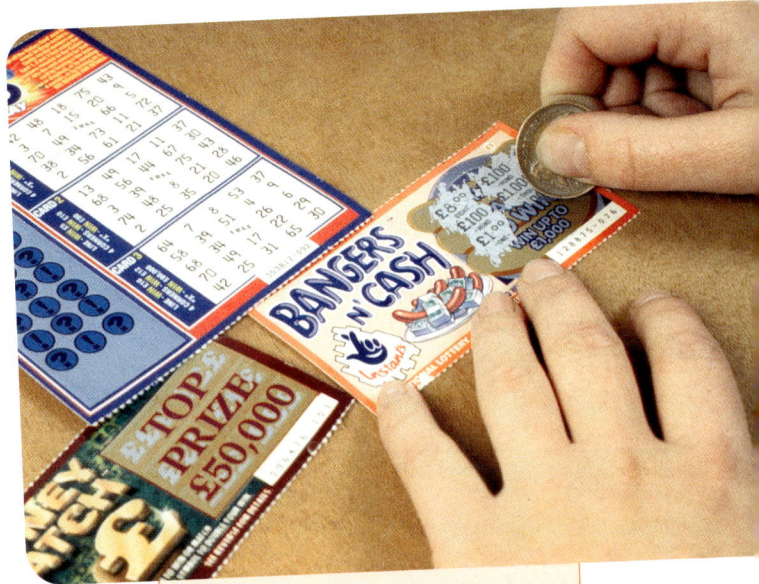

▲ Gambling of any kind is built upon a simple love of money.

TASKS

1. **a.** What do Catholics believe should be the attitude of all Christians to wealth and poverty?

   b. Give two examples from the Bible that a Catholic might use to support his or her point of view.

2. Why do you think a wealthy Christian might feel unhappy with his or her wealth?

✳ **DISCUSSION POINT**

What evidence can you bring forward to support the assertion of Paul that the love of money is the root of all evils?

41 CATHOLIC TEACHINGS ON WEALTH AND POVERTY (2)

We need to take the teaching of the Catholic Church on wealth and poverty a little further here. There are many topics connected with wealth and poverty on which the teaching of the Church is very clear including:

1. Possessions, the uses and abuses of wealth

The desire to be happy is a natural and proper one. It comes from God himself, who has placed it in the human heart. His intention is to draw us to himself who, alone, is able to satisfy the desire. The Catechism states that "God alone satisfies" (1718). Part of the search for human happiness is to discover those things that are unable to satisfy the human heart and bring happiness. One of these is wealth and possessions.

As the Catechism reminds us, the desire for possessions and wealth leads us to envy those who have them while we do not. The tenth Commandment forbids envy. It forbids the person who has wealth from spending all their energy simply in amassing more and more possessions. As the Catechism puts it:

> **A** "Our thirst for another's goods is immense, infinite, never quenched. Thus it is written, 'He who loves money never has money enough.'"
> (CCC 2536)

2. Almsgiving

Catholics are expected to give to the Church and other needy causes generously from the wealth that God has given them. In the Old Testament the rule was that Christians gave 1/10 of their wealth to God (a **tithe**) but were expected to give 'generously'. As the early Christians were reminded by Paul 'God loves a cheerful giver' (2 Corinthians 9.7). To give generously is both an act of charity and an act of penance.

▶ Giving to God part of one's wealth is a very important part of Christian worship.

3. Stewardship

The Catechism points out that in the beginning God entrusted the earth and all its resources to the common stewardship of mankind to:

- take good care of them;
- master them by human labour so that they are fruitful;
- enjoy the fruits of the earth.

It points out that the goods of creation were always intended by God to be for the benefit of the whole human race. However, a large part of the world's population is endangered by poverty and threatened by violence. This is very bad stewardship, a failure for which those who have much will be called on by God to give an account.

4. Charity

'Charity' means being willing to give freely to those in the greatest need. It should be a characteristic of the Catholic Church and of all who would follow the teachings of Jesus Christ. Charity is the path that recognises the need to love God and also to love one's neighbour. This is why the Catechism calls it 'the greatest social commandment' (1889).

5. Compassion and justice

'Compassion' is a very deep sense of pity. It was an emotion that Jesus often felt when he was confronted by a sea of needy people who had so many spiritual and physical needs. He not only felt their needs but also took their needs on himself. Catholics are called upon to feel compassion for those in the world who do not even have their basic human needs. It is unjust that human beings should be treated in this way and so Catholics will seek a way of putting such injustices right.

At the moment the relationship between rich and poor is completely unfair and unjust. Catholics should be in the forefront of those working to put such injustices right.

TASKS

1. Describe what the Catholic Church teaches about:
   a. the uses and abuses of wealth
   b. almsgiving and charity
   c. compassion and justice
   d. stewardship

✳ DISCUSSION POINT

Do you think that the Catholic Church has got it about right when it comes to understanding human responsibility for those who have few of the earth's resources?

42 THE NEED FOR WORLD DEVELOPMENT

As far as the distribution of wealth in the modern world is concerned, countries can be divided into two groups.

- *The northern developed world.* This consists of countries that have a high standard of living, referred to as **developed countries**, and includes North America, western Europe, including the UK, Japan and Australasia. These areas only have 25% of the world's population and yet they consume 75% of the entire world's resources – energy, food, medical supplies and so on. These countries used to be called the First World.

- *The southern, developing countries.* This group of countries can be divided into two:

  - The Communist and ex-Communist countries – the Eastern European countries, Russia, China and so on. It also includes countries in South and Central America, such as Mexico and Brazil, and countries in the Far East, such as Malaysia. These countries are fast catching up the developed nations. Until recently this was called the Second World.

  - The **less developed countries** (LDCs) that still struggle with a high level of poverty and hunger. In recent years the struggle of Sudan to feed its own population has made headline news. This used to be called the Third World.

Five facts about developing countries

Following are five facts about the LDCs. They highlight the differences between the rich (developed countries) and the poor countries in the world. LDCs have:

1. A high level of malnutrition. In the world's poorest nations, such as Mali and Sudan, up to 75% of the people try to make a living out of agriculture compared with fewer than 5% in the UK. This is largely 'subsistence' farming with people simply trying to grow enough to meet their own needs and those of their family. They have little left to sell to buy the things they cannot grow.

2. A low standard of education and literacy. There is a direct link between the level of poverty and the level of literacy (the ability to read and write). People who are illiterate (at least 850 million in the world) can find no way out of the poverty trap.

3. A high level of illness and disease. If children in LDCs survive the hazards of birth and infancy they find that their living conditions leave them vulnerable to illness and disease for the whole of their life. Twenty-five million people a year die from water-borne diseases; about 2.4 billion (30% of the world's population) do not have adequate sanitation and 2 billion do not have access to clean drinking water. There are few doctors and nurses in LDCs. Some 30 million people worldwide are suffering from HIV/AIDS – the vast majority living in the LDCs. They cannot afford the drugs that patients need to keep them alive.

4. A high rate of infant mortality. Children are most vulnerable in the first few years of their life. Over 15 million children under the age of five die from malnutrition each year. Malnourished mothers are unable to provide milk for their underfed babies and so the cycle of poverty continues.

5. A low life expectancy. In the UK, on average, a man can hope to reach the age of 77 and a woman 82 years. In many developing countries men barely have a life expectancy of forty years and women a year or two more.

There are many reasons why some countries are underdeveloped. Some countries are much more prone to natural disasters – earthquakes, floods, droughts and so on – than others. When they strike they have few resources to fight the destruction that they bring. Many developing countries are saddled with huge debts that they owe the richer countries. In many countries war, either with another country or a civil war, has proved extremely costly. Often land is used to grow cash crops (coffee, tea, cotton and so on) to service debts rather than to feed the population. The end result is that many LDCs are simply getting poorer as other countries grow richer. The gap between them is getter larger all the time.

▲ There is a great amount of malnourishment in less developed countries (LDCs).

TASKS

1. Into which groups can the nations of the world be divided?
2. What is a LDC and what are its characteristics?
3. Make a list of the characteristics of the less developed countries.

❋ **DISCUSSION POINT**

Do you think that people in developed countries would be willing to lower their standard of living so that people's lives in less developed countries might be improved?

43 RELIEVING POVERTY IN THE UK

The main Catholic organisation working in the UK to relieve poverty and other social problems is the St Vincent de Paul Society, which was established in 1833 by a young college student. Challenged to put his faith into action, Frederick Ozanam created the Society and named it after Vincent de Paul, a saint noted for his work among the poor.

The work of the St Vincent de Paul Society

The St Vincent de Paul Society is an international Christian organisation. Catholic in origin and character it is dedicated to helping all those in need. It interprets this very widely, organising the visiting of the sick, the lonely, the addicted and those suffering from different disabilities. Visits are made to families, the sick at home or in a hospital or hospice, to residential homes and to offenders in prison.

Loneliness, especially among the elderly, is a growing problem, so members spend a great deal of time with the housebound to prevent them from feeling isolated. Many appreciate a friendly face and enjoy a chat over a cup of tea, knowing that someone cares. Support may extend to doing shopping, decorating, gardening or filling in official forms to make sure the person receives any benefits that are due to them.

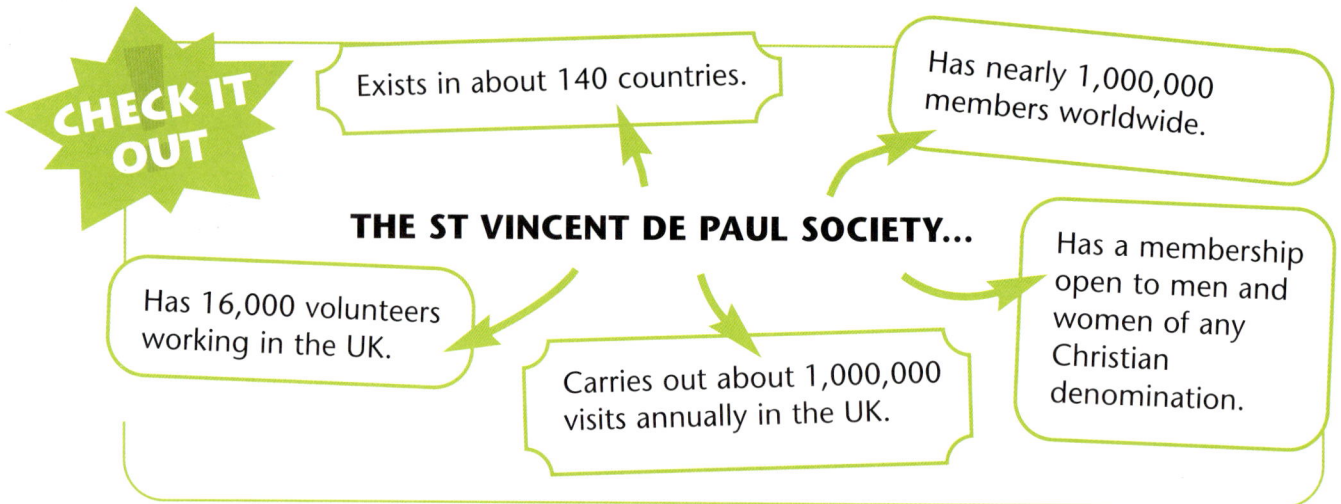

CHECK IT OUT

THE ST VINCENT DE PAUL SOCIETY...

Exists in about 140 countries.

Has nearly 1,000,000 members worldwide.

Has 16,000 volunteers working in the UK.

Carries out about 1,000,000 visits annually in the UK.

Has a membership open to men and women of any Christian denomination.

How the Society works

The St Vincent de Paul Society is a grass-roots organisation. This means that it works through local groups, called Conferences, that are set up in each parish. These meet regularly to review their work as well as allocating future work in the spirit of prayer. Much of its work focuses on visiting needy people in their homes, operating from the local parish. Other aspects of its work are largely based in large towns and cities:

- Children's camps – organised in several dioceses including Hexham, Liverpool, Nottingham, Shrewsbury (covering the Wirral) and most of the London dioceses (Brentwood, Southwark and Westminster).

- Furniture stores – where furniture, donated by supporters, is renovated and then sold at a very reasonable price. These stores exist in Merseyside (3), Doncaster, Leeds, Sheffield and South Wales, with more planned in the future.

- Housing Associations – established in London, Greater Manchester and Lancashire with the intention of providing reasonably priced housing.

- Drop-in centres – these exist in Leeds, Newcastle upon Tyne and Sheffield, providing opportunities for those in need to find practical help and advice. Soup runs are also provided in several places for those who are homeless and living on the street.

- Holiday schemes – operate in several dioceses including Birmingham and Leeds.

- Hostel accomodation – provided in Newcastle upon Tyne, Nottingham, London and Birmingham, for vulnerable people.

- Community shops – providing employment and help for isolated communities.

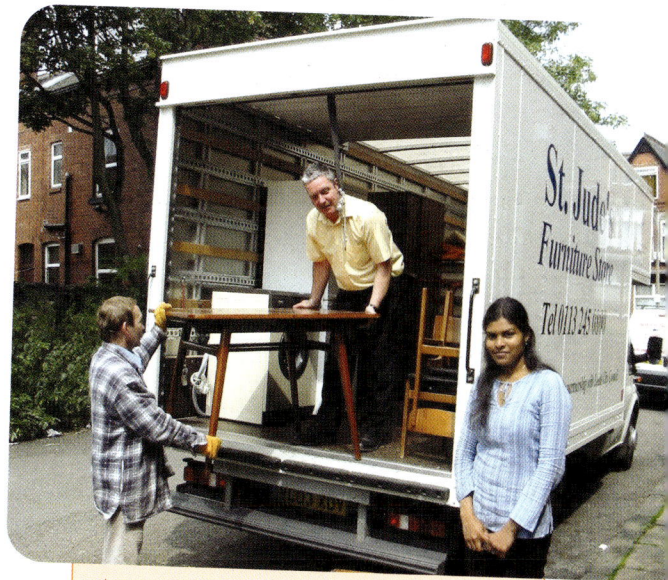

▲ *The Society finds that it can often supply pieces of furniture to make life more comfortable for those in need.*

TASKS

1. What is the motivation behind the work of the St Vincent de Paul Society?
2. Describe the extent of the work of the St Vincent de Paul Society.

✳ DISCUSSION POINT

Why do you think there is a need for the work of an organisation like the St Vincent de Paul Society in the 21st century?

44 CAFOD

There are many Christian charities that work among the poor and needy in today's world. One such organisation is CAFOD – the Catholic Fund for Overseas Development. It was set up by Catholic bishops in 1962 to assist the poor and disadvantaged to help themselves. Projects financed by CAFOD attempt to tackle the causes, as well as the symptoms, of disease, ignorance and poverty.

CAFOD now supports well over 500 different projects in 75 countries. The Irish equivalent of CAFOD is TROCAIRE ('Mercy') and the two often work alongside each other in their projects.

> **A** **"**The duty of making oneself a neighbour to others and actively serving them becomes even more urgent when it involves the disadvantaged, in whatever area this might be. 'As you did to one of the least of these my brethren, you did it to me.'**"**
>
> (CCC 1932)

Tackling world development

CAFOD tackles some of the most pressing issues in the world today by working along three lines:

1. By raising funds. To bring home the link between the money it raises and the problems it tackles, CAFOD sponsors special fasts during October and Lent each year. Worshippers are encouraged to go without food for a day and give the money they would have spent to CAFOD projects. Each year, more than £20 million is raised in this way to help the poor. This encourages people to see the work as a spiritual as well as a material necessity.

2. By sending aid. CAFOD carries a fund that can respond quickly if a natural disaster strikes. It can gather food, medicines and shelter together in a few days. It joins with other charities in making a joint appeal for funds (short-term aid). It also supports the work of Caritas, an international Catholic organisation, by channelling money to be used on long-term projects, such as healthcare, irrigation, food production and education amongst children and adults (long-term aid). In countries such as Brazil, there are thousands of children living on the streets of most large cities without a home and CAFOD supports workers who take education and food to them.

3. By educating people. The educating of people in the UK about development issues is a very important part of the work of CAFOD. Five pence in every £1 raised is spent on educating Catholics in the UK. CAFOD workers go into schools to speak to classes about various overseas projects.

Why get Involved?

The struggle for equality and justice in the many poor parts of the world is one that should engage all Christians, including Catholics. There are four reasons for believing this:

- Christians believe that the love of God needs to be taken everywhere;
- treating people with care and compassion is an essential part of the Gospel;
- Christians are called to work towards a world that is less selfish and self-centred;
- the Gospel is not only about personal salvation, but also the working out of God's will for equality and justice in the world.

TASKS

1. Describe three ways in which CAFOD helps people in developing countries.

2. Go to the website www.cafod.org.uk/ and find out about two projects, one short-term and one long-term, in which CAFOD is involved. Make notes so that you can answer a question about CAFOD in your exam.

3. "The amount of help that organisations like CAFOD can give is tiny compared with the need in today's world. It is hardly worth making the effort." Do you agree with this comment? Give reasons for your answer, showing that you have thought about more than one point of view.

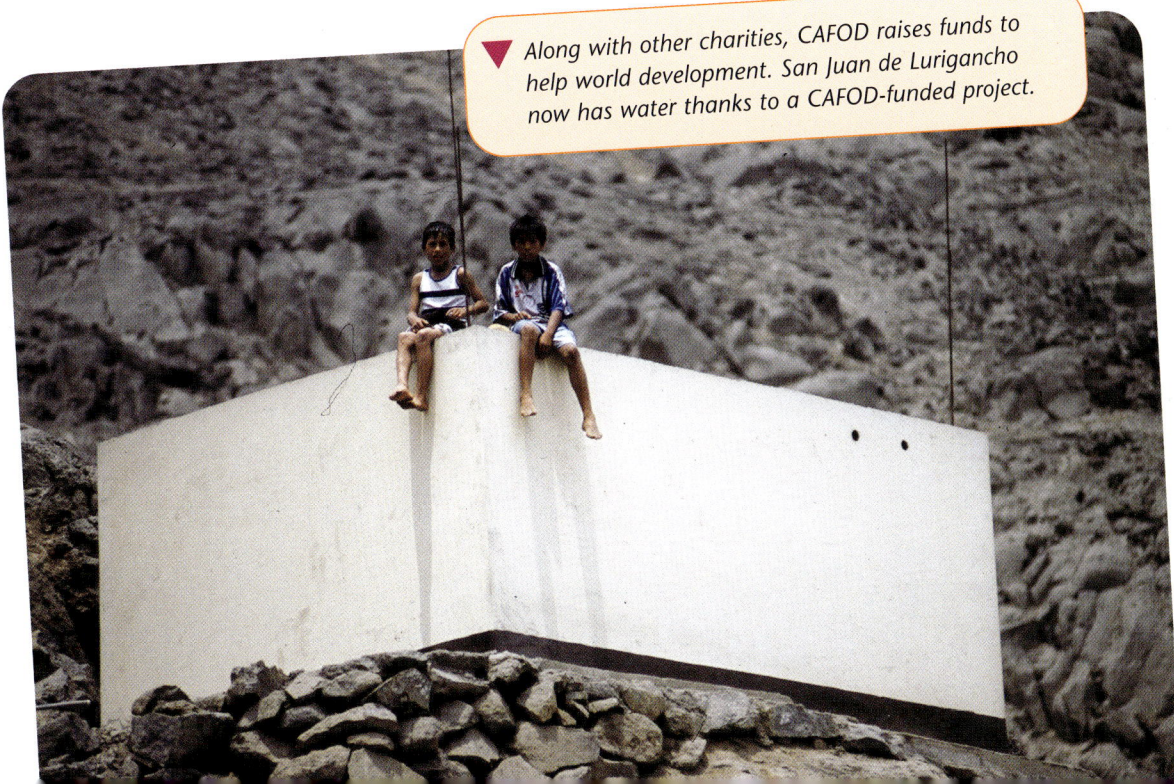

▼ Along with other charities, CAFOD raises funds to help world development. San Juan de Lurigancho now has water thanks to a CAFOD-funded project.

EXAM HELP

In the examination

Make sure that you know about:

WEALTH AND POVERTY

- The Catholic teachings about wealth and poverty. Two important incidents in the life of Jesus – the rich young ruler and the widow's mite. The danger of loving money – a warning in the teaching of Paul. The correct approach to possessions. The uses and abuses of wealth. The principle of almsgiving. The importance of stewardship: sharing out God's good gifts. Charity. The meaning of compassion and justice. The unequal division of resources in the world.

- The need for world development. The rich world and the LDCs (less developed countries). The five facts about LDCs – malnutrition, poor education and literacy, high level of illness and disease, high rate of infant mortality, and low life expectancy.

- Relieving poverty in the UK – the St Vincent De Paul Society. How the Society works.

- Relieving poverty in the world – CAFOD. Ways of tackling world development. Reasons why Catholics should be involved in world development.

Sample exam questions

1. What do Catholics believe to be the attitude that they should adopt to world poverty?

2. Describe two incidents in the life of Jesus that illustrate the attitude his followers should adopt towards money and wealth.

3. St Paul said, "The love of money is the root of all evil." Do you agree with him? Give reasons for your answer, showing that you have thought about more than one point of view.

4. **a.** What is a less developed country (LDC)?

   b. Describe five characteristics of LDCs and explain why they are important.

5. Describe in detail one Catholic organisation working among the poor and needy in the UK.

6. **a.** Why was CAFOD set up in the first place?

   b. What are the different aspects of the work of CAFOD?

   c. How does CAFOD set about its work?

Beliefs and values

In this topic you will find out about:

- the beliefs of the Catholic Church as expressed in the Apostles' Creed;
- the Church's belief in God, the Father;
- the Church's belief in Jesus;
- the Church's belief in the Holy Spirit;
- the Church's teaching about sin and salvation;
- Christian values.

KEY WORDS

Christ The name given to Jesus to show that he was God's **Messiah**, the one 'anointed by God'.

Crucifixion The Roman method of execution suffered by Jesus.

Dove A symbol for the Holy Spirit to suggest God's peace.

Faith A willingness to trust in the power of God.

Fire A symbol to indicate the purifying power of the Holy Spirit.

Forgiveness The power of God to forgive a person for the sins they have committed.

Incarnation The Christian belief that Jesus was both fully God and fully human: God in human flesh.

Monotheism A belief in one God.

Reconciliation Bringing together people who are separated, also bringing together a sinner and God.

Repentance An expression of a sorrow for one's sins and a willingness to change.

Resurrection Refers to Jesus being brought back to life by God and also to all believers being brought back to life when Christ returns.

Trinity The Christian belief that God is one in three Persons.

Virgin Birth The belief that Jesus was conceived in Mary's womb by the Holy Spirit and that Mary remained a virgin.

Wind A symbol for the Holy Spirit to indicate his power.

45 THE BELIEFS OF THE CHURCH

The basic beliefs of the Catholic Church are those expressed in the **Apostles' Creed**. The origin of this Creed was not the original apostles of Jesus. Instead it was a baptismal confession of faith that summed up the teaching of the apostles and the early Church (extract A). New converts to the faith used it to declare that they genuinely believed in Jesus and accepted the teachings of the Church.

> **A** ❝*I believe in God, the Father Almighty, Creator of heaven and earth.*
>
> *I believe in Jesus Christ, his only Son, our Lord. He was conceived by the power of the Holy Spirit and born of the Virgin Mary. He suffered under Pontius Pilate, was crucified, died and was buried. He descended to the dead. On the third day he rose again. He ascended into heaven, and is seated at the right hand of the Father. He will come again to judge the living and the dead.*
>
> *I believe in the Holy Spirit, the Holy Catholic Church, the communion of saints, the forgiveness of sins, the resurrection of the body and the life everlasting.*❞
>
> (The Apostles' Creed)

Like other early Creeds, the main content of the Apostles' Creed fell into three parts:

1. I believe in God

The Apostles' Creed begins with a very short statement of belief in God. Christianity is very much a **monotheistic** faith: believing in one God. It believes that this God is both the Father (close to all who believe) and yet Almighty (all-powerful, and beyond all human reach and understanding). He is eternal (without beginning or end) and infinite (without any restriction or limit).

Jesus taught his disciples to refer to God as their Father. This underlined to them that they owed their very existence to God. He is the great Creator God who brought the heavens, the earth and all life – with whom he has a close relationship similar to the one they have with their earthly father – into existence. At the same time he does not fail them or let them down as their human father might do.

2. I believe in Jesus Christ

The major part of the Creed is taken up with describing the life and death of Jesus, the only Son of the Father and our Lord. His birth was extraordinary; he was conceived by the power of the Holy Spirit and born to the Virgin Mary. He suffered at the hands of the Roman governor, Pontius Pilate, was crucified, died and was buried. While dead he descended into hell. On the third day after dying he rose again from the dead and ascended into heaven, where he is seated at the right hand of his Father. From there he will return to judge the living and the dead at some future time – an event known as the Second Coming.

3. I believe in the Holy Spirit

The Church states its belief in the Holy Spirit, the third member of the **Trinity**, although it does not actually use that word. The Church believed in a Trinity of three Persons, each of them divine and equal, joined together in perfect unity but not separate Gods. In one way it is a Trinity of revelation – God is revealed to the world as the Father Creator, Jesus is revealed to the world as the Saviour and the Holy Spirit is revealed as God in action in the world today.

The Creed ends with further statements of belief.

I believe:

- in the Holy Catholic Church
- in the communion of saints (the mystical bond that links the living with the dead)
- in the forgiveness of sins
- in the resurrection of the body
- in the life everlasting.

▶ *The Apostles' Creed was mainly concerned with providing a summary of the life, death and resurrection of Jesus.*

TASKS

1. What was the original intention of the Apostles' Creed?
2. Sum up what the Apostles' Creed says about:
   a. God, the Father
   b. God, the Son

✳ DISCUSSION POINT

The Creeds are very old. Do you think that it would be a good idea for the Catholic Church, and others, to come up with a modern Creed? Do you foresee any major problems in attempting to do this?

46 GOD, THE FATHER

From the Apostles' Creed we learn three things about God.

1. The Oneness of God

As the Apostles' Creed begins with the fundamental statement - "I believe in God, the Father Almighty, Creator of heaven and earth" – so we encounter the basis for the Roman Catholic belief in God. The belief in the oneness (the unity) of God, a belief called monotheism, is firmly rooted in the Old Testament. The Jews acknowledged that there was one God who had to be worshipped with the whole heart, soul and strength. This faith was later confirmed by Jesus (source A).

> **A** ❝This is the first [commandment]: Listen, Israel, the Lord our God is the one, only Lord and you must love the Lord your God with all your heart, with all your soul, with all your mind and with all your strength.❞
>
> (Mark 12.29–30)

2. The Fatherhood of God

The favourite description by Jesus of God was to refer to him as his Father. He taught his disciples that they should address God this way as well. We can see this clearly in the prayer that Jesus taught his disciples to use – the Lord's Prayer or the 'Our Father' (extract B). By using this term to refer to God, Jesus was drawing on a familiar word to his followers – the word 'father' – but also expanding it beyond its normal meaning.

▶ The Bible account of creation emphasises that human beings are different from the remainder of creation – they alone are capable of worshipping God.

B ❝*He said to them, 'When you pray, this is what to say: Father, may your name be held holy, your kingdom come; give us each day our daily bread, and forgive us our sins, for we ourselves forgive each one who is in debt to us. And do not put us to the test.'*❞
(Luke 11.2–4)

God is like a normal father and yet different. Just like an earthly father he is intensely concerned for the welfare of his children: he feeds them, clothes them and provides a roof over their heads. He takes every opportunity to show his love for them. He tries to protect them from all dangers. Yet he never lets them down – as an earthly father sometimes does. Most important of all, he sent his Son into the world to give the perfect example of his love for them – to die so that their sins might be forgiven.

The Apostles' Creed calls God the 'Almighty Father' and that is important. If the idea of God as Father stresses his close interest in all his children then this emphasises that God is also all-powerful and that nothing lies beyond his power and authority. Christians recognise this at the end of the Lord's Prayer when they say "For yours is the kingdom, the power and the glory".

3. God the creator

Catholics believe that God is the Creator of the heavens and the earth – the creator of all life, as the Apostles' Creed says. This does not mean that Catholics reject the theory of evolution as an explanation of how life began. They believe that science answers the question: "What kind of world do we live in and how did it begin?" The Biblical story of creation answers another question: "Why is there a world of any kind to live in?" Everything that we discover about the natural world should increase our sense of wonder and awe.

The story of creation in the opening chapters of the Bible (Genesis 1.1– 2.3) makes it clear that the creation of the first human beings was the summit of God's creative activity – his masterpiece. This is because the first man and woman were made 'in the image of God'. This means that they were given a spiritual capacity – a soul or spirit – that was not given to any other part of creation. They alone are capable of worshipping their Creator.

As we say in unit 45, Christians believe that God is a Trinity. They do not believe that there are three Gods but that God has revealed himself in three different Persons: as God, the Father, God, the Son and God, the Holy Spirit. In other words, God is a Unity.

1. What do Christians believe about God, the Father?

2. What do Christians believe about God, the Creator?

3. "It is important that Christians believe that God created the world in six days. If this conflicts with the findings of science, then it's too bad." Do you agree with this comment?

TASKS

47 JESUS (1)

Most of the Apostles' Creed is taken up with stating the beliefs of the early Christians about Jesus. In the opening sentence there are four references to Jesus that are important.

1. Jesus

There are two accounts of the birth of Jesus in the Gospels – in Matthew's Gospel and Luke's Gospel. In Luke's account the Angel Gabriel tells Mary, in an event known as the Annunciation, that she is going to conceive and bear a son – and that she must call him Jesus (God saves). The angel then went on to explain the reason for his name: "He will be great and will be called the Son of the Most High" (Luke 1.32). This was a clear reference to the reason for the coming of Jesus – he was going to save the people from their sins.

▲ *The basic belief held by Christians about Jesus is that he was both God and man.*

2. The Christ

The Greek word 'Christos' is the equivalent of the Hebrew title 'Messiah' and means 'the anointed one'. It was the name given by the Jews to the One they believed God would send as their King and Saviour. He would be God's agent in bringing into being the new age of righteousness and peace. The title summed up all the expectations that were expressed in the Jewish Scriptures.

The disciples of Jesus came to recognise, with the help of divine illumination, that Jesus was the Christ. A supreme moment of insight came to the Apostle Peter at Caesarea Philippi and you can find his declaration in extract A.

> **A** ❝*'But you' he said 'who do you say I am?' Then Simon Peter spoke up and said, You are the Christ, the Son of the living God. Jesus replied, 'Simon son of Jonah, you are a blessed man! Because it was no human agency that revealed this to you but my Father in heaven.'*❞
>
> *(Matthew 16.15–17)*

After the resurrection of Jesus from the dead, the disciples were confident that he was the Christ and they proclaimed this message to the Jews. It became common for the early Christians to speak of Jesus, the Christ, which was shortened to 'Jesus Christ' or 'Christ Jesus'. The Church soon began to use the title 'Christ' as the one word that contained the other names and titles of the One that they served and worshipped.

3. The only Son of God

The Catholic Catechism draws our attention to the fact that in the Old Testament the title 'sons of God' was given to angels, the Jews themselves and their kings. It underlines the very close relationship that exists between God and his creatures. Applied to Jesus, however, the title reminds us that Jesus was both fully human and yet fully divine. As a human being he shared with us all the human feelings and emotions that we experience. As God he had a relationship with God that no human being could possibly experience. After his resurrection from the dead the full extent of his divine sonship was made clear.

4. Lord

This is a title for God from the Old Testament and it is used in the New Testament to refer both to the God of Israel and also Jesus when he had ascended into heaven. In Christian worship it can apply to God in general and to Jesus in particular. It is, therefore, recognition that Jesus is God.

Although not mentioned in the Apostles' Creed, an important description of Jesus in the Gospels is that of 'the Word of God' (the Logos). This description was first used by John in his Gospel (1.1). The Catholic Catechism explains the word as describing Jesus, the eternal Son of God, who existed with God, the Father from the beginning of time. The Word became incarnate (took on human flesh) when Jesus was born.

> **B** **❝At the time appointed by God; the only Son of the Father, the eternal Word, that is, the Word and substantial Image of the Father, became incarnate; without losing his divine nature, he has assumed human nature.❞**
> (CCC 479)

TASKS

1. What is the meaning of:
   a. Jesus?
   b. Christ?
2. What do Christians mean when they call Jesus 'Lord'?

48 JESUS (2)

In unit 47 we saw four different names or titles that are given by the Christian Church to Jesus. Now we look at the different statements that are found in the Apostles' Creed about Jesus which cover both the beginning and the end of his life.

1. Conceived by the power of the Holy Spirit and born of the Virgin Mary

Roman Catholics believe that as Jesus was divine he could not have been conceived like every other human being. Instead he was conceived supernaturally in the womb of Mary by the power of the Holy Spirit. As the eternal Son of God, Christians believe that Jesus was not conceived normally through sexual intercourse. If Jesus had been conceived normally he would have inherited original sin and so could not have been sinless. Catholics also believe that Mary herself was 'immaculately conceived' and so could not have passed on the taint of original sin to her son. The unique birth of Jesus is called the Virgin Birth.

The pregnancy of Mary followed the usual course and so the birth of Jesus was perfectly normal. Catholics believe that Mary was a virgin when Jesus was born and that she remained a virgin throughout her life. The birth of God as a human being is called the Incarnation.

2. Suffered under Pontius Pilate, was crucified, died and was buried

We believe that Jesus was put to death in either 29 or 30BCE during the time that Pontius Pilate was the Roman governor of Judea. He was arrested in the Garden of Gethsemane, taken before the Jewish leaders who accused him of blasphemy, appeared before Pilate where he was accused of treason, condemned to death and then crucified (the crucifixion). Christians believe that the death of Jesus was not an accident of history but part of God's plan for the salvation of the world.

3. Descended into hell

Jews at the time of Jesus believed that hell was a real place of darkness and punishment under the earth. It has always been a part of the Church's belief that Jesus visited hell between the time that he was put to death and the time that he rose from the dead.

4. On the third day he rose again

Christians believe that death was not the end for Jesus. Because he was God, his Father in heaven brought him back to life on the third day. This is the most important event in the Christian faith. By his death Jesus secured the forgiveness of the human race and his resurrection was final proof of this. Soon after his resurrection, Jesus appeared to many of his followers. Paul told them in his letters that the resurrection of Jesus from the dead was the guarantee to every believer that they, too, would rise from the dead. Jesus was the first of countless numbers who would also rise again (extract A).

Christians believe that it was by the death of Jesus that the forgiveness of their sins is made possible.

> **A** **"**Christ, 'the first-born from the dead' is the principle of our own resurrection.**"**
>
> (CCC 658)

5. Jesus ascended into heaven and is seated at the right hand of the father

Jesus spent forty days with his disciples after his resurrection before being taken up from the earth in an event known as the Ascension. Christians believe that he is now in heaven interceding with God on behalf of his followers on earth. To say that Jesus is 'seated on the right hand of God, the Father' is simply a way of saying that he has been given the place of supreme power and authority by God.

6. Jesus will come again to judge the living and the dead

Christians believe in the Second Coming (the **Parousia**). It will be a time of judgement when the eternal destiny of all human beings will be decided. As the parable of the sheep and the goats (Matthew 25.31–46) makes clear, people will finally be judged on how they have treated other needy human beings.

TASKS

1. Describe Christian beliefs about Jesus of Nazareth.
2. "Both the birth and the end of the life of Jesus were supernatural." Do you agree? Give reasons for your answer, showing that you have thought about more than one point of view.

✳ DISCUSSION POINT

Why do you think that the resurrection of Jesus is the most important Christian belief – or maybe you don't?

49 THE HOLY SPIRIT

The Roman Catholic Church is totally committed to its belief in the Trinity – God, the Father, God, the Son and God, the Holy Spirit. The order in which they are placed here, and in which they are presented in worship, does not represent in any sense an order of importance. The three Persons of the Trinity are absolutely equal with one another and one does not have precedence over the others. It simply indicates the order in which they have been revealed and made known to the world through the Bible:

- God, the Father, created the world in the beginning and continues to give it the life which sustains it day by day.

- God, the Son, was revealed through the Incarnation and given the task of redeeming the world. He did this by offering up his life to save it. After rising from the dead, Jesus returned to his Father in heaven.

- God, the Holy Spirit, although present in both the Creation and the Incarnation, is primarily the One who was promised by Jesus to come alongside those who were witnessing to their faith in front of hostile crowds after Jesus left the earth. He was revealed to the world on the **Day of Pentecost** when he was given to the early Christians (see below). He continues to be the power of God in action in the world today. Catholics believe that the Holy Spirit now works through the Church bringing life and breath to every part of the Church's witness in the modern world.

▲ *This banner reminds us that the Holy Spirit came like a mighty, rushing wind on the Day of Pentecost.*

A **"***The Trinity is One. We do not confess three Gods, but one God in three persons, the 'consubstantial Trinity'. The divine persons do not share the one divinity among themselves but each of them is God whole and entire. 'The Father is that which the Son is, the Son is that which the Father is, the Father and the Son that which the Holy Spirit is, i.e. by nature one God.'***"**
(CCC 253)

The giving of the Holy Spirit

In Acts 2 we discover how the disciples were huddled together in the city of Jerusalem after Jesus ascended into heaven – a very dispirited group of people without any real hope or direction. Suddenly they heard the sound of a mighty rushing wind blowing through the room where they were meeting and saw tongues of fire sitting on each one of them. They had been given the Holy Spirit as Jesus promised they would. On this day the Church was born and the Church is the place where Catholics can know the life-giving Holy Spirit today:

In the Holy Scriptures.

In Church tradition.

CHECK IT OUT

In prayer.

WHERE THE HOLY SPIRIT IS FOUND TODAY...

In the Church's **Magisterium**.

In the charisms and ministries of the Church.

In the signs of the apostolic and missionary life.

In the witness of the saints.

When Catholics profess their faith in the statement of the Apostles' Creed – "I believe in the Holy Spirit" – they are really stating their need for God's help and power to live out the Christian life in the world today. They receive that help through the inspiration of the Scriptures, which they hear being read in church and read in their own personal devotions. They also receive help through the continuing teaching ministry and authority of the Church. Even as they pray and look for inspiration in the lives of those who have lived and died before them (the saints) so they are recognising that the work of the Holy Spirit goes on, unbroken, from age to age.

TASKS

1. Outline the beliefs that Christians hold about the Holy Spirit.
2. What do Christians mean when they say that they believe in the Trinity?

✱ DISCUSSION POINT

How do you think that Christians today might be aware of the Holy Spirit's power in their everyday lives?

50 THE SYMBOLS OF THE HOLY SPIRIT

Throughout the New Testament different symbols or images are provided to help us to understand the work of the Holy Spirit. Here are three of the most important.

1. Fire

In the Old Testament, fire was used as a symbol in two ways:

1. It covered – masked – the appearance of God. When God appeared to Moses, for instance, he did so in a burning bush that appeared to be on fire and yet was not burned. God then spoke to Moses out of the burning bush so that he would not be able to see God himself.

2. It purified. Metals were placed in the burning fire to burn away the dross, the base elements, so purifying the metal itself.

Christians believe that speaking of the Holy Spirit as a fire is very appropriate. When the Holy Spirit was given to the disciples on the Day of Pentecost he appeared as tongues of fire sitting on each of them. God uses the Holy Spirit to purify his followers before they are considered fit to enter heaven. The Holy Spirit is the purifier who cleanses the hearts of all Christians and gives them God's power for living the Christian life. For Catholics this work of purification begins with **baptism** and continues through the sacrament of confirmation.

2. Wind

In the Old and New Testaments the wind was a mystery. People knew that it was blowing because they felt it and, if it blew strongly enough, it could be highly destructive. The problem, though, was that the wind could not be seen. One writer in the Old Testament said that life could be as meaningless as trying to chase after the wind (Ecclesiastes 2.11). This is why the wind was thought to be a good symbol for the presence of God – people knew when they had experienced it but they could never see it.

It is noticeable that when the Holy Spirit was given to the early Christians (Acts 2) he came to them with the sound of a mighty rushing wind. For them the Holy Spirit was the source of God's power. Until this time, the disciples were huddled together behind closed doors and frightened of being arrested by the Romans. Now, with the Holy Spirit, they were transformed into a fearless group willing to lay down their lives for what they believed.

3. The dove

The dove, released by Noah after the flood, brought back an olive-tree branch as a sign that the waters had receded from the earth (Genesis 8.8–12). The dove was a symbol of peace and of the promise by God that he would never again seek to destroy the earth that he had created. After his baptism by **John the Baptist**, the Holy Spirit came to Jesus in the form of a dove (Matthew 3.16) to show what kind of ministry Jesus was going to perform. He was to be the Prince of Peace. Peace is an important theme running through the New Testament:

- The father of John the Baptist looked forward to the coming of Jesus as the one who would give light to those who live in darkness and guide their feet in the way of peace (Luke 1.79).

- In the Beatitudes, where Jesus listed the spiritual characteristics required of those who would enter God's kingdom, we read:

A **"Blessed are the peacemakers: they shall be recognised as children of God."**
(Matthew 5.9)

- Paul listed peace among the many 'fruit of the Spirit' (Galatians 5.22).

The Catechism recognises the importance of the Catholic Church working to bring about peace in the world. It also recognises that injustice will need to be removed before peace can be experienced (extract B).

▲ The dove is a powerful image of peace and has been adopted by many modern agencies, including the United Nations, to convey this clear message.

B **"Injustice, excessive economic or social inequalities, envy, distrust and pride raging among men and nations constantly threaten peace and cause wars. Everything done to overcome these disorders contributes to building up peace and avoiding war."**
(CCC 2317)

TASKS

1. What can we learn from the symbols of fire, wind and the dove about the work of the Holy Spirit?

2. What can the symbol of the dove, when applied to the Holy Spirit, teach us about peace in the modern world?

51 SIN AND SALVATION

What is sin?

In Roman Catholic teaching the word 'sin' is used to describe two separate realities:

1. Original sin – the sin of Adam that has brought such evil effects on the human race. Each person inherits a natural tendency to do wrong, when they are born, and this is translated into actual sinful actions throughout his or her life.

2. Actual sin – a fundamental choice to act against the laws of God, a free and willing turning away from God's love and laws as they are found in the Bible. In Catholic teaching actual sins might be:

    – mortal (grave and serious), a deliberate going against the will of God.

    – committing a sin in a grave matter

    – venial (less serious).

Any sin, however, is a challenge to the law of God and is damaging to the Church (extract A).

> **A** ❝Sin is before all else an offence against God, a rupture of communion with him. At the same time it damages communion with the Church. For this reason conversion entails both God's forgiveness and **reconciliation** with the Church, which are expressed and accomplished liturgically by the sacrament of Penance and Reconciliation.❞
> (CCC 1440)

Repentance and faith

John the Baptist was the cousin of Jesus and born just a short while before him. The Gospels make it clear that, just as Jesus was called by God to be the Messiah, John was called to be the Forerunner of the Messiah – the one who went before him to prepare the hearts and the minds of the people. Luke summed up the ministry of John as he began to baptise people in the River Jordan – we are told that John went through the whole Jordan area proclaiming "a baptism of repentance for the forgiveness of sins" (Luke 3.3).

Repentance means a person showing a genuine sorrow for the sins they have committed – and then going further by taking steps to put matters right. This is the only way that a person can demonstrate that his or her repentance is genuine. John told those listening that they must share what they had with those who had nothing. Tax collectors must only take from people what they owed – and no more. Soldiers should not extort money from people just because they were powerful enough to do so. To put things right is a sign that the repentance has been genuine.

Forgiveness of sins and reconciliation

Forgiveness of Sins

The teaching in the letters of Paul and the teaching of the Roman Catholic Church are very clear – everyone has sinned and fallen short of God's glory. This places them firmly under the judgement of God, since a holy God must always judge sin. Human beings can never offer God anything to persuade him to overlook their sinful behaviour. This is why the death of Jesus was the only hope for humankind. Jesus was perfect, without sin, and so his sacrifice for sin was acceptable to God. The sins of the world can be forgiven because of the perfect sacrifice that God himself provided by offering up the life of his own Son on the cross.

▲ In the Catholic Church, the confession of sins to a priest is an important spiritual discipline.

Reconciliation

Sins break relationships. It breaks relationships between people. Most importantly, it breaks any relationship between God and human beings. The death of Jesus brought together (reconciled) God and humanity. Catholics believe that God is able to offer the world his reconciliation through the sacrament of baptism and it can then be renewed day by day through the sacrament of penance and a regular celebration of the Mass.

This is how the Catechism explains this:

> **B** 66 *The confession (or disclosure) of sins, even from a simply human point of view, frees us and facilitates our reconciliation with others. Through such an admission man looks squarely at the sins he is guilty of, takes responsibility for them, and thereby opens himself again to God and the communion of the Church...* 99
> (CCC 1455)

TASKS

1. What does the Catholic Church mean when it uses the word 'sin'?
2. How would you explain the meaning of the word 'repentance'?
3. What is meant by forgiveness and reconciliation?

52 CHRISTIAN VALUES

Loving God and loving others

A Jewish leader listened, on one occasion, to Jesus debating with his enemies and was very impressed by the answers that he gave (Mark 12.28–34). He asked Jesus which was the greatest of all the commandments in the Jewish Scriptures and in reply Jesus gave him the two commandments that summed up the whole of the Jewish law – extract A.

> **A** **"**Listen, Israel, the Lord our God is the one, only Lord, and you must love the Lord your God with all your heart, with all your soul, with all your mind and with all your strength. The second is this: You must love your neighbour as yourself.**"**
> (Mark 12.29–31)

We can see from this that when we are talking about Christian values the most important of them is love – a love for God and a love for others. We turn to the apostle Paul for an expansion on this theme, when he looks at the three great Christian values of faith, hope and love, concluding that love is the greatest of them all. In 1 Corinthians 13 he tells us what the characteristics of this love are:

- Love is always patient and kind.
- Love is never jealous.
- Love is not boastful or conceited.
- Love is never rude nor seeking its own advantage.
- Love does not take offence or store up grievances.
- Love does not rejoice in wrongdoing but finds its joy in the truth.
- Love is always ready to make allowances, to trust, to hope and to endure whatever comes.
- Love is eternal.

Loving others

Jesus told two parables that sought to explain what it meant in practice to love one's neighbour.

The Good Samaritan (Luke 10.25–37)

This parable was told to answer the direct question "Who is my neighbour?" The point that Jesus was making here is simply that my neighbour is anyone who is in need. The centuries-long antagonism between the Jews and the Samaritans, which forms the background to this parable, would have made it even more surprising to the listeners of Jesus. Jesus was simply saying that a people's needs take precedence over everything else – including their nationality, religion or colour. He was also making the point that true love is a very practical thing – it is not a warm feeling inside or kind words but it is actually doing something practical.

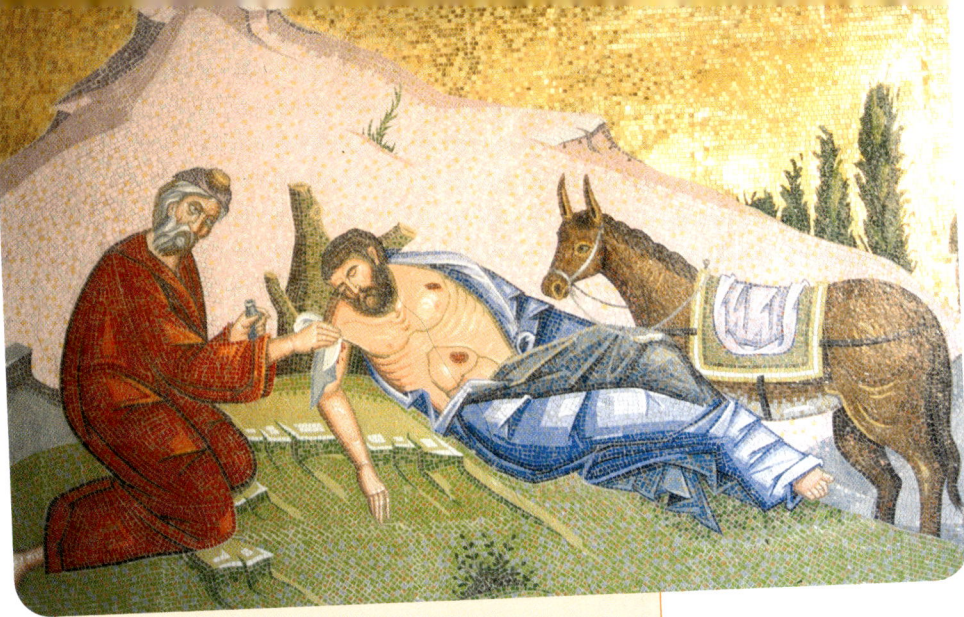

▲ *The parable of the Good Samaritan was one of the parables that Jesus told to teach that love is much more a matter of action than feelings.*

The Sheep and the Goats (Matthew 25.31–46)

Here Jesus is speaking of the Judgement on the Last Day, when Jesus returns to the earth with his angels. He explains that this judgement would only be based on one thing – how individuals have treated Jesus:

- Did they give food to him when he was hungry?
- Did they give water to him when he was thirsty?
- Did they take him in and make him welcome when he was a stranger?
- Did they give him clothes when he was naked?
- Did they look after him when he was sick?
- Did they visit him when he was a prisoner?

Those who were chosen for heaven were surprised to find that they had done these things for Jesus. Jesus, though, explained that just as they had done them for others so they had done them for him. This is true love and an explanation of what it means to love one's neighbour in practice.

TASKS

1. What did Jesus say were the two great Christian values?
2. Describe two parables in which Jesus seeks to explain what is involved in loving one's neighbour.

✳ DISCUSSION POINT

What do you think might be involved in loving one's neighbour in the modern world?

EXAM HELP

In the examination

Make sure that you know about:

GOD THE FATHER

- The three basic beliefs of the Catholic Church. The Apostles' Creed and its origin. The belief in God – Christianity is a monotheistic religion – believing in one God. God is both the Father of all and the Almighty One – eternal (without beginning or end) and infinite (without limit). The Creator God. Belief in Jesus – a supernatural birth to the Virgin Mary; that he suffered under Pontius Pilate, was crucified, died, descended into hell, was buried – and rose from the dead. Left earth to ascend into heaven. The Second Coming, a time of judgement. Belief in the Holy Spirit, the holy Catholic Church, the forgiveness of sins, the communion of saints and everlasting life. A Trinity of Retribution.

- God, the Father. The Oneness of God. Christianity is very strongly a monotheistic religion. The Fatherhood of God as in the Lord's Prayer. Similarity and differences between God, the Father, and a human father. God the Father, Almighty. God the Creator – the Bible answers why God made everything while science answers the question of how. Human beings given a spiritual capacity by God that makes them unique. God is a Trinity – not three Gods but God in three persons.

- Jesus. The importance of the names Jesus (Saviour), the Christ (God's 'anointed one' or Messiah), the only Son of God (the importance of this phrase in the Old Testament highlights the fact that Jesus was fully God and fully man), Lord (a recognition that Jesus was God as it was applied to God in the Old Testament). Also an important description of Jesus as the Logos (the Word of God).

- Further statements about Jesus in the Apostles' Creed – conceived in the womb of Mary by the Holy Spirit; born to the Virgin Mary, the Virgin Birth; the Incarnation, the birth of God in human form; suffered under Pontius Pilate, accused of blasphemy by the Jews and of treason by the Romans; was crucified, died and was buried; descended into hell; rose again on the third day. The importance of the resurrection to the Christian Church; Jesus ascended into heaven and seated on the right hand of God, the Father. The Ascension; Jesus will come again to judge everyone, called the Second Coming.

THE TRINITY AND THE HOLY SPIRIT

- The Trinity. The importance of the Christian belief in the Trinity. Equality of the three Persons of the Trinity. God, the Father – the Creator, who made and sustains the world. God, the Son – the Redeemer – He was revealed through the Incarnation. God, the Holy Spirit – the power of God in the world, given to the Christian Church on the Day of Pentecost. The order of importance.

- God, the Holy Spirit. The giving of the Holy Spirit on the Day of Pentecost. The birth of the Christian Church. Where the Holy Spirit is found today – in the Scriptures, Church tradition, magisterium, Sacraments, prayer, the ministries of the Church, signs of apostolic life, the witness of the saints. To say "I believe in the Holy Spirit" is a plea for God's help.

- Three important symbols in the Bible for the Holy Spirit: fire, which appeared on the Day of Pentecost, as God's purifier; wind, as the divine presence that can be felt but not seen, of God's power to give the followers of Jesus courage to speak out and witness; the dove, the bringer of peace, very important in the New Testament.

SIN, SALVATION AND CHRISTIAN VALUES

- Sin and salvation. The difference between original and actual sin. Catholics divide actual sin into mortal and venial. Repentance and faith. The baptism, offered by John the Baptist, of repentance. The meaning of repentance. The forgiveness of sins – everyone needs to seek God's forgiveness. Only possible through the death of Jesus, the perfect sacrifice. Reconciliation – the bringing together of God and the human race – again through the sacrifice of Jesus.

- Christian values – loving God and loving others. The most important Christian virtue is love – Paul's hymn of praise to love in I Corinthians 13. Two parables that show the importance of loving one's neighbour – the Good Samaritan ("Who is my neighbour?") and the sheep and goats ("In loving the least of these my brethren you have loved me").

EXAM HELP

Sample exam questions

1. If you were asked to describe the beliefs of the Catholic Church what would you say?

2. Outline the beliefs that Catholics hold about God, the Father.

3. Explain the significance of each of these titles of Jesus:

    a. Jesus

    b. the Christ

    c. the only Son of God

    d. the Lord

4. "Jesus was both divine and human." Do you agree with this comment? Give reasons for your answer, showing that you have thought about more than one point of view.

5. Outline the teaching of the Apostles' Creed on Jesus and explain the meaning and importance of each phrase.

6. What do we learn about the nature of the Holy Spirit from the symbols of fire, wind and the dove?

7. What do Catholics believe about sin and salvation?

8. What do we learn from the parable of the sheep and goats about the importance of loving others?

Community and tradition

In this topic you will find out about:

- the purpose of Jesus in founding the Christian Church and choosing his disciples to continue his work;
- the 'high' view the Catholic Church holds of the Church believing that it is central to God's plan for human salvation;
- the Church encouraging the growth of the first shoots of faith and nurturing this faith through the sacraments of baptism and confirmation;
- the Church preparing us for the journey of death at the end of our life.

KEY WORDS

Apostolic Applied to the Church, this means that its authority and teaching goes back to the apostles of Jesus.

Apostolic Succession The authority of the disciples of Jesus passed down through the laying on of hands to bishops in the Church.

Bible The holy book for all Christians.

Bishops Priests chosen to be responsible for the churches in an area called a diocese.

Body of Christ A term often applied to the Church to show that it is made up of many different people, each with their own gifts.

Catholic Applied to the Church, meaning 'universal'.

Celibacy The requirement that Catholic priests do not marry.

Communion of Saints A term used in the Apostles' Creed to indicate that the Church is a fellowship of all believers, alive and dead.

Deacons People ordained to serve the Church, usually at the stage before they are ordained as priests.

Dogmas Beliefs that are held and taught by the Catholic Church.

Faith The trust that believers place in God, the body of belief of which the Church is the custodian.

Holy One of the characteristics of God, which all believers are expected to emulate.

Laity Members of the Church who are not ordained.

Magisterium The Pope and the bishops of the Church receiving the inspiration of the Holy Spirit to decide what the Church should believe and teach.

Ordination The anointing of someone to serve the Church as a bishop, priest or deacon.

Papacy The office of the Pope.

Priests Men called to be responsible for a church and for administering the Sacraments to its members.

53 THE CHURCH

Through his life and teaching, Jesus began God's work on earth as he started to build up the divine kingdom. He knew, however, that his time on earth was going to be very brief and so one of the first things that he did was to choose 12 disciples to continue with the work after he returned to his Father in heaven. The movement that Jesus began soon grew into the Christian Church (extract A).

For a time there was only one Church, although it was not long before Christian believers began to disagree among themselves. They disagreed over the way that the Church should be organised and who should be allowed to join – and on what terms. Should the Church still be attached to the Jewish faith out of which it had grown – or should it have a totally independent existence? That matter was soon settled when the early Christian leaders met together in Jerusalem around 49BCE. There were soon, however, far more serious disagreements over Christian belief, or doctrine.

> **A** *"The Church in her doctrine, life and worship, perpetuates and transmits to every generation all that she herself is, all that she believes."*
> (CCC 98)

In the 11th century, the first major split occurred in the Church when the Eastern Orthodox Churches split away from the Western Roman Catholic Church. Since then there have been many other splits, including the Reformation in the 16th century, and today the one Christian Church is divided into many different Churches.

The Church – our Mother

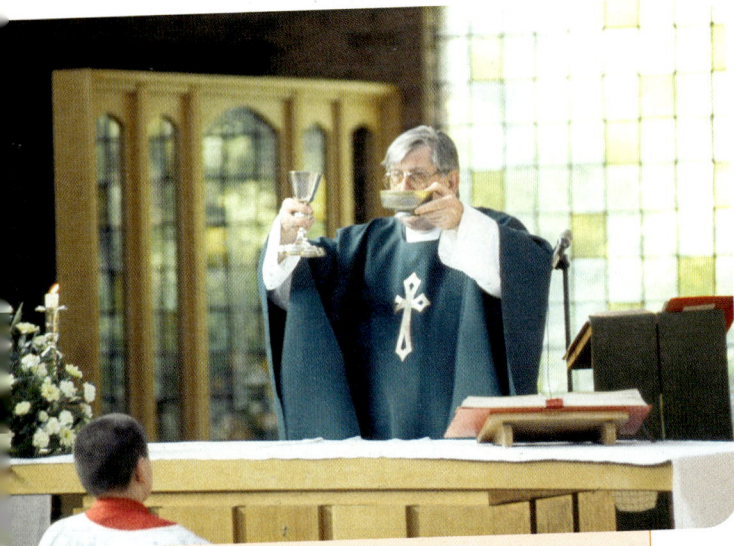
▲ *Worship in church is an essential part of the Christian life for most Catholics.*

Catholics have a very 'high' view of the Church and its place in the salvation of humankind. God has achieved the salvation of the human race through the death and resurrection of Jesus. Human beings are sinful creatures and can do nothing to save themselves through their own efforts. They can only receive the life of faith that God offers to them with the promise of free forgiveness. This offer comes to them through the worship and especially the sacraments of the Church.

B 〝*Salvation comes from God alone; but because we receive the life of faith through the Church, she is our mother. We believe the Church as the mother of our new birth, and not in the Church as if she were the author of our salvation.*〞
(CCC 169)

The Church is the transmitter of our salvation. It nurtures and encourages the first shoots of faith in us that are the fruits of the new birth that we experience through baptism. It provides the means by which that faith is 'confirmed' and encourages its growth as we are given opportunities to serve God through the Church. In later life, the sacrament of Anointing prepares us for the journey that is called death. These are the different ways in which the Church can be called our Mother. It exists to guide and help each believer towards a mature and adult faith in God.

Salvation, then, is something that grows and matures throughout life. The Church plays a central role in the process. That is why Catholics refer to the Church as God's 'means of salvation'. Eventually it will guide all Catholics to heaven.

▲ *Most Catholics think of their church as a spiritual family in which they can grow in their faith along with other people on the same spiritual journey.*

TASKS

1. What kind of problems did the Church have to face in the early centuries of its existence?

2. In what sense do you think that Catholics speak of 'Mother Church' and what do they mean by it?

✳ DISCUSSION POINT

In what sense do you think that Catholics feel that they 'need' the Church?

54 THE FOUR CHARACTERISTICS OF THE CHURCH

According to the Creed there are four distinctive characteristics of the Christian Church:

1. The Church is one

Although it takes many forms, the Christian Church is essentially one. The Catholic Church offers itself to all other Churches as the focus of that unity under the leadership of the Pope. It is a unity that stems from the oneness of the Trinity. It is shown by the profession of one faith received directly from the Apostles: the celebration of a single worship – especially the sacraments – and the unbroken line of bishops appointed by apostolic succession.

This is why the bishops at the Second Vatican Council insisted that 'the one true Church' is found in the Catholic Church, which is governed by the successors of St Peter and the bishops who are in communion with him. The fact is, however, that there are few signs of the different Churches even moving closer together let alone uniting. Divisions in the Church arose because of deep disagreements over doctrine and worship, and it seems that those are destined to remain.

▲ *The Church may not be perfect but it is God's chosen instrument to build up the new kingdom on earth.*

> A **"***The Church is one: she acknowledges one Lord, confesses one faith, is born of one Baptism, forms only one Body, is given life by the one Spirit, for the sake of one hope, at whose fulfilment all divisions will be overcome.***"**
> (CCC 866)

2. The Church is holy

The Church is 'the holy people of God' and its members are 'saints'. It is through belonging to the Church and sharing in its worship that people are made holy. Through the Church they share in God's love and love God, and others, in return. The Church is made up of imperfect people but they have the sacraments and the prayers of the saints, especially the **Virgin Mary**, to help them as they struggle with their faith.

> B **"***The Church is holy: the Most Holy God is her author; Christ, her bridegroom, gave himself up to make her holy; the spirit of holiness gives her life… Her holiness shines in the saints…***"**
> (CCC 867)

3. The Church is catholic

The Catechism explains that the word 'catholic' here is used to mean 'universal, according to the whole, totality'. Christ is to be found everywhere in the Church because he is its head. The Catholic Church is the true Church because:

- It alone has the orthodox, and correct, profession of faith. This goes all the way back to the origins of the Church.

- It has the full complement of the Sacraments and uses them to deepen the faith of its members.

- It has a ministry directly descended from the apostles of Jesus.

> **C** ❝*The Church is catholic: she proclaims the fullness of the faith. She bears in herself and administers the totality of the means of salvation…She speaks to all men.*❞
>
> *(CCC 868)*

4. The Church is apostolic

Jesus began by choosing 12 disciples (learners). After Jesus left the earth they became apostles (those who are sent). These were the men chosen by Jesus to take the Christian Gospel to all quarters of the Roman Empire. They were later joined in their mission by the greatest leader in the early Church – Paul. The Catholic Church believes that the bishops of the Church today are the successors of the early apostles. The leader of the early apostles was Peter and he has special significance for all Catholics. He was the first Bishop of Rome: the Pope. The office of the Pope is called the Papacy. His authority was handed down to the present holder of the post by apostolic succession.

> **D** ❝*The Church is apostolic. She is built on a lasting foundation…She is upheld infallibly in the truth: Christ governs her through Peter and the other apostles, who are present in their successors, the Pope and the college of bishops.*❞
>
> *(CCC 869)*

TASKS

1. What is meant by 'apostolic succession'?
2. What is meant when the Church is described as:
   a. One?
   b. holy?
   c. Catholic?
   d. apostolic?

55 TWO IMPORTANT PICTURES OF THE CHURCH

There are two pictures or images of the Church that figure prominently in the New Testament. They give us an insight into how the early Christian believers saw the Church.

1. The Church as the body of Christ

It was St Paul who spoke of the Church as being 'the Body of Christ'. This conjures up a picture of the Church being like a human body with Christ himself as its head and all its members as part of the body. This image emphasises two important points about the Church:

1. The importance of each part of the body. The human body is made up of many parts and each one of them has a crucial part to play – the arms, legs, feet and so on. Similarly there are many parts to the Church and each one is as important as the others. You can read what Paul had to say about this in extract A.

> **A** *There is one Body, one Spirit, just as one hope is the goal of your calling by God. There is one Lord, one faith, one baptism and one God...*
>
> *(Ephesians 4.4–6)*

▶ Christians of all denominations believe that they are part of the universal Church and belong to the Communion of Saints.

2. The importance of the head. Just as the head and the body need each other, so there is a very close link between Christ (the head) and the Church (the body). The head fulfils an essential role in the well-being of the body. It provides the sense of direction as well as being the basis of the body's unity and strength. In the same way Christ is the head of the Church and gives the body its strength and direction.

The Communion of Saints

After confessing its belief in the 'Holy Catholic Church' the Apostles' Creed adds "... and in the communion of saints". Above everything else, the Church is a fellowship of believers. It is a fellowship brought into being by the Father, in Christ and through the power of the Holy Spirit. By speaking of the Communion of Saints the Catechism is drawing our attention to the facts that:

- All faithful Christians belong to the fellowship of the Church. God gives his grace to those who are on earth through the sacraments.

- This fellowship, to which all Christians belong, is not broken by death. The Communion of Saints links together all those who are faithful in this life with those who have entered the life beyond. The Catechism spells this idea out more clearly:

  – There are those who are, at the present time 'pilgrims on earth'. Our pilgrimage is hard and we need all the help we can get from those who have gone on ahead of us.

  – There are those who 'have died and are being purified'. This refers to the people who are currently in purgatory. This intermediate place of purification is discussed in unit 8.

  – There are those who are 'in glory, contemplating in full light, God himself triune and one, exactly as he is…'. These are those members of the Communion of Saints who have passed from purgatory into the full glory of heaven.

- Believing that there is a communion that links those on earth with those who have gone beyond, means that Catholics can offer their prayers to God through the saints in heaven. The saints are those who have passed beyond the fires of purgatory into the presence of God himself – heaven. Prayers can also be offered for the dead as all distinctions between heaven and earth have been broken down. The prayers of the saints in heaven contribute in many ways to the building up of the Church on earth.

> **B** **❝***We believe in the communion of all the faithful in Christ, of those who are pilgrims on earth, of the dead who have achieved their purification, of the blessed in heaven, who together form one Church and we believe that in this communion the merciful love of God and of his saints will always hear our prayers.***❞**
> (Credo of the People of God, Pope Paul VI)

56 THE CHRISTIAN MINISTRY (1)

The Second Vatican Council stressed that all believers, both ordained and lay people, are called by God to be 'priests'. All Christians have a vocation (calling) to serve God wherever they have been placed – whether as a nurse, a teacher, a doctor or a taxi-driver. Some Christians, however, believe that they have a special vocation to serve God as a priest, a nun or a monk.

Within the Catholic Church, there are three Orders (levels) in which those who have been ordained to the Christian ministry can serve God. They are:

- *Bishops.* Sometime between the time of Paul and the end of the 1st century, bishops became an important part of the Church's ministry. While Paul, in his letter to Titus, talks of elders as Church leaders (extract A), by 100BCE, St Ignatius wrote about the control that bishops had over Church life (extract B). By the end of the 1st century, it was bishops who had authority in the Christian community and they alone could administer the sacraments. The source of this authority was passed down from the apostles through the 'laying on of hands' (Apostolic Succession). This was underlined by the Second Vatican Council. As long as the Christian community remained small, the bishops could keep this power in their own hands. As the Church spread, however, so the work of the 'presbyter' or priest developed:

> **A** *"...each of them [elders] must be a man of irreproachable character; he must not have been married more than once, and his children must be believers and not uncontrollable or liable to be charged with disorderly conduct."*
>
> *(Titus 1.6)*

> **B** *"From the earliest days of the Church the first place has always been accorded to the bishops because of the life-giving contact between them and the apostles, because of the unbroken succession that links them."*
>
> *(Second Vatican Council)*

- *Priests.* The Order below that of bishop is priest. A priest can celebrate the sacraments, including the Eucharist. A priest can also give a blessing and absolve people from their sins (**Absolution**).
- *Deacons.* The lowest of the three Orders of Christian priesthood. A deacon can lead services and preach the homily. He can take funerals, marry couples and baptise babies. He cannot, however, celebrate **Holy Communion**. For most people, being a deacon is the first step to becoming a priest.

Religious Orders

There are many religious Orders, both male and female, and these can be either contemplative and closed, or open and active in the outside world. The contemplative Orders, such as the Cistercians (male) and the Carmelites (female), give themselves over to a life of silence, prayer and solitude. People who enter these Orders leave their family and all earthly possessions behind, seeking only Jesus. The active Orders also follow lives based on prayer but they are active in education, medical or social work in the community. Members of most religious Orders take the traditional vow of poverty, chastity and obedience.

▶ *Many convents are ageing communities with little sign of new life coming through.*

TASKS

1. What do Catholics mean when they use the word 'vocation'?
2. What particular authority is given to bishops by the Catholic Church?
3. What do you think is the role of religious Orders in the modern world?

✳ DISCUSSION POINT

The number of people offering themselves for ordination to the priesthood and for entry to the Religious Orders has declined drastically in recent years. What explanation can you offer for this and what do you think can be done about it?

57 THE CHRISTIAN MINISTRY (2)

Ordination is the service in which God's help is sought for those about to become bishops, priests and deacons. Ordination shows that the ministry of the Church is always linked with that of Christ and his apostles. It also shows that anyone called to the service of the Church needs the help of God's Holy Spirit.

The ordination of priests

The ordination of priests takes place within the Liturgy of the Eucharist, celebrated by a bishop. Members of the priest's new church must be present since it is among them that the priest has been called by God to serve. In the service that follows:

- the priests are called forward by name. They are asked whether they wish to serve God's people, to which each candidate replies, 'I am ready and willing';

- the bishop obtains confirmation that the person is suitable to serve the people. The congregation shows its approval by responding with the words, 'Thanks be to God';

- the bishop then asks for confirmation that each man is prepared to care for God's people; celebrate the sacraments; dedicate his life to building up God's kingdom and obey the bishop;

- the bishops lay their hands on each candidate as a prayer is offered up (extract A). The hands of the priest are anointed with oil and the symbols of his office are handed over – vestments, a chalice holding bread and wine and a paten on which rests the bread to be consecrated;

- the ceremony ends with the exchange of the Sign of Peace;

- the liturgy ends with the newly ordained priest celebrating Mass with the bishop and fellow priests.

▲ *During the ordination service, priests lie flat on their faces to show that they are placing themselves at the service of everyone and God.*

The ordination of a bishop

The consecration of a bishop confers on him responsibilities given by Christ – to teach, to rule and to sanctify (make holy) the people entrusted to his care. During his ordination, the bishop is given the Gospel book, his episcopal ring, a mitre, a staff (crozier) and the Bishop's Chair. As the successor to the apostles, the bishop is expected to act as a good shepherd to those who have been entrusted to his care.

Celibacy

The Orthodox Church allows married men to become priests although it does not allow priests to marry after they are ordained. Orthodox bishops have to be unmarried. In the Nonconformist Churches, no restrictions are placed on ministers, who may be married or not. In fact, such Churches believe that married people can minister better to the needs of their congregations. Women also can be ministers. The Anglican Church in this country admits women to the priesthood, although to date (2006), no woman has been ordained to be a bishop.

Since the 4th century, it has been characteristic of the Roman Catholic Church to have celibate priests. It became Church law in 1139. The last Pope, John Paul II, made it very clear that he was opposed to the idea of opening the priesthood to married men. He stated that a priest always represents Christ when he is standing at the altar giving the Eucharist; or preaching and administering the sacrament to someone who is ill. As such, he must be male and celibate.

> **A** *"Almighty Father, grant to this servant of yours the dignity of priesthood. Renew within him the spirit of holiness. As a co-worker with the order of bishops, may he be faithful to the ministry that he receives from you, Lord God, and be to others a model of right conduct."*
>
> *(Prayer at ordination of a priest)*

TASKS

1. What is ordination?
2. Describe the service in which deacons and priests are ordained.
3. In Titus 1.5–9, Paul describes the kind of person that he would expect to be appointed an elder (priest). Describe just what those qualities are.

58 THE LAITY

The role of the laity in the Church

The laity is a term that describes all those members of the Catholic Church who are not in the priesthood nor members of a Religious Order. These people, the vast majority of the Church, are essential members of the Body of Christ (the Church) and have their part to play in carrying the Gospel to the world. This was one of the basic messages of the Second Vatican Council.

Just as those who enter the priesthood or a Religious Order have a vocation from God so do the laity. This was made clear in 1946 by Pope Pius XII (extract A).

> **A** 	*…the laity is the front line of Church life…they, in particular, ought to have an ever clearer consciousness of belonging to the Church, that is to say, the community of the faithful on earth under the leadership of the Pope, the common Head, and of the bishops in communion with them. They are the Church.*
>
> *(Pope Pius XII)*

The Catechism applauds the words of Pope Pius XII and makes the following points:

1. For the true believer the whole of life – work, prayer, married life and relaxation – can be offered as a spiritual sacrifice to God. So, too, can any suffering.

2. The whole of a person's life can be offered as a sacrifice to God every time they take the Eucharist.

3. Every Church member must look out for opportunities to share the Gospel of Christ with others.

4. Within the local church, all members are expected to offer their best gifts to God for the benefit and blessing of the Church as a whole.

The ordination of women

Ordination is a sacrament through which a man is given the authority to share the sacraments with members of his congregation. The clear teaching of the Catholic Church is that only men can be ordained because only a man can represent Christ before God as he stands at the altar. The Catholic Church has been strongly opposed to the ordination of women since earliest times and re-emphasised it in 1976 and again in 1994.

This opposition to women priests is based on the following arguments:

1. When Jesus chose twelve disciples to continue his work after he left the earth he only chose men for the task.

2. When the disciples (apostles) later chose bishops and priests to take over the work of leading the developing Christian Church they only chose men.

3. The Church cannot change anything to do with any of the seven sacraments and this would involve a change to the sacrament of ordination.

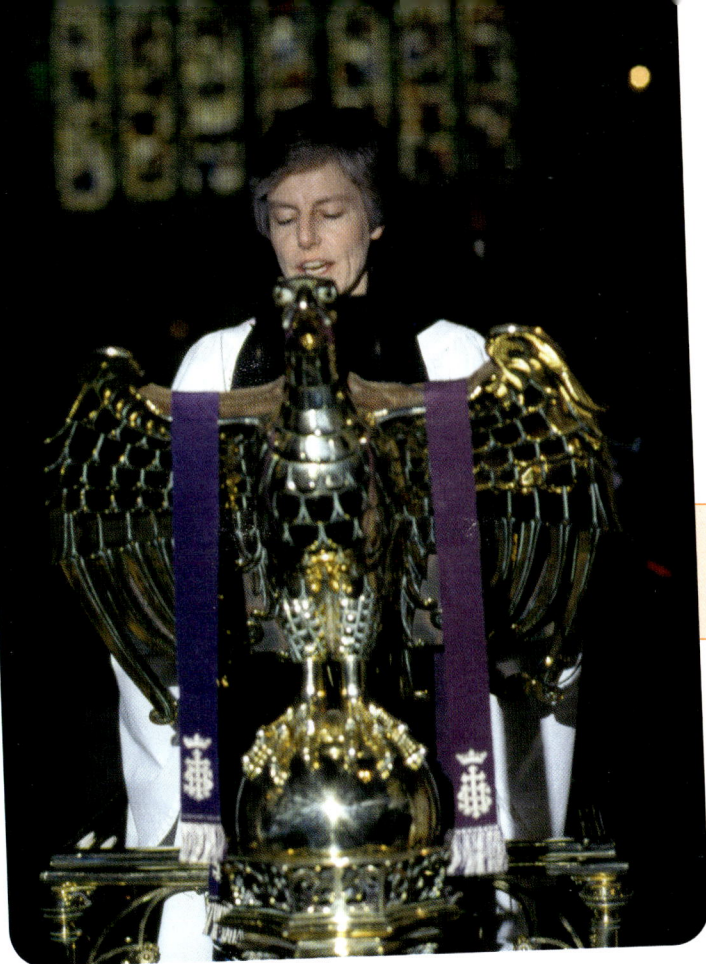

The Anglican Church was the last major Christian Church to admit women to the priesthood.

4. Church tradition, 2000 years old, does not yield a single example of a woman being ordained.

All of the other Christian Churches now admit women into the priesthood. The decision of the Anglican Church to admit women in the early 1990s was stated by Pope John Paul II to be a major obstacle standing in the way of a closer relationship between the two Churches and a major hindrance to Church unity.

TASKS

1. **a.** What is the laity?
   b. What role does the Catholic Church expect its laity to carry out in the modern Church?

2. What are the main reasons that the Catholic Church puts forward for refusing to ordain women to the priesthood?

3. "As most of the members of a congregation will be married, so it is clearly better for their priest to be married as well. He can understand them and their problems better." Do you agree with this comment? Give reasons for your answer, showing that you have thought about more than one point of view.

59 THE BIBLE

The word 'Bible' comes from a Latin word meaning 'the books'. The Bible is a collection of books written in many styles and by many different people over a period of more than 1000 years. Christians, however, regard the Bible as a single unit, since they believe the whole book to have been inspired, in some way, by God. It is this that gives the Bible its special authority and makes it different from any other book for Christians. The books included in the Bible are on a list or canon (standard), which the Church regards as being divinely inspired. The official canon of the Bible was settled in the 4th century, although it was not officially recognised by the Catholic Church until 1546.

The Bible

There are three sections to the Roman Catholic Bible:

1. The Old Testament

The early Christians were almost all Jews and they naturally turned to their own Scriptures to understand the life and teachings of Jesus. This is why all of the Jewish Scriptures, written originally in Hebrew or Aramaic, are included in the Christian Bible (the Old Testament).

The Jewish Scriptures fall into three sections:

- The **Torah** – the five books of the Law (Genesis, Exodus, Leviticus, Deuteronomy and Numbers). These are the most precious books in the Jewish Scriptures as they tell the story of the Jews, from the creation of the world and the formation of the Jewish people, through the time they spent in Egyptian slavery, to the **Exodus**. It was on this journey that the Jews received their precious laws, including the Ten Commandments, from God.
- The **Prophets** – prophets were men and women who told the people how God expected them to live. The followers of the most important prophets recorded their words and preserved them carefully. Much later, they were written down and included in the Scriptures.
- The **Writings** – these books contain a wide range of religious and moral teachings. The songs contained in the book of Psalms, for example, were used in worship in the Temple in Jerusalem, while the book of Job is a long examination of the problem of suffering.

For centuries, God prepared the people for the coming of a very special leader, the Messiah, who would deliver the Jews from their enemies. Christians believe that the Old Testament points to the coming of Jesus, God's spiritual Messiah.

2. The Apocrypha

The **Apocrypha** is a collection of books that were left out of the Jewish Scriptures because they were not considered to be inspired by God. When the Jewish Scriptures were translated from Hebrew into Greek in the 1st century BCE (a translation called the Septuagint), these books were included and they are found in modern Catholic Bibles.

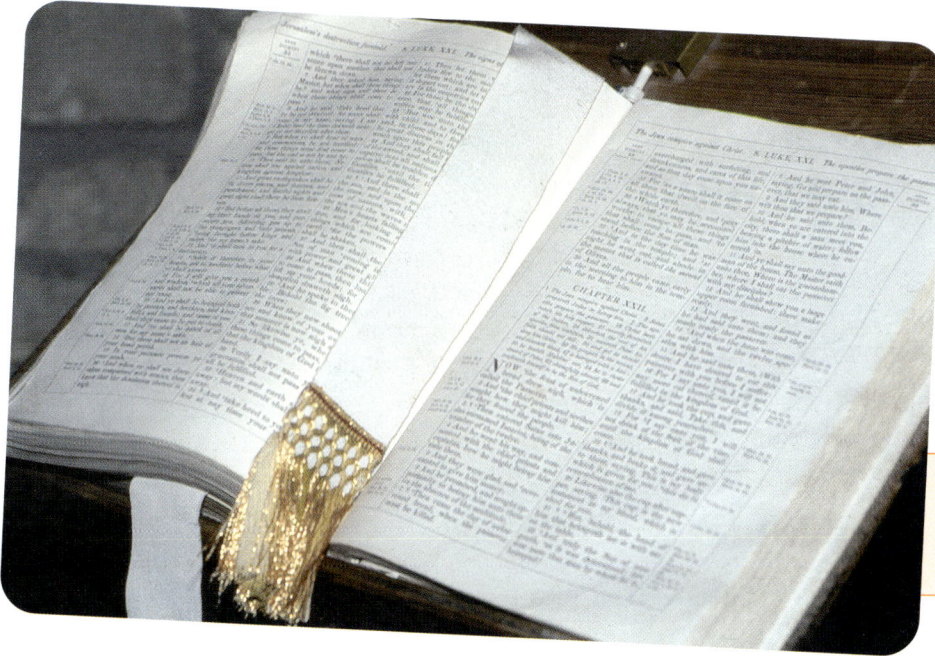

◀ *The Bible is at the centre of the spiritual life and worship of all Christians.*

3. The New Testament

The New Testament contains books written by early Christian leaders and includes:

- The Gospels – records of the life and teaching of Jesus. There are four Gospels in the New Testament – Matthew, Mark, Luke and John.
- The Acts of the Apostles – describes the beginning of the Christian Church.
- The **Epistles** – letters written by early Christian leaders, such as Peter, Paul and John.

There are 27 books in the New Testament altogether and they were all written in the years following the death and resurrection of Jesus. Just as the Gospels occupy a unique place in the New Testament, so they do in Catholic worship.

> **A** ❝*All scripture is inspired by God and can profitably be used for teaching, for refuting error, for guiding people's lives and teaching them to be holy. This is how the man who is dedicated to God becomes fully equipped and ready for any good work.*❞
>
> *(Paul, 2 Timothy 3.16)*

Explain what Christians understand by:

- **a.** the Bible
- **b.** the Canon
- **c.** the Old Testament
- **d.** the Apocrypha
- **e.** the New Testament

TASK

60 THE INSPIRATION AND AUTHORITY OF THE BIBLE

The Catholic Church believes, and teaches, that God has spoken to humankind through the Bible. Because the Bible contains the words that God has spoken, it is a holy book that must be treated with the greatest respect. In particular, it must be given a central place in the Church's worship life.

The inspiration of the Bible

Christians regard the Bible as being great literature that is able to bring spiritual enlightenment to those who read it. Their belief in the Bible, however, goes further than this. They believe that the Bible was inspired by God working through the Holy Spirit and it is this that gives it its unique authority. This does not mean that the writers of the different books were only empty channels that God filled with words because each of them has left his own imprint on his work – as any reader of the Bible can see for themselves. Christians believe that what they wrote in their own language and time was directed by God so that it carries his divine authority (extract A).

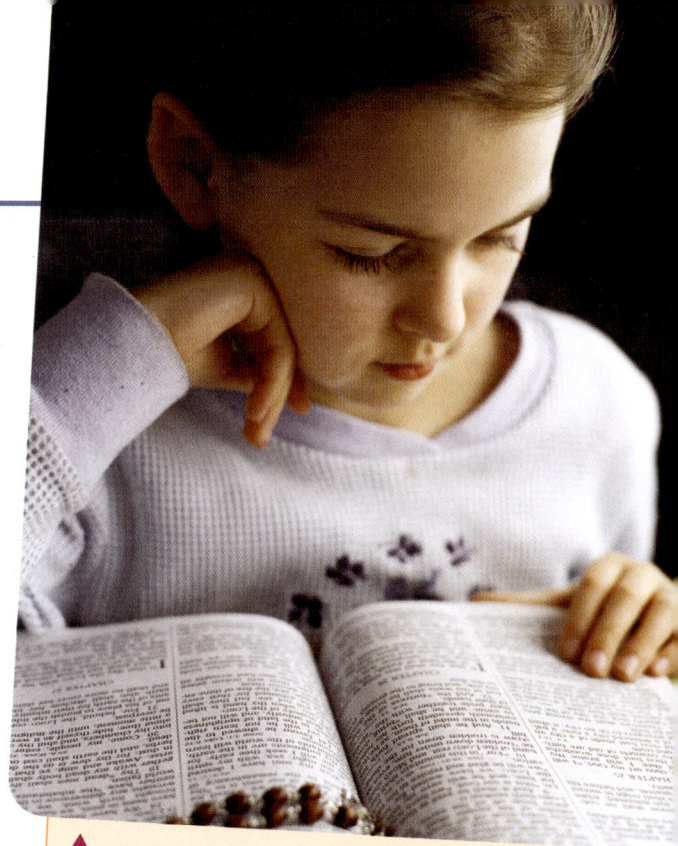

▲ Catholics bring up their children to read the Bible from an early age so that they become familiar with its stories and teachings.

> **A** **"**In Sacred Scripture, God speaks to man in a human way. To interpret Scripture correctly, the reader must be attentive to what the human authors truly wanted to affirm, and what God wanted to reveal to us by their words.**"**
> (CCC 109)

The authority of the Bible

Most Christians agree that the Bible has authority both in the forming of their beliefs and in guiding their behaviour. Along with the teaching ministry of the Church, the magisterium (see unit 61) and the traditions of the Church, the Bible is the main source of authority for all Catholics. Catholics read and study the Bible in a number of different ways:

- During their own personal devotions. Many Catholics set aside a time each day when they read a passage from the Bible and meditate (think deeply) about it. They usually combine this with prayer, during which they remember the needs of the world, their own local community, their church and its members, their family and friends, and themselves. Catholics believe that this time of quiet reflection provides an opportunity for God to speak to them and guide them through the Holy Spirit.

- As a central part of every act of Catholic worship. In many services there are three readings from the Bible – one from each of the Old Testament, the Gospels and the Epistles. The Gospel reading is the most important and this is given by the priest from the centre of the church to underline this. Readings each week are taken from a calendar of readings, a **lectionary**, so guaranteeing that most of the Bible is heard in public over a period of time.

- In house-groups. This is most likely to happen during Advent, in the run-up to Christmas, and during Lent, the time of spiritual preparation before Easter. Time is spent studying the relevant parts of the Bible in order to understand these two great Christian festivals.

- It is the basis for the sermon or homily in most services during which the priest explains the meaning of a passage from the Bible to help members of the congregation in their everyday Christian lives. The sermon is, however, more important in Protestant services that are centred on the Bible, the Word of God, rather than the sacraments as in Catholic worship.

▲ *Christians from all denominations regularly hear the Bible being read in their church services.*

TASKS

1. What do Catholics mean when they describe the Bible as being 'inspired'?

2. "In order to be a good Catholic and a good Christian it is important to take every opportunity to know the Bible better." Do you agree with this comment? Explain your reasons, showing that you have thought about more than one point of view.

61 THE APOSTOLIC TRADITION AND THE MAGISTERIUM

The Apostolic tradition

When Jesus departed from the earth it was left to his disciples, now called apostles, to pass on the Good News of the Gospel. This Good News was that Jesus had died for the sins of the world and had risen from the dead. In the years that followed this Gospel was passed on in two forms:

- In an oral form. For many years after the departure of Jesus, the apostles were the only link that the early Christians had with Jesus. His memory was kept alive for them through the preaching of the apostles. This was passed by the apostles through the bishops of the Church to become part of the teaching of the Catholic Church. It is kept alive in the teaching and worship of the Church today.

- In written form. As the apostles were martyred or simply died, the fear was that many of the memories of Jesus would die with them. This was the motivation to commit those memories to writing. Before this happened, however, Paul, who was the leader of the early Christians but was not an apostle, wrote many books that were highly treasured. Matthew, Mark, Luke and John then wrote four accounts of the life of Jesus – the Gospels.

Tradition and the Bible form the twin sources of authority for all Catholics (extract A). It is the responsibility of the Church to pass on and interpret them for Christians today. This it does through the Magisterium.

> **A** **❝**What Christ entrusted to the apostles, they in turn handed on by their preaching and writing, under the inspiration of the Holy Spirit, to all generations...**❞**
> (CCC.96)

The Magisterium

The Latin word 'magister' means 'teacher'. Magisterium is the word used to describe the teaching role that the Catholic Church has in the light of the clear teachings of the New Testament – "Anyone who listens to you listens to me" (Luke 10.16). Although this teaching role belongs to all Christians who preach Christ through their daily lives, it is reserved in the Catechism for bishops who are exercising their official role as preachers of the Gospel. It takes one of two forms:

- The 'ordinary' magisterium – the day by day teaching of the bishops.

- The 'extraordinary' magisterium – when the bishops gather together in Council, as at the Second Vatican Council. On these rare occasions, when such a Council is called, the Church teaches that the Holy Spirit will keep the bishops from lapsing into error of any kind.

There is no higher authority in the Catholic Church than the Pope and the bishops working together in the magisterium. The magisterium is responsible for looking after and safeguarding the dogmas – the most important beliefs – of the Catholic Church. Although the Pope is the first among equals, as a bishop it has been accepted, since the Second Vatican Council, that he should accept a 'collegiate' style of leadership – he should confer with the bishops before making any attempt to interpret the beliefs and practices of the Church for its members. Individual Catholics must follow the teachings of the Magisterium (see extract B).

B 	**"The Roman Pontiff and the bishops, as authentic teachers, preach to the People of God the faith which is to be believed and applied in moral life… The infallibility of the Magisterium of the Pastors extends to all the elements of doctrine, including moral doctrine, without which the saving truths of the faith cannot be preserved, expounded or observed."**

(CCC 2050–51)

TASKS

1. How has the Catholic Church preserved traditions going all the way back to the original apostles?
2. **a.** What is the Magisterium?
   b. Why is the Magisterium very important to the Roman Catholic Church?

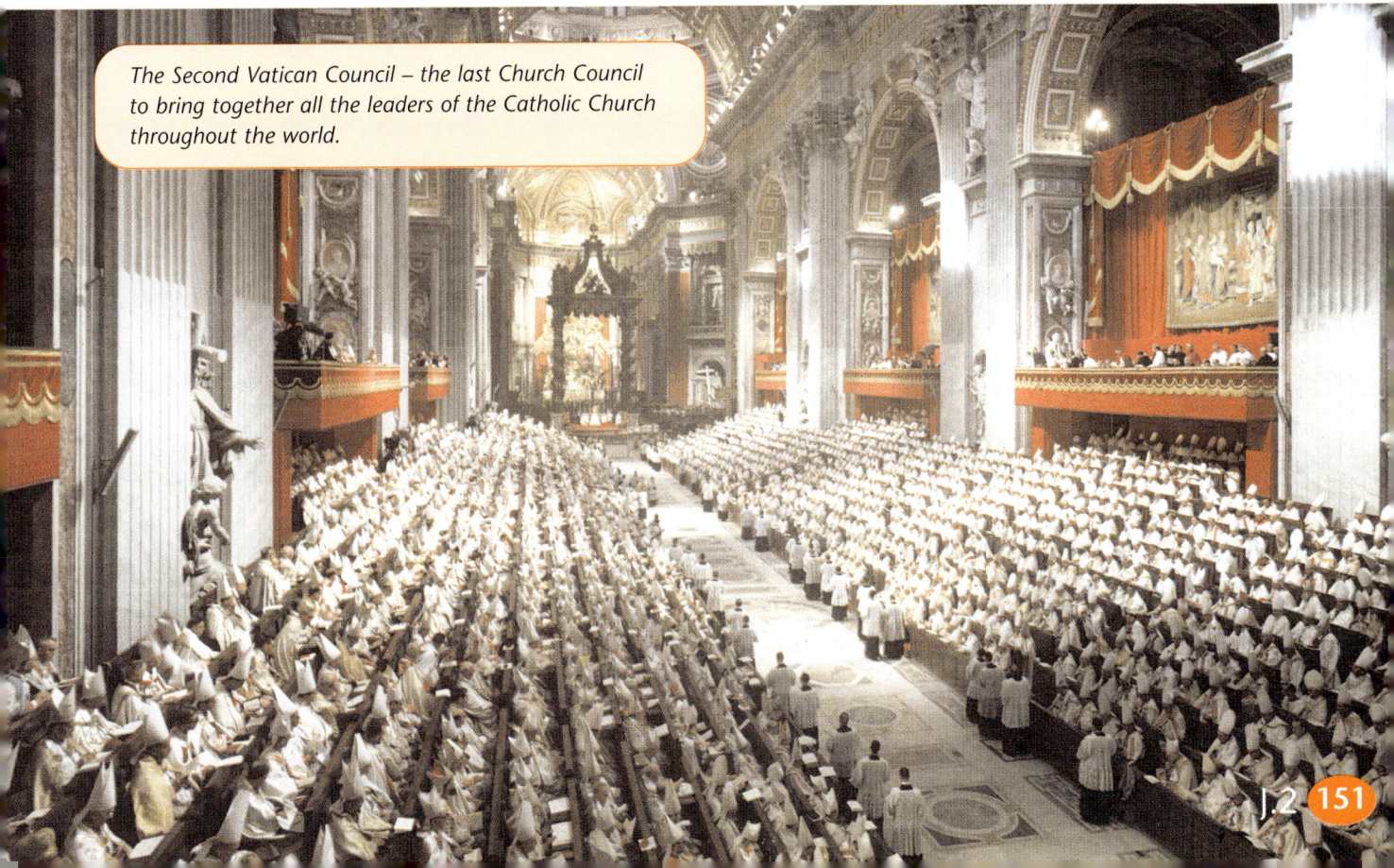

The Second Vatican Council – the last Church Council to bring together all the leaders of the Catholic Church throughout the world.

62 THE VIRGIN MARY

Of all the saints in the Christian Church none is more highly honoured than Mary, the mother of Jesus, in both the Catholic and Orthodox traditions. Catholics call her 'the Mother of God' – an extraordinary title because all Christians believe that God was without beginning. She has this title because Christians believe that the fullness of God dwelt in Jesus – "…God wanted all fullness to be found in him" (Colossians 1.19) – and yet Mary gave birth to him. This is why Orthodox Christians call Mary 'Theotokos', the God-bearer.

Three important Catholic beliefs about Mary

There are three important beliefs that Catholics hold about Mary:

1. The Immaculate Conception of Mary

The Catholic Church teaches that Mary was conceived without sin. This means that from the first moment of her existence she was full of grace and free from any separation from God brought about by original sin. Mary lived a blameless life since she played a central part in God's plan of salvation. The **Immaculate Conception of Mary** is celebrated by Catholics on 8 December.

2. The Perpetual Virginity of the Virgin Mary

The Catholic Church has always taught about the perpetual virginity of Mary, that she was a virgin 'before, during and after' the birth of Jesus. The Catechism describes this belief as 'beyond all human understanding and possibility' (CCC 497). It can only be understood with the gift of faith. God alone took the initiative in the Incarnation since he alone is the Father of Jesus, the Saviour of the world.

3. The Bodily Assumption of the Virgin Mary

Although this has only been the belief of the Catholic Church officially since 1950 its roots are found much earlier. Mary was preserved from the decay of death, which affects all human beings, and became the first to share in the fruits of the resurrection of Jesus. Her assumption into heaven is an anticipation of our own future resurrection. This festival is celebrated on 15 August.

▲ Catholics believe that the Virgin Mary can help them to pray to God because she is already interceding for them even before they pray.

Mary, the model for all Christians to follow

Catholics believe that Mary is able to intercede with God on their behalf and this is the reason why they pray to her. They call her the 'Mediatrix' (mediator). The Hail Mary is the most important Catholic prayer because it expresses this belief (extract A).

> **A** "Hail Mary, full of grace, the Lord is with you. Blessed are you among women and blessed is the fruit of your womb, Jesus. Holy Mary, Mother of God, pray for us sinners now and at the time of our death."
>
> (The Hail Mary)

Mary is the supreme example (model) for all Catholics to follow. She freely agreed to bear God's Son describing herself as 'the hand-maiden of the Lord'. She supported him throughout his life and ministry. At the end of his life she was one of a handful of women who stayed with him and shared his suffering. She continued to support the apostles and the early Church with her prayers and she does the same for the Church today.

Many Catholics remind themselves regularly of the example of the Virgin Mary by using a rosary to help them pray. As they pass the beads of the rosary through their fingers they recite the Hail Mary 50 times and meditate on the joyful, sorrowful and glorious mysteries of the life of Jesus – you can find out more about the rosary in unit 7.

▶ The beads on the rosary are a help for many Catholics to reflect on the most important events in the life of Jesus and also to remember some important Catholic prayers.

TASKS

1. What are three important beliefs that Catholics hold about the Virgin Mary?
2. Why do you think that Catholics hold up the Virgin Mary as an example for all to follow?

EXAM HELP

In the examination

Make sure that you know about:

THE CHURCH

- The importance of the Church in God's plan for the salvation of the human race. The building of the Church on the teaching of the twelve disciples of Jesus. The splintering of the Church – most important divisions being between the Catholic and Orthodox Churches (11th century) and Catholics and Protestants in the Reformation (16th century). The 'high' view of the Church held by Catholics – God's grace to all comes through the Church. The importance of the Church – nurtures faith through baptism and allows it to grow through confirmation and the sacraments. The picture of the Church as our Mother. The Church nurtures our faith. The Church accompanies all believers from birth through to death.

- The four characteristics of the Christian Church. The Church is One. The focus of unity for all Churches. Others based on one faith, worship, apostolic succession. The Church is holy – members are saints, made holy by sacraments and prayers of those in heaven. The Church is catholic-universal. The Church is apostolic. Twelve disciples. Past. Inportance of Peter. The Papacy.

- Two important 'pictures' of the Church. The Church as the body of Christ – Christ being the Head and the Church members the body. Each part of the body, all the members, is equally important. The overwhelming importance of the head – the source of the body's unity and strength.

- The Communion of Saints – the fellowship of all members, alive and dead. Links together those who are still pilgrims on earth, with those in purgatory and those who have already reached heaven. Belief in the communion of saints means that prayers can be offered through the saints in heaven – especially the Virgin Mary.

- The Christian ministry. A universal vocation for all to serve God. Special vocations to the Christian ministry – three Orders (Bishops, Priests and Deacons). Bishops carry great responsibility for the Church as a whole, with apostolic authority through the laying on of hands. Priests carry spiritual responsibility for individual churches; their most important task is to administer the Sacraments. Becoming a deacon is usually the first step towards becoming a priest. Religious orders divided between contemplative and active. Male and female orders. Prayer is the most important monastic activity – even for those in an active order. The three vows – poverty, chastity and obedience.

- The ordination of bishops and priests. The elements in the service of ordination – the laying on of hands in particular.

- The role of the laity – those who are not ordained and do not belong to a religious order. Laity have a true vocation in the Church. The importance of the Church service as a spiritual offering to God.

- The ordination of women: rejected by the Roman Catholic Church because Jesus only chose male disciples, the Church cannot change anything to do with the Sacraments including ordination, and sacred tradition is against women priests. All Protestant Churches now admit women to priesthood – a major obstacle to closer union.

Sample exam questions

1. What do Catholics believe about the Church and why do they think it is so important?

2. Explain what Catholics mean when they describe the Church as being:
   a. one
   b. Holy
   c. Catholic
   d. apostolic

3. "One of the most helpful images is to speak of the Church as being the Body of Christ." Do you agree with this comment? Explain your answer, showing that you have thought about more than one point of view.

4. In the Catholic Church there are three Orders of ministry. Explain the role that deacons, priests and bishops are expected to play in the Church.

5. "Married priests would make better priests because they would understand most of their parishioners better." Do you agree with this comment? Give reasons for your answer, showing that you have thought about more than one point of view.

EXAM HELP

THE BIBLE, THE MAGISTERIUM AND THE VIRGIN MARY

- The Bible. The Old Testament (the Torah, the Prophets, the Writings), the Apocrypha and the New Testament (the Gospels, the Acts and the Epistles). The inspiration of the Bible – by God through the Holy Spirit. The authority of the Bible – used by Catholics in private devotions, in public worship, in house-groups and in homilies. The difference between Catholics and Protestants in their attitudes to the Bible.

- The apostolic tradition and the magisterium. The tradition from the apostles lived on in oral and written form. Bible and tradition are the twin sources of authority for Catholics. Magisterium – the teaching role of the Church through the Pope and bishops. The ordinary magisterium (day by day teaching of bishops) and extraordinary magisterium (the bishops and Pope in special council).

- The Virgin Mary: Mother of God. Three beliefs about the Virgin Mary – immaculate conception, perpetual virginity and bodily assumption. Mary – the model for all Catholics. The Hail Mary. The rosary.

Sample exam questions

1. **a.** What is the Magisterium?

    b. Why do Catholics believe that they should follow the teachings of the Magisterium?

2. Describe the teachings of the Catholic Church about the Virgin Mary?

3. What do you think the Catholic Church has in mind when it describes the Virgin Mary as the perfect example for all Catholics to follow?

Worship and celebration

In this topic you will find out about:

- the Sacraments;
- the Catholic services of Infant baptism and Confirmation;
- the Jewish Passover festival as background to the Mass;
- the Jewish Passover and the **Last Supper**;
- the Catholic service of the Mass and its spiritual importance;
- the ways that other Christians celebrate Holy Communion;
- the Sacraments of healing – Penance and Reconciliation/Anointing of the Sick;
- the Liturgical Year – the Christmas, Easter and Pentecost cycles;
- Lent, **Palm Sunday** and **Maundy Thursday**; **Good Friday**; Easter Sunday; Ascension Day; and Pentecost.

KEY WORDS

Absolution The granting of God's forgiveness by a priest after the confession of sins.

Chrism The oil that is used as part of the sacraments of baptism, confirmation and ordination.

Christmas The festival that celebrates the birth of Jesus.

Contrition A deep feeling of sorrow felt by people for their sins.

Easter The time when Catholics remember the death and resurrection of Jesus.

Eucharist Meaning 'thanksgiving': another term for the Mass.

Holy Week The time before Easter running from Palm Sunday through to Good Friday.

Lent A time of spiritual preparation before the festival of Easter.

Liturgy of the Word The centre of the Mass that is based on readings from the Bible and the homily of the priest.

Penance A penalty given by a priest so that Catholics can show their sorrow for their sins.

Penitential rite The confession of sin and the absolution that come at the beginning of the Mass.

Real Presence The Catholic belief that Jesus is 'really' present in the bread and wine during the Mass.

Renewal of baptismal vows Solemn promises made by parents and godparents when a baby is baptised; these are renewed when the baby grows up and he or she is confirmed.

Rite of Communion The act of receiving the bread and wine at the Mass.

Sacrifice The act by Jesus of offering himself to God when he died on the cross.

Tabernacle The cupboard to one side of the altar that holds the blessed bread and wine to share with those people unable to attend church for the Mass.

Transubstantiation The Catholic belief that the bread and wine on the altar become the actual body and blood of Jesus during the Mass.

Vows Solemn promises that are made to God as part of different sacraments.

Water Used in baptism to indicate the washing away of sin and spiritual purification.

63 WHAT ARE THE SACRAMENTS?

What is a sacrament?

1. Christians believe that God is the supreme mystery. This does not stop them, however, from trying to find words and symbols to express something of this divine mystery. They look for signs and symbols that they can use to remind themselves of the God who is beyond human understanding. These signs or symbols are called sacraments. The word 'sacrament' means 'a signpost which points a way to God'.

2. A sacrament is also a God-given service that brings God closer to the worshipper. It uses material elements – such as bread, water, oil and wine – to bring God closer to the worshipper. The sacraments can do this because the world itself is holy and so God can work through earthly elements to bestow a spiritual blessing on human beings. To enjoy God's grace is to share in the divine life through which human beings can know and love God – calling Him their Father.

The seven sacraments

There are seven special ways, or sacraments, in which Catholics celebrate the good news that Jesus brought God closer to them through his death and resurrection. The Orthodox Church also recognises seven sacraments although it calls them 'mysteries'. The Anglican Church only recognises two of them as sacraments – baptism and the Eucharist. Most Nonconformist Churches also celebrate baptism and the Eucharist, although the **Quakers** and the **Salvation Army**, alone among the major Christian Churches, do not celebrate any of the sacraments.

CHECK IT OUT

THE SACRAMENTS CELEBRATED BY THE CATHOLIC CHURCH

- Baptism
- Confirmation
- Penance
- The Eucharist
- Anointing the sick
- Matrimony
- Ordination to the priesthood

Christ and the Church as sacraments

1. *Christ and the sacraments.* The sacraments are services by which Christians can receive God's grace. Through celebrating them, they are able to receive God's power into their daily lives. Some of the sacraments, such as baptism and confirmation, are only received once in a person's lifetime. Others, such as the

Eucharist, can be received many times – even daily. Through celebrating the Eucharist, Christians discover that Jesus was the supreme sacrament because he made God known to the people.

2. *The Church and the sacraments.* The power of God is also experienced in the Church. When Jesus left the earth, he established his Church as the living sacrament that continues to make God known in the world. The Church does this through its life and witness. Just as the sacraments make God known to those who believe, so the Church makes God known in the world (extract A).

A *"Christ instituted the sacraments of the new law... The seven sacraments touch all the stages and all the important moments of Christian life: they give birth and increase, healing and mission to the Christian's life of faith... The purpose of the sacraments is to sanctify [make holy] men, to build up the Body of Christ and, finally, to give worship to God. Because they are signs they also instruct. They not only presuppose faith, but by words and objects they also nourish, strengthen and express it."*
(CCC 1210; 1123)

▶ Anointing the sick with oil is one of the seven sacraments celebrated by the Catholic Church.

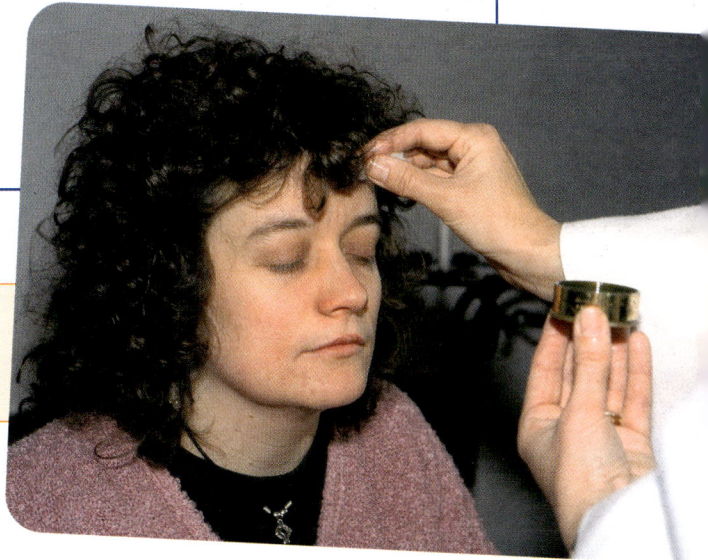

TASK

Read the extract from the Catechism in extract A.

a. Explain the three purposes of the sacraments.

b. Apart from strengthening the faith of believers, the sacraments also serve another purpose. What is it?

c. Why do you think that the sacraments are called 'sacraments of faith'?

✳ **DISCUSSION POINT**

The Orthodox Church prefers to use the term 'mysteries' to describe the sacraments. Why do you think this is?

64 INFANT BAPTISM

Baptism in the early Christian Church was for adults, but soon there was a demand for a form of baptism that included children as well. Christians wanted their children to grow up as part of the Christian family. From the 4th century onwards, Infant baptism began to replace adult baptism as the norm.

The Catholic service of Infant baptism

In the Church today, Infant baptism is the most widespread 'initiation' ceremony as the Orthodox, Catholic, Anglican and other Protestant Churches practise it. In the Orthodox and Catholic Churches, an older convert to Christianity, or someone who was not baptised as a child, can be baptised later in life.

When the Catholic priest greets the parents and the child at the door of the church, he is welcoming them into the family of faith. The service that follows usually takes the form of a Mass.

1. The priest begins by asking for the child's name. To call a child by his or her name underlines his or her uniqueness in the sight of God, who knows us all by name.

2. The parents and godparents – who must be Catholics – are asked questions, called vows, about their own religious faith. By bringing the child to be baptised, they are showing their willingness to bring the child up in the Christian faith. The priest welcomes the child into the Christian family and makes the 'sign of the cross' on his or her forehead.

3. The Liturgy of the Word includes readings from the Old Testament and New Testament. It also includes the Prayers of the Faithful and the Litany of the Saints.

4. Satan is exorcised from the child in a symbolic act. This takes place before the child is anointed with the Oil of Catechumens, symbolising the healing and strength of God. The priest lays his hands on the child's head, calling on the blessing of God.

5. After the water in the **font** has been blessed and the parents and godparents have made their final confession of faith, the priest baptises the child by pouring water over his or her head:

   In the name of the Father and of the Son and of the Holy Spirit.

   In baptism, Catholics recognise that:

   God is our Father (Abba), Jesus is our brother, the Holy Spirit lives within us.

6. Finally, the child is anointed with **chrism** (consecrated oil); the parents are presented with a candle which is lit from the **paschal candle** (a symbol of the suffering and death of Jesus) and a white shawl (representing new life) is placed around the child.

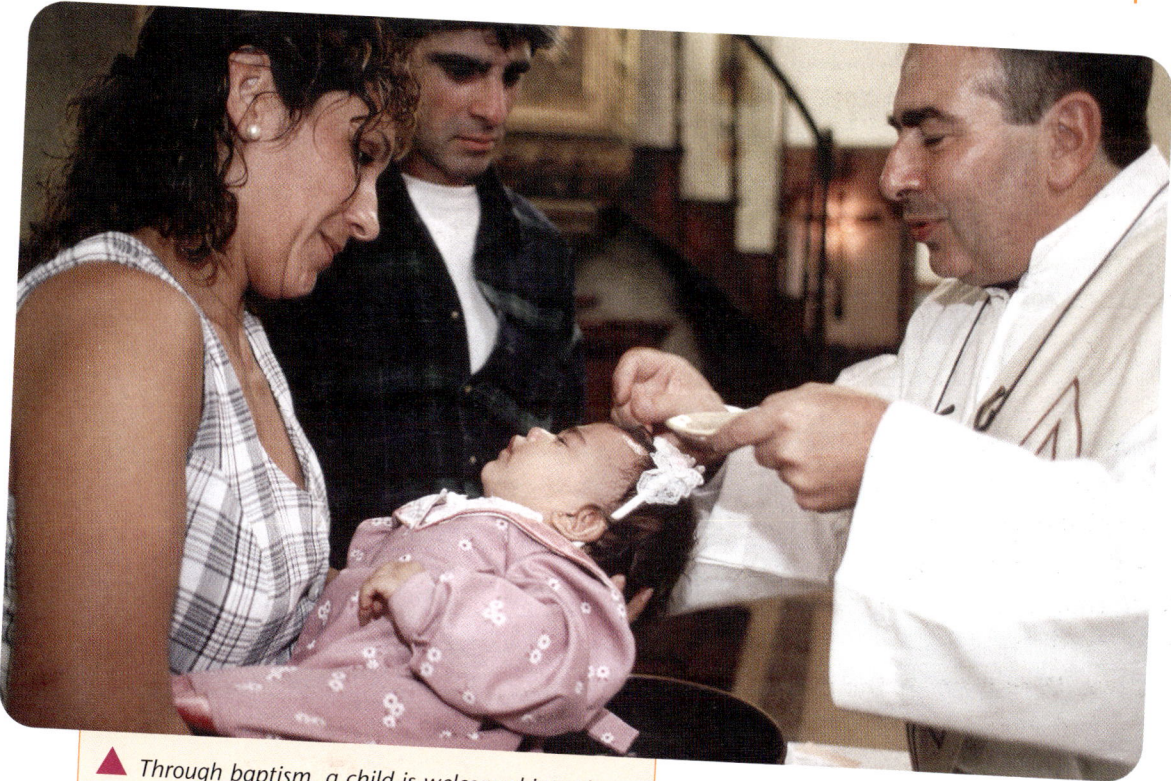

▲ *Through baptism, a child is welcomed into the Church family and given every opportunity to grow up as a Church member.*

The meaning of Infant baptism

Infant baptism is a very important doctrine in the Catholic Church.

1. It cleanses the child from original sin. This is the belief that everyone is born with a sinful nature and even the youngest of children can go against the will of God. The cleansing of baptism and the entry of the Holy Spirit into a child's life show that sin will be resisted as the child grows up.

2. It welcomes the child into the Christian family – the Church. This is why most babies and children are baptised during the Mass because that is when the Church family is most likely to be together.

3. Baptism marks the time when a child is 'born again' and begins the Christian life. Catholics believe that it is very important that a baby is baptised as soon as possible after birth – especially if he or she is weak or unwell.

TASKS

1. How does a priest indicate that a baby is special in the sight of God and in the eyes of the Church?

2. What does the Church believe actually happens when a baby is baptised? Does any 'change' take place in a child or is it all symbolic? If it is symbolic, what does the actual symbolism mean?

65 CONFIRMATION

Confirmation gives people who have been baptised the opportunity to renew their baptismal vows and commit themselves to the Christian faith. Traditions that baptise babies also offer confirmation – notably the Orthodox, the Catholic, the Anglican, the Methodist and the United Reformed Churches. Confirmation is a service of Christian initiation. During confirmation, a person receives the Holy Spirit in a special way through the 'laying on' of the bishop's hands.

Preparing for confirmation

Parish programmes designed to prepare candidates for their confirmation vary but they are likely to include:

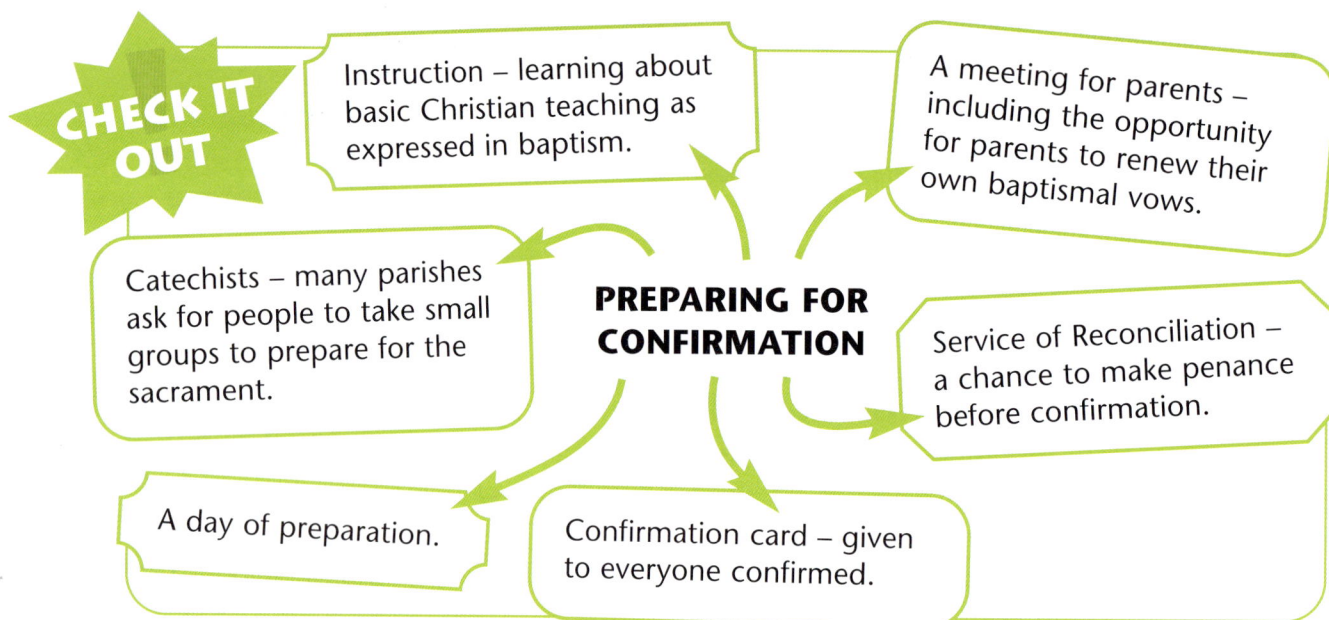

CHECK IT OUT

Instruction – learning about basic Christian teaching as expressed in baptism.

A meeting for parents – including the opportunity for parents to renew their own baptismal vows.

Catechists – many parishes ask for people to take small groups to prepare for the sacrament.

PREPARING FOR CONFIRMATION

Service of Reconciliation – a chance to make penance before confirmation.

A day of preparation.

Confirmation card – given to everyone confirmed.

The age at which people are confirmed varies from Church to Church. In the Anglican, Methodist and United Reformed Churches, people can be confirmed from about the age of 11, with Holy Communion following afterwards. In the Catholic Church, children can begin receiving Communion as early as seven, with confirmation following three or four years later. In the Orthodox Church, however, babies are confirmed at the same time as being baptised in a service called **Chrismation**.

The Catholic sacrament of confirmation

Although a bishop usually presides at confirmation, this is not essential. The most popular times for people to be confirmed are Easter and Pentecost. Confirmation normally takes place during a celebration of Mass and includes the following:

- The renewal of baptismal vows. At baptism, these vows were taken by other people (parents and godparents), but now they are made by each person for themselves and include a rejection of all that is evil and a profession of faith in God.

- The bishop extends his hands over those wishing to be confirmed and prays that they might be given the gifts of the Holy Spirit. This is an ancient way of calling down the power of God on a person. It was often done in Old Testament times to consecrate a prophet or a king after God had given them a special task to carry out.

> **A** *"Send your Holy Spirit upon them to be their Helper and Guide. Give them the spirit of wisdom and understanding, the spirit of right judgement and courage, the spirit of knowledge and reverence. Fill them with the spirit of wonder and awe in your presence."*
>
> *(Prayer of bishop)*

- Each candidate approaches the bishop in turn together with his or her sponsor. The sponsor places his or her hand on the candidate's shoulder as a sign of support. Placing his or her hand on the candidate's head, the bishop anoints him or her with oil and makes the sign of the cross on his or her forehead. This is the heart of the confirmation service. The bishop says: "Be sealed with the Holy Spirit."

> ▶ *Christians believe that confirmation is the beginning of a person's lifetime of service to God and to the Church.*

TASKS

1. Explain the significance of:
   a. the laying on of hands
   b. the anointing with oil in the sacrament of confirmation
2. Explain the link between baptism and confirmation.
3. Explain what lies at the heart of the service of confirmation.

✳ DISCUSSION POINT

Why do you think that a person who was baptised as a baby might want/not want to be confirmed when he or she is older?

66 BACKGROUND TO THE MASS

You can find out the details of the Roman Catholic Mass and how it is celebrated in unit 67.

READ: Luke 22.7–23

The Eucharist (the Mass) is the most important sacrament of the Roman Catholic Church. While baptism and confirmation, the other two sacraments of initiation, can only be celebrated once in a lifetime, Catholics are encouraged to celebrate the Eucharist as often as possible. Properly celebrated, it provides a Catholic with spiritual nourishment throughout his or her life.

The Jewish Passover

Celebrated by Jews for centuries, down to the present day, the Passover retells the events of the Exodus – the release of the Jews from Egyptian slavery over 3000 years ago. Before the final plague, the killing of the eldest son in every Egyptian home, the Jews were told to sprinkle the blood of a lamb on the doorposts of their homes. The Angel of Death 'passed over' every house marked in this way.

Each year, at the Passover meal, Jewish parents retell this story to their children. In this way, the memory of this ancient event, the most important in Jewish history, is kept alive. During the retelling, everyone shares, through eating different foodstuffs, the event as if they were there.

The Last Supper

When Jesus met with his disciples for the Last Supper, it was the traditional Passover meal. The unleavened bread and the goblets of wine were on the table as for each Passover meal. Jesus used this Passover meal to teach his disciples something very important about his forthcoming death. To do this, he used the bread and the wine on the table and these were later to become the central elements in the Church's celebration of the Eucharist:

- the bread was to be the symbol for the body of Jesus, broken on the cross;
- the wine was to be the symbol for the suffering and sacrifice of Jesus.

To Roman Catholics, the Mass is, above all else, a sacrifice. This is why, in the Mass, Jesus is called 'the Lamb of God'.

> **A** 	*'Christ Jesus who died, yes, who was raised from the dead, who is at the right hand of God, who indeed intercedes for us', is present in many ways to his Church: in his word, in his Church's prayer 'where two or three are gathered in my name', in the poor, the sick and the imprisoned, in the Sacraments of which he is the author, in the sacrifice of the Mass, and in the person of the minister. But 'he is present…most especially in the Eucharistic species.'*
>
> *(CCC 1373)*

▼ *The Mass, and other celebrations of Holy Communion, are based on the last meal that Jesus enjoyed with his disciples.*

TASKS

1. What is the difference between the Eucharist and the other sacraments of initiation – baptism and confirmation?

2. a. What kind of meal was the Last Supper?

   b. What use did Jesus make of the bread on the table?

   c. What use did Jesus make of the wine on the table?

67 THE MASS

Catholics believe that they should prepare themselves spiritually before sharing in the Mass. Those who have committed a grave (mortal) sin should make a personal confession of what they have done to a priest. As the Mass begins with the Penitential Rite so this deals with lesser, venial, sins.

On entering, church worshippers dip their fingers in the holy water which is in a receptacle (the **stoup**) just inside the door and make 'the sign of the cross' on their body. Worshippers can also use some special prayers in the Sunday **Missal** to prepare themselves spiritually for the service.

Celebrating the Mass

There are four parts to the Mass:

1. *The Penitential Rite.* The congregation confesses to God that they have sinned and ask for divine forgiveness. The priest then grants them absolution.

2 *The Liturgy of the Word.* As you can see below, the Liturgy of the Word has six parts. This part of the Mass has its origins in the old Jewish synagogue services that brought the people together to pray, and study their Scriptures.

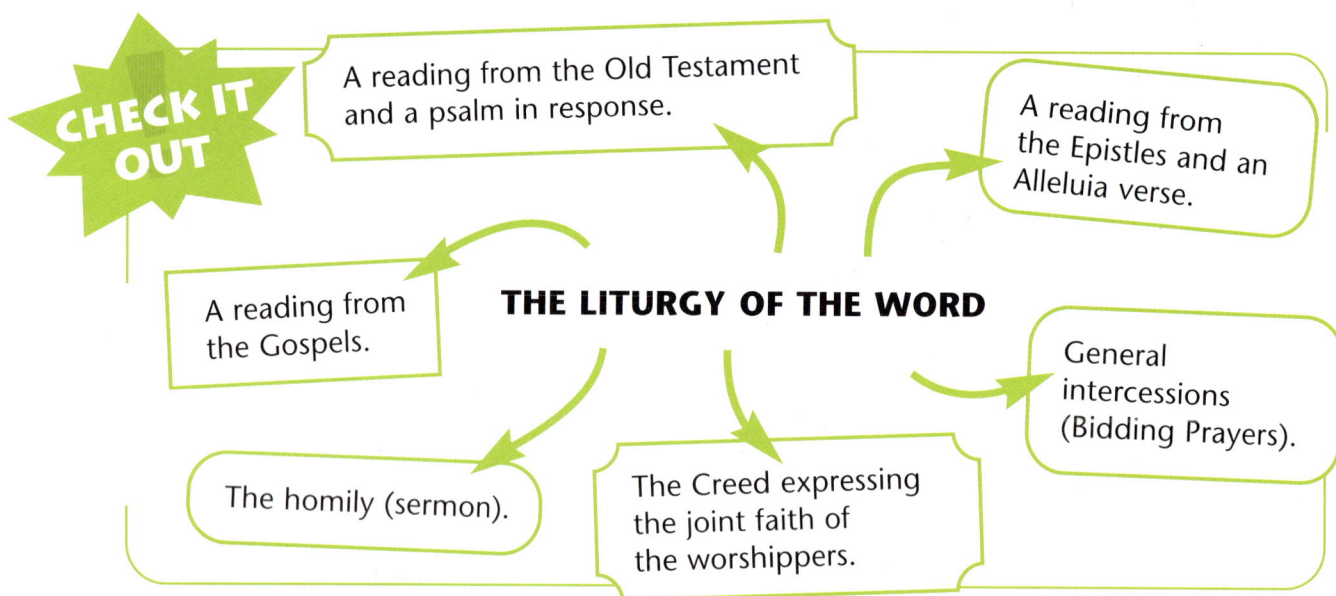

CHECK IT OUT

A reading from the Old Testament and a psalm in response.

A reading from the Epistles and an Alleluia verse.

A reading from the Gospels.

THE LITURGY OF THE WORD

General intercessions (Bidding Prayers).

The homily (sermon).

The Creed expressing the joint faith of the worshippers.

The readings are based on a lectionary that follows a three-year cycle to cover the four Gospels of Matthew, Mark, Luke and John and other Biblical passages over this time.

3. *The Liturgy of the Eucharist.* The Liturgy of the Eucharist begins with members of the congregation bringing up the people's offerings of bread, wine and gifts for the poor to the altar. The Mass is the people's offering to God and, since the symbols of bread and wine show God's goodness to us, it is right for us to offer some of God's gifts back to him.

The Eucharistic Prayer is at the heart of the celebration of the Mass. Everyone is reminded of their duty to thank God through Jesus Christ in the power of the Holy Spirit. The priest repeats the words of Jesus at the Last Supper and it is during the saying of this that the bread and wine are changed into the actual body and blood of Jesus. This is indicated by a bell being rung.

> **A** *"...by the consecration of the bread and wine there takes place a change of the whole substance of the bread into the substance of the body of Christ our Lord and of the whole substance of the wine into the substance of his blood. This change the holy Catholic Church has fittingly and properly called transubstantiation."*
>
> *(CCC 1376)*

During the Church Year the Church uses four different Eucharistic prayers and they all:

- call upon the power of the Holy Spirit;

- recount the words of Jesus spoken at the Last Supper;

- ask God's blessing on the Church – the living, the dead and saints from all ages;

- end with the Great Amen, where everyone responds to what has been said with a resounding 'Yes'.

4. The Rite of Communion. The people prepare themselves to receive Christ by saying the Lord's Prayer (the 'Our Father') together and offering one another the Sign of Peace. The priest breaks the consecrated host and places a piece of it in the wine in the chalice. After taking the bread and wine himself, the priest shares them with the congregation. After a time of brief meditation, the Mass ends with the people being blessed and dismissed.

▲ *The Mass has a meaning for Catholics that is not shared by most of the other Christians.*

TASKS

1. Describe what happens during the Mass.
2. What is the difference between the Liturgy of the Word and the Liturgy of the Eucharist?

68 WHAT THE MASS MEANS TO CATHOLICS

St Thomas Aquinas taught that the Eucharist does for the spiritual life of every Catholic what food does for their bodies. Catholics often speak of the Eucharist as 'regenerating' their spiritual lives. This is why the Catechism says that Catholics "…receive in the Eucharist the food of eternal life…" (1212). Elsewhere the Catechism tells us that the Eucharist "remains at the centre of the Church's life" (1343).

The spiritual importance of the Mass

Regularly celebrating the Mass is of immense spiritual importance to every Catholic. When it is celebrated believers can expect that:

- They have been cleansed from their past sins and preserved from committing many future sins.

- The gifts of the Holy Spirit – faith, hope and love – are developed within them by the power of God's same Spirit. St Paul expanded on this theme by referring to the further gifts of wisdom, knowledge, healing, miraculous powers, prophecy, discernment, speaking in tongues and interpreting tongues (1 Corinthians 12.7–11) as all being gifts from "the one and the same Spirit".

- It gives them the spiritual energy needed to complete their pilgrimage to heaven.

- There is a close link between the celebration of the Mass and eternity (see extract A).

▶ Catholics believe that each time the Mass is celebrated the death of Jesus on the cross is renewed.

> **A** *Almighty God, we pray that your angel may take this sacrifice to your altar in heaven. Then as we receive from this altar the sacred body and blood of your Son, let us be filled with every grace and blessing.*
>
> (Eucharistic Prayer; The Sunday Missal)

Catholics believe that the Mass gives worshippers an insight into what heaven is like and unites everyone with the 'Church triumphant' – believers in heaven and on earth. This is an insight that Catholics share with believers from the Orthodox Church.

- It puts people into contact with the saving effects of the death of Jesus – eternal life. Each time the Mass is celebrated the sacrifice of Jesus which was offered to God is renewed. It is then offered by the Church to its Father in heaven. The faithful are spiritually nourished by feeding on the body and blood of Jesus.

> **B** *In the Eucharist Christ gives us the very body which he gave up for us on the cross, the very blood which he 'poured out for many for the forgiveness of sins.' The Eucharist is thus a sacrifice because it re-presents (makes present) the sacrifice of the cross...*
>
> (CCC 1365–66)

- It is an act of Holy 'Communion'. It unites worshippers with God through Jesus. It also unites worshippers with each other in an act of spiritual communion. This takes place through the sharing of bread and the act of giving each other 'the sign of peace'.

TASKS

1. Describe three spiritual blessings that Catholics enjoy by celebrating the Mass together.
2. "Christians should not need the symbols of bread and wine for them to experience the presence of God." Do you agree? Give reasons for your answer, showing that you have thought about more than one point of view.

✳ DISCUSSION POINT

'The Mass is so important that it is impossible to imagine anyone being a good Catholic without regularly attending the service.' Do you agree with this comment? Produce arguments on both sides of the divide.

69 HOLY COMMUNION AND OTHER CHURCHES

Among the major Christian Churches only the Salvation Army and the Quakers (the Society of Friends) do not celebrate Holy Communion. They simply do not believe that this sacrament is spiritually necessary. Among the other Churches there are variations in the way that Holy Communion is celebrated and even in the names that the service is given.

The Anglican Church (Holy Communion or the Eucharist)

1. In the **Anglican Church**, of which the Church of England is a part, there are two basic approaches to this service. Some members of this Church hold beliefs that are similar to the Roman Catholic Church and these people are called High Church or Anglo-Catholics. There is also a growing group, called Low Church or Evangelicals, who hold beliefs that are like other Protestants such as Methodists and Baptists.

2. Anglicans call the service the 'Eucharist', which means 'thanksgiving', and this underlines the main thrust of the service for them – an act of thanksgiving for the death and resurrection of Jesus.

The Orthodox Church (the Divine Liturgy)

1. A liturgy is a service that follows an ancient and prescribed pattern. The **Divine Liturgy**, followed by the different Orthodox Churches, goes all the way back to the 5th century. It follows a similar pattern to that of the Catholic Mass, with a confession of sins followed by the Liturgy of the Word, the Liturgy of the Eucharist and the taking of communion.

2. Much of the Divine Liturgy takes place behind the **iconostasis**, a screen hiding the High Altar. This screen symbolises the distance between God and the human race, and also, during the Eucharist, their coming together in the act of communion.

3. Like Catholics, Orthodox Christians believe in transubstantiation – that the bread and wine become the body and blood of Jesus.

▲ As they eat the bread in the service of the Lord's Supper, worshippers are meditating on and remembering the death of Jesus to save them from their sins.

Protestant churches

1. Churches such as the Baptist and Methodist Churches hold similar beliefs about the meaning of this service and also have their own names for it. The two most common names used are:

- the **Lord's Supper**. This expression was used by St Paul in 1 Corinthians 11.20. The Lord's Supper was, in the early Church, a time for sharing and fellowship.

- the **Breaking of Bread**. This is a term taken from the Acts of the Apostles: "On the first day of the week we met for the breaking of bread" (Acts 20.7). It describes the practice of the earliest Christians who frequently met together to share an ordinary meal. Apart from being an act of worship this also fed those who were hungry and needy in the Christian community.

2. In most churches there are four parts to the service: a confession of sins to God and a reading from the Bible; the consecration of the bread and wine to God; the receiving and the eating of the bread and wine; and the sending out of worshippers into the world to serve God.

3. Protestants believe that the bread and wine are symbols and no more. They prompt each worshipper to remember the death of Jesus and to be thankful for it. At no time do they become the actual body and blood of Jesus. This area of disagreement was the major cause of the Reformation in the 16th century, which led to the separation of the Church of England from the Roman Catholic Church.

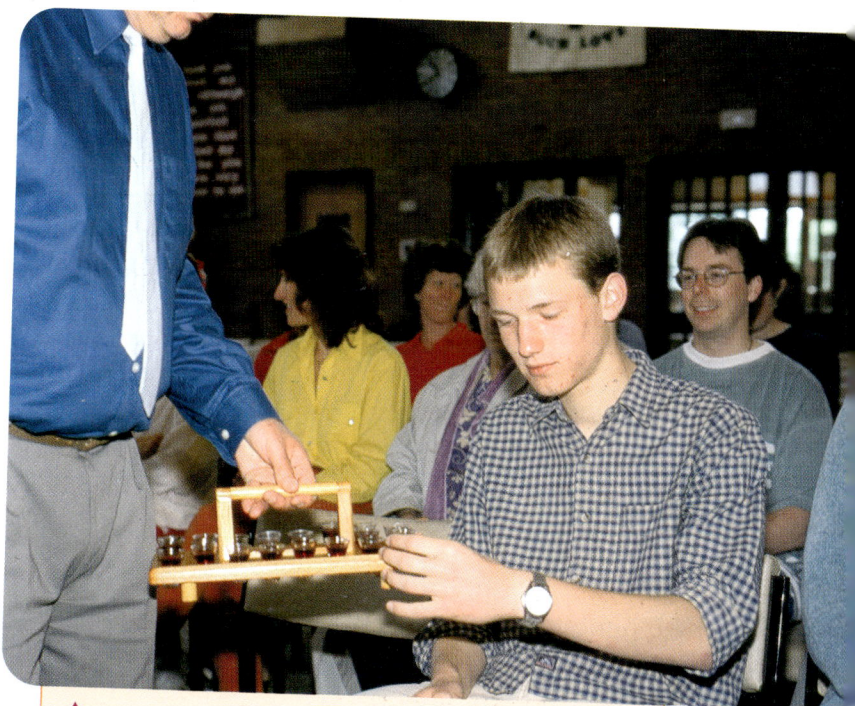

▲ *In Baptist churches people hold on to their wine and drink together as a symbol of their unity in Christ.*

TASKS

1. Which two terms do Protestants use for the service of Holy Communion?
2. What is the meaning and significance of each of these terms?

70 THE SACRAMENTS OF HEALING

There are two Sacraments of Healing in the Catholic Church:

1. The sacrament of penance and reconciliation (confession)

Although the sacrament of penance has been practised by the Catholic Church for centuries, it was given a fresh focus by the Second Vatican Council (1961–65). The Council declared that its purpose was to obtain "pardon from the mercy of God" and to be:

A *"... reconciled with the Church whom (sinners) have wounded by their sin, and who, by its charity, example and prayer, collaborates in their conversion."*
(Dogmatic Constitution on the Church n.11)

▲ *The old method of hearing confession with the priest and the penitent separated from each other.*

In the 17th century the 'confessional box' was introduced to ensure the privacy of penitents. Confession became concerned with confessing sin and receiving absolution from the priest. The Second Vatican Council, however, opened the way to face-to-face conversation, with the priest allowing the penitent to receive more direct counselling and help. Although the priest now knows the identity of the person, he is still bound by the 'seal of confession', which means that he cannot reveal anything that is said during confession.

During the act of making a confession the following happens:

1. The penitent is reminded by the priest that God will always forgive the person who is genuinely sorry for his or her sinful behaviour.

2. After the penitent has confessed his or her sins, the priest offers words of encouragement.

3. Once confession has been made and the penance accepted, the 'act of sorrow' takes place. Forgiveness can only be offered to those who are genuinely sorry for their past actions (contrition) and show that they are ready to amend their life in future (a firm purpose of amendment).

4. The priest then uses the ministry of forgiveness: a ministry which Jesus gave to his Church. It is not the priest who forgives the penitent but God. The priest pronounces absolution (extract A) and the sacrament of penance is given. The sign of the cross is made over the penitent.

> **A** **"** *God, the Father of mercies, through the death and resurrection of his Son had reconciled the world to himself and sent the Holy Spirit among us for the forgiveness of sins; through the ministry of the Church may God give you pardon and peace, and I absolve you from your sins in the name of the Father and of the Son and of the Holy Spirit.* **"**
>
> *(The Prayer of Absolution)*

2. The sacrament of anointing the sick

Pope Paul VI announced the new sacrament of anointing the sick in 1972. This is intended to assure sick people that they are not alone in their suffering because God is always with them. They can know that through their suffering they are sharing in the sufferings of Jesus and playing a part in the redemption of the world. There are three parts to this sacrament:

1. The priest sprinkles the sick person with holy water as a reminder that he or she first started to follow Jesus after baptism. After Bible readings, the priest lays his hands on the person.

2. The priest anoints the person, using olive oil that was blessed by the bishop at the **Chrism** Mass held on the previous Maundy Thursday.

3. The person takes Holy Communion. The believer's suffering draws them close to God in a special way through this celebration. If the person is dying then the act of communion is called the '**viaticum**' ('food for the journey') and the person is assured that he or she is travelling to his or her Father in heaven.

TASKS

1. What events lead up to the pronouncement of absolution by the priest in the Sacrament of Penance?
2. What are the three main parts to the sacrament of anointing the sick?

✳ DISCUSSION POINT

Both of these sacraments are full of symbolism. Why do you think this is very important?

71 THE LITURGICAL YEAR

With worship in mind, the Catholic Church divides the year into three seasons or cycles. Each season has at least one major festival that commemorates a very important event either in the life of Jesus or in the history of the Christian Church. The three cycles in the liturgical year are as follow.

1. The Christmas cycle

The liturgical year begins around the end of November with Advent. This period of four weeks leads up to the celebration of Christmas and during this time Christians prepare themselves to welcome the coming of Jesus into the world. This time of preparation has been part of the liturgical year since the 6th century. Christmas is the most widely celebrated of all Christian festivals. The name comes from the Old English for 'Christ's Mass' and is a time for Christians of all denominations to celebrate the birth of Jesus.

▲ The resurrection of Jesus from the dead is the foundation on which the whole religion of Christianity is built.

The Christmas cycle ends with the festival of **Epiphany** (manifestation or showing). In western churches this day, 6 January, focuses on the visit of the Magi (Wise Men) to the infant Jesus. This was important because the Wise Men were the first non-Jews (Gentiles) to share in the Incarnation, the birth, of Jesus.

2. The Easter cycle

Although Christmas is the most popular Christian festival, Easter is the most important spiritually. It begins with Lent, when Catholics enter into a time of spiritual reflection and preparation before Easter. The last week of Lent is called **Holy Week**. There are four important celebrations during Holy Week.

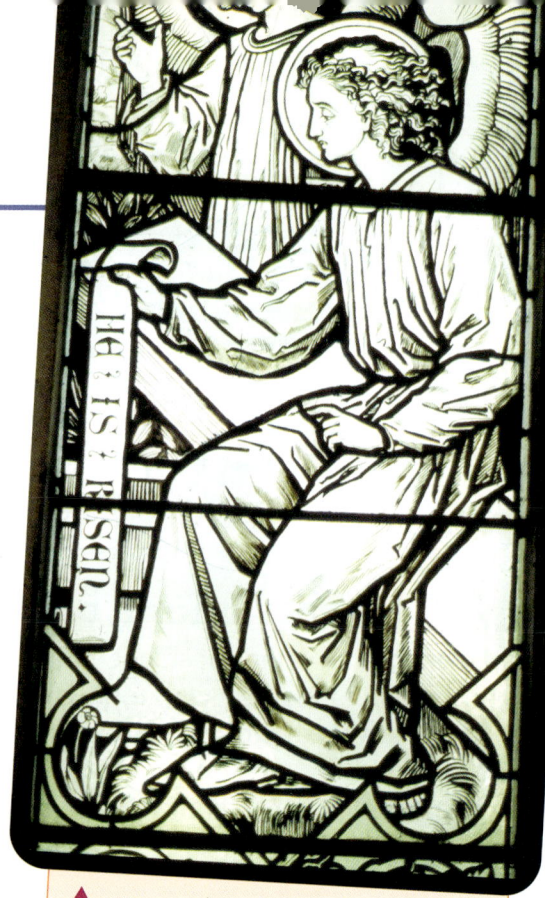

CHECK IT OUT

Palm Sunday – when Jesus entered Jerusalem riding on a donkey.

Maundy Thursday – when Jesus washed the feet of his disciples and ate his last meal.

THE EVENTS OF HOLY WEEK

Good Friday – the day on which Jesus was crucified.

Easter Saturday – the day on which the body of Jesus lay buried in the tomb.

The day after the end of Holy Week is called Easter Sunday. This is the most joyful day in the liturgical year as it is the time when Christians celebrate the resurrection of Jesus from the dead. The resurrection of Jesus is the cornerstone of the Christian faith and it stands at the very centre of Catholic faith.

3. The Pentecost cycle

With Easter completed, only one major Christian festival remains before the cycle starts again the following November. This is the festival of Pentecost (sometimes called **Whitsun**), which follows 40 days after Easter Day. This is when Christians celebrate the giving of the Holy Spirit to the first Christians on the day of Pentecost in Jerusalem. For centuries this was the traditional time for baptising new converts to Christianity, a ceremony for which they dressed in white – hence 'Whitsun'.

Ascension Day is a festival that celebrates the ascension of Jesus into heaven. To begin with, this event was celebrated at Pentecost but it has been a separate festival since the 6th century. There are also special Saints' Days such as All Saints' Day (1 November) and All Souls' Day (2 November) but these are not major Christian festivals.

> **A** *" … the Church, especially during Advent and Lent and above all at the Easter Vigil, re-reads and re-lives the great events of salvation history in the 'today' of her liturgy. "*
> (CCC 1095)

TASKS

Before we look at the festivals individually it would be good for you to carry out some research to discover:

a. Which traditions and customs are associated with Advent?

b. What is the significance of Shrove Tuesday and Ash Wednesday at the beginning of Lent?

c. Which event in the life of Jesus is the model for the Christian celebration of Lent?

d. Any special events or customs in the Catholic Church associated with Lent and Easter.

e. How the Catholic Church celebrates Pentecost.

72 ADVENT

The Church year begins with Advent. This time of preparation for Christmas begins on the fourth Sunday before Christmas and is then celebrated on the three following Sundays.

The three 'comings'

For all Christians, the coming of God into the world, the Incarnation, was a momentous event. So momentous, in fact, that many churches set aside four weeks to prepare their members to celebrate this event properly. The hymns, Bible readings and sermons during Advent tell of three 'comings':

1. The coming of God's promised Messiah. Throughout the Old Testament, God led the Jews to expect that He would send them a divine leader who would deliver them from their enemies – and set up God's kingdom on earth. The prophets, in particular, looked forward to the coming of the Messiah and readings from one of them, Isaiah, play a prominent role during Advent.

2. The coming of John the Baptist. John was important because he played a very valuable role in the early ministry of Jesus. He prepared the people for the coming of Jesus and baptised him before his ministry started.

3. The Second Coming of Christ at the end of time. Because this event is still awaited, it is timely that Christians should be reminded of it at Advent.

Three symbols of Advent

The Advent Wreath

This is sometimes called an 'Advent crown' and is an old custom associated with the Advent season. Five candles are placed in an evergreen wreath and these are lit on the four Sundays of Advent – one in the middle of the wreath and the others around the outside. The central candle, often called the 'Christ candle', is white and the others are purple.

◄ The crown of holly in the Advent wreath is a reminder to Christians of the crown of thorns that was placed on the head of Jesus shortly before his crucifixion.

The **Advent wreath** is a good example of the use of symbolism in Christian worship:

- Evergreen plants are a symbol of eternity – the eternity of God. The circle of the wreath is a reminder of the love and mercy of God, which are never-ending.

- As John reminds us in his Gospel (John 8.12), Jesus was called 'the Light of the World' and this is symbolised by the candles, especially the one in the centre. The white candle is lit for the first time on Christmas Day to remind everyone that Jesus, the Saviour of the world, has been born. It is then lit for all services leading up to **Epiphany**. White is the symbol of joy and happiness, while purple symbolises penitence for one's sins.

- The crown is made of holly. Christians believe that the holly represents the crown of thorns that was placed on Jesus' head before his crucifixion, while the red berries symbolise the blood of Jesus that was shed for the sins of the whole world.

Advent Candle

You will find an Advent candle in many churches and homes in the days before Christmas. The numbers 1 to 24 are printed down the candle so that it can be lit during the days of Advent. In Christian homes, a prayer and a reading from the Bible often accompany the burning of the candle. Its burning helps to build up the anticipation for Christmas Day.

Advent Calendar

Advent calendars are popular with children in the run-up to Christmas. Inside the calendar, there are 24 windows which, when opened, show a picture with some kind of Christmas theme. This may be religious, although nowadays many Advent calendars show non-religious Christmas themes. Again, anticipation is built up as Christmas approaches.

TASKS

1. Describe each of the three 'comings' that are traditionally associated with the season of Advent.
2. Describe an Advent wreath.
3. Describe three pieces of symbolism found on an Advent wreath.
4. Why do you think that Advent calendars are very popular with children?

✴ TO TALK ABOUT

What do you think is the real message of Advent?

73 CHRISTMAS AND EPIPHANY

The story of the birth of Jesus is told in two of the four Gospels in the New Testament – Matthew and Luke. Both tell us Jesus was born to a virgin mother as the result of a miraculous conception.

Two Gospel accounts

- Matthew writes his description from the point of view of Joseph, the human father of Jesus. He saw the birth of Jesus as the fulfilment of prophecies from the Old Testament. An angel appeared to him in a dream and announced:

> **A** **"***Joseph, son of David, do not be afraid to take Mary home as your wife, because she has conceived what is in her by the Holy Spirit. She will give birth to a son and you must name him Jesus, because he is the one who is to save his people from their sins.***"**
>
> *(Matthew 1.20–21)*

- Luke tells the story from Mary's point of view. An angel appeared to her in an event that Catholics know as the Annunciation and you can find the angel's words in extract B.

> **B** **"***You are to conceive and bear a son, and you must name him Jesus. He will be great and will be called Son of the Most High.***"**
>
> *(Luke 1.31)*

No one knows exactly when Jesus was born, although it was probably around 4BCE. 25 December was the date of the Roman festival of Saturnalia. When Christianity became the official religion of the Roman Empire, it took over this date to celebrate the birth of Jesus.

▶ *For many people, the crib is the best symbol of Christmas.*

The crib and other Christmas celebrations

In the days leading up to Christmas, churches have **carol** services at which special hymns that celebrate the birth of Jesus are sung. There are nativity plays in schools and churches. People exchange Christmas cards with friends and relatives. At midnight on Christmas Eve, many Christians meet for a special service to greet the birth of Jesus and this ends early on Christmas morning.

Many homes and churches have cribs which show the stable scene and the main characters in the Christmas story. This becomes the main focus of prayers and worship over the Christmas time. The idea was originally used by St Francis of Assisi in the 13th century to teach the Christmas story to members of his congregation, and it has become an important part of Christmas celebrations ever since.

The meaning of Christmas

Christians believe that God came to the world in a special way at Christmas – in the form of His Son. God showed His love for the people by sharing their lives and showing them how He expected them to live. By setting up God's kingdom on earth, Jesus showed the nations of the world how they could live together in peace.

Epiphany

The word 'Epiphany' means 'to show forth'. In the Gospels, Jesus is 'shown forth' as the Son of God and the festival of Epiphany, following 12 days after Christmas, commemorates three 'showings' of Jesus:

- the showing of Jesus to the Wise Men, the first Gentiles to meet him (Matthew 2.1–12);
- the baptism of Jesus (Mark 1.9–11);
- the Transfiguration of Jesus (Mark 9.2–13).

Catholics celebrate a special Mass on the feast of Epiphany and another Mass on the Sunday following remembers the baptism of Jesus.

> **C** ❝*The Epiphany is the manifestation of Jesus as Messiah of Israel, Son of God and Saviour of the world.*❞
>
> *(CCC 528)*

TASKS

1. What are the main differences between the accounts of the birth of Jesus by Matthew and Luke?

2. What celebrations show that Christmas is a special time for Christians?

3. The Apostles' Creed says that "Jesus was conceived by the power of the Holy Spirit and born to the Virgin Mary." Do you think that it is important for Christians to believe that the conception and birth of Jesus is special?
Give reasons for your answer, showing that you have thought about more than one point of view.

74 LENT

Easter is the most important of all the Christian festivals. For this reason, Catholics believe that a period of solemn spiritual preparation is necessary before the festival. This time of reflection lasts for 40 days and is called Lent.

Why Lent?

The length of time for which Lent lasts is significant. In the Gospels Jesus spent 40 days in the desert after he had been baptised by John the Baptist (Mark 1.12). While he was there, he prayed and fasted. During this time, he was tempted three times by the Devil:

- to turn the stones around him into bread to relieve his hunger and break his fast;

- to throw himself down from the Temple to show that God would take care of him;

- to be given all the kingdoms of the world so that he would be all-powerful.

Significantly, Jesus rejected each of these temptations by quoting the Jewish Scriptures to the Devil.

For Christians, Lent is the time for penance and repentance – a time to prepare the soul for the despair and joy of Easter. By going through the ordeal of Lent, Christians are preparing themselves for the task of sharing the Christian Gospel with others. They are also spiritually preparing themselves for the events that are celebrated within the Church during Holy Week. The days of Holy Week carry a very special spiritual significance and the solemnity of it builds up as each day passes. During Lent Christians:

▲ *The ash cross on the forehead is a sign that someone is genuinely sorry for their sins and wishes to make amends in the future.*

1. *Read the Bible and pray.* Although these two activities are regular ingredients of Catholic devotion, people try to set aside more time for them during Lent.

2. *Study.* Often during Lent, Catholics, and other Christian groups, come together into study groups. Time is then spent studying an appropriate topic from the Bible.

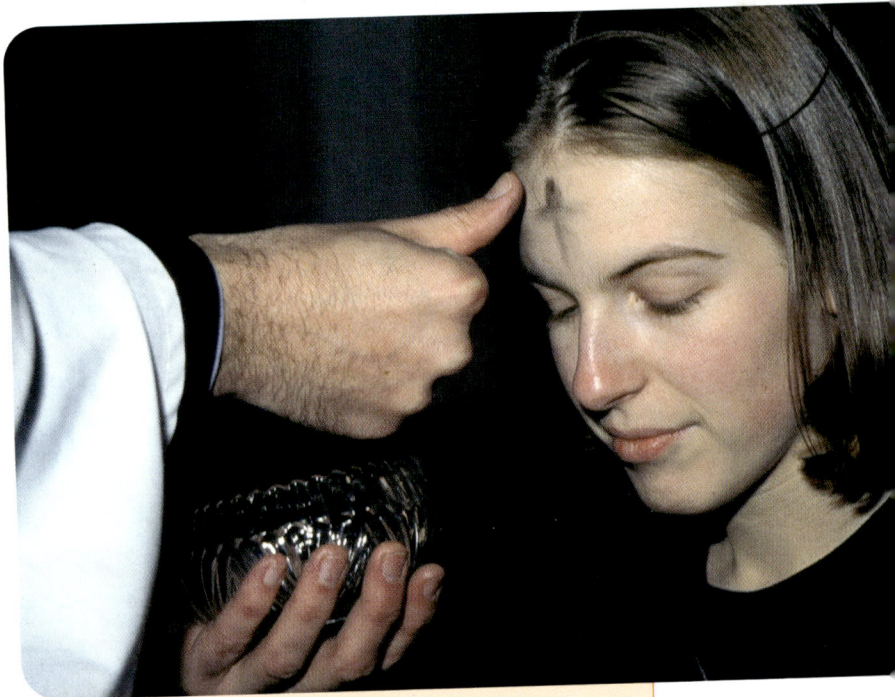

3. *Fast.* Some Christians take fasting seriously during Lent by giving up certain kinds of much-loved food. They may also try to remedy certain defects in their character in this time. Self-denial has always been an important part of taking Lent seriously for many Christians.

4. *Carry out good work.* Christians often increase their contributions to charity or other forms of social work during Lent. The festival is a time for remembering the poor, the homeless and other needy people.

Shrove Tuesday and Ash Wednesday

Shrove Tuesday is the day before the beginning of Lent. In the past, people came to church on this day to make their confession and receive absolution from the priest. Many still do. In the past, all fat in the house was put out or used up before the fast of Lent began. In this country, the fat was used to make pancakes – a custom that is still popular today on Shrove Tuesday.

Ash Wednesday marks the beginning of Lent. People come to church on this day to be marked on the forehead with the 'sign of the cross'. The sign is made of ash which has been made from the burning of the previous year's palm crosses. In Old Testament times, people used to put on 'sackcloth and ashes' as a sign that they were genuinely repentant for their sins. It is also a reminder that each human being only has a brief time on earth (extract A).

> **A** ❝With sweat on your brow shall you eat your bread, until you return to the soil, as you were taken from it. For dust you are and to dust you shall return.❞
> *(Genesis 3.19)*

TASKS

1. Describe four spiritual activities that many Christians are likely to pursue during Lent.
2. When you give up important things, do you think that it is a good idea to have some time to think about the spiritual aspects of life?

✳ DISCUSSION POINT

Do you think that it is a good idea to have a time each year when you devote yourself to serious thought about your own faith and spend time with other Christians who are doing the same?

75 PALM SUNDAY AND MAUNDY THURSDAY

Holy Week is the last week of Lent. During this week, Christians remember events that took place in the last week of the life of Jesus before he was put to death in Jerusalem. Holy Week begins on Palm Sunday and ends at midnight on Holy Saturday.

Jesus entering Jerusalem

As Jesus approached the city of Jerusalem with his disciples, he sent two of them to find a colt, the foal of a donkey, that someone had left tethered nearby.

▲ *By riding on a donkey into Jerusalem, Jesus was announcing that he was the peaceful Messiah.*

They brought the animal to him and he sat on it. Many people saw what he was doing and spread their cloaks and palm leaves on the road in front of him. Everyone began shouting:

> **"** *Hosanna! Blessings on him who comes in the name of the Lord. Blessings on the coming kingdom of our father David!* **"**
>
> *(Mark 11.9–10)*

In this way Jesus entered the courts of the Temple in Jerusalem.

The meaning of the event

This simple event had a profound meaning for his disciples and those who were watching the event:

- The people who cheered Jesus as he entered Jerusalem on a donkey were welcoming him as their Messiah. The donkey was an animal of peace. If he had been coming as the warrior Messiah, as the people were hoping, he would have been riding a horse. The people were hoping that 'the kingdom of King David' was going to be restored. David was a much-loved Jewish king who had united the many tribes of Israel into a mighty nation. Jesus, however, was announcing that he was the Prince of Peace – but still the Messiah.

- The palm leaves that the people were waving were signs of victory as they were traditionally waved after a victory had been gained in battle.

- By his actions, Jesus was fulfilling a verse from the Jewish Scriptures (see extract A).

> **A** **"** *Say to the daughter of Zion: Look, your king comes to you, he is humble, he rides on a donkey and on a colt, the foal of a beast of burden.* **"**
>
> *(Zechariah 9.9. quoted in Matthew 21.5)*

Maundy Thursday

On Holy Thursday, the Thursday of Holy Week, Christians remember two important events in the life of Jesus:

- The institution of the service of Holy Communion at the Last Supper.

- The washing of the feet of the disciples by Jesus to teach them about humility and service. This task was usually undertaken by the most menial of the servants in a household. Jesus was encouraging his disciples to follow his example.

The name 'Maundy Thursday' comes from the Latin word *mandatum*, meaning commandment. This refers to the new commandment that Jesus gave to his disciples on this day (extract B).

▲ *The bread and wine are two of the most important Christian symbols, reminding everyone of the death of Jesus.*

> **B** **"**I give you a new commandment: love one another; you must love one another just as I have loved you.**"**
>
> *(John 13.34)*

At the Last Supper, Jesus:

- broke a loaf of bread in front of his disciples and told them to eat bread together to remember him;

- shared a goblet of wine with his disciples telling them that the wine symbolised his own blood which was going to be offered up to God for them.

The Last Supper is re-enacted by Christians in the most important of all services – Holy Communion. This is the service that Catholics refer to as the Mass (you can find out more about this service in units 66–69). A special Mass is held in Catholic churches on this day and the priest may follow the example of Jesus by washing the feet of some members of his congregation.

1. What was the significance of the entry of Jesus into Jerusalem on a donkey?
2. Which two events in the life of Jesus are remembered on Maundy Thursday?

TASKS

76 GOOD FRIDAY

Good Friday is the most important day of Holy Week. On this day, Christians look back to the crucifixion of Jesus in Jerusalem. Each Gospel devotes at least 30% of its space to telling this story, from the arrest of Jesus through to his death alongside two criminals (extract A).

> **A** 	*"They brought Jesus to the place called Golgotha, which means the place of the skull... Then they crucified him, and shared out his clothing... It was the third hour when they crucified him... And they crucified two robbers with him, one on his right and one on his left."*
> (Mark 15.22–27)

On Good Friday

The sombre and dark mood of the first Good Friday is reflected in the decor of many churches as all pictures, wall hangings and statues are either removed or covered by a black cloth on Good Friday. There are no flowers in the church building and the Eucharist is not celebrated between Maundy Thursday and Easter Sunday. All of this reminds the worshippers that Good Friday is a day set aside for serious meditation on the death of God's Son.

Marches of witness

Often, the shared grief of Christians at the death of Jesus draws them together across denominational divides to take part in a combined act of witness to their Christian faith on this day. This usually takes the form of a procession behind someone carrying a large wooden cross, re-enacting the journey of Jesus up the Via Dolorosa (the Way of Sorrows) in Jerusalem to Calvary. On the way, an open-air service is held in which members of the public are invited to join.

Church Services

Most Christians try to spend some time in church on Good Friday worshipping and meditating on the death of Jesus. Different denominations have their own ways of doing this.

1. In Roman Catholic and some Anglican churches, there is a special service running from noon to 3:00pm. These were the last hours of Jesus' life before he died and the people are sharing them with him. The accounts of the Crucifixion from all four Gospels are read, since each of them brings a different perspective. A wooden cross is then laid in front of the congregation and each person comes forward to kiss it – an act of devotion that is called 'venerating the cross'. The priest says:

> *"This is the wood of the cross on which the Saviour of the world died."*

All Roman Catholic churches have fourteen **Stations of the Cross** around the walls of the building that illustrate, with paintings or sculptures, the different places where Jesus stopped on the way to his execution. These Stations were originally placed in churches when it became too dangerous for pilgrims to make the actual journey to the Holy Land to walk in the footsteps of Jesus. Now, visiting the Stations is a kind of 'pilgrimage' as Christians try to share the pain and suffering of Jesus. Each person slowly visits each Station, kneeling and saying a prayer before moving on to the next.

2. In Orthodox churches, Good Friday is known as 'Great Friday'. The special Orthodox Good Friday liturgy is held in the evening, with the priest carrying an **icon** of the dead Christ, wrapped in burial clothes. The people gather around holding candles as if they are at a funeral. They come forward and kiss the icon to show their love for Jesus. Later, the icon is carried around the outside of the church in a funeral procession as church bells toll.

3. Nonconformist churches do not have a special ritual associated with Good Friday. They do, however, have a service in which readings from the Gospels figure prominently. God is thanked for sending Jesus to die so that the sins of the people can be forgiven.

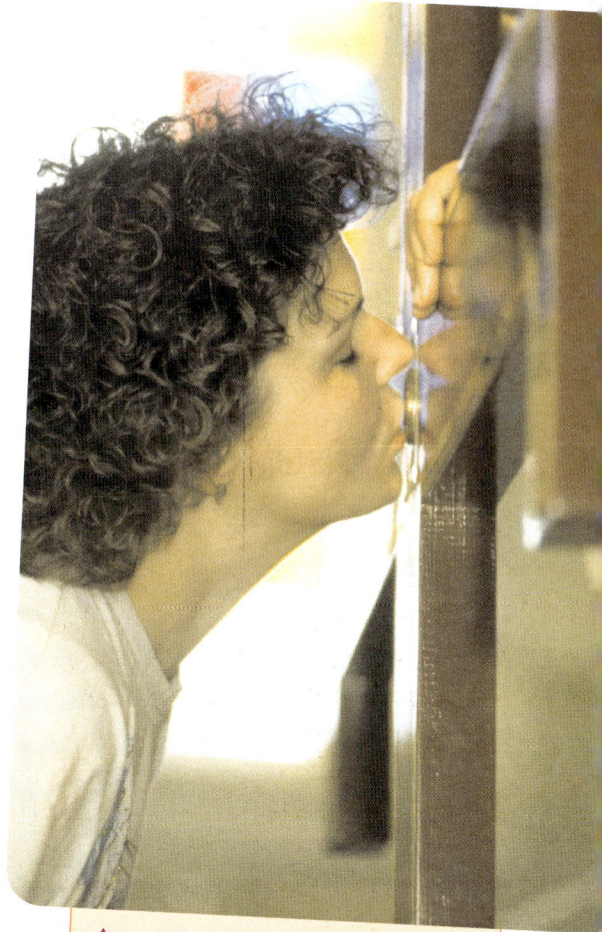

▲ *By venerating the cross, Christians show their deep love and respect for Jesus and his sacrifice.*

TASKS

1. What events in the life of Jesus are specifically remembered on Good Friday?
2. The day on which Jesus died is called Good Friday. In what way do you think the events of this day could be called 'good'?
3. Describe how either Roman Catholics or Orthodox Christians celebrate Good Friday.

✳ **DISCUSSION POINT**

What do you think is the meaning of the death of Jesus?

77 EASTER DAY

This is the day when Christians celebrate the resurrection of Jesus from the dead. It is the most important day in the Christian year. On the third day after Jesus was put to death, some of his female followers went to the tomb to anoint his body. They found that the tomb was empty and a man dressed in white clothes, an angel, told them that Jesus had risen from the dead (extract A). He told them to go and inform the disciples, especially Peter who had denied Jesus, that Jesus was alive. This they did. Jesus then appeared to groups of his followers before he left the Earth.

> **A** **The Resurrection of Jesus is the crowning truth of our faith in Christ, a faith believed and lived as the central truth by the first Christian community.**
> *(CCC 638)*

The paschal candle

In Catholic and Orthodox churches, celebrations begin late on the Saturday night when worshippers gather outside a dark church called the Easter Vigil. The paschal candle ('the candle of suffering') is lit and carried into the darkened church. This symbolises the 'Light of the World' (Jesus) who has brought light into a sinful world by conquering death and bringing light to all. Some worshippers light the candles they are holding before passing the light on to others. This happens until the whole church is glowing with light. This symbolises the passing on of the Good News of the Gospel from person to person.

Apart from the obvious symbol of light that the paschal candle represents, it also contains two Greek letters – Chi and Rho. These are the first two letters of the word 'Christ'. Five grains of incense are placed in the centre of the candle to commemorate the five wounds of Christ. The candle has the year printed on it and the first and last letters of the Greek alphabet – Alpha and Omega.

Easter Day services

On Easter Day, the clergy wear their brightest vestments for Mass. Church bells are rung for the first time since Good Friday and the service opens with a rousing resurrection hymn. The readings tell the story of the Resurrection and the homily draws the attention of the people to the new life that is theirs through the rising of Jesus from the dead. Worshippers often join in the ancient response:

"The Lord is risen! The Lord is risen indeed!"

During the Mass, three important events are remembered:

- the death of Jesus;
- the rising of Jesus from the dead;
- the Second Coming – the return of Jesus in glory.

These events are linked together with the prayer:

> *Dying you destroyed our death, rising you restored our life. Lord Jesus, come in glory.*

With these words, the Church summarises its Easter faith. It is the faith which forms the core of the Gospel to which the Catholic Church it totally committed.

Easter eggs and Easter gardens

Easter eggs, the most popular of all symbols for this season, are used to represent God's new life in bringing Jesus back from the dead. Orthodox Christians dye boiled eggs red to represent the blood of Jesus, which was shed for the sins of all. Chocolate Easter eggs became popular because the fast of Lent was broken on Easter Day. Easter gardens are a traditional way of teaching about the resurrection of Jesus. Moss, twigs and stones are used to create a garden in which a tomb stands with its stone rolled away from the entrance. Surrounding it is a garden which uses spring flowers to symbolise the new life of Easter. Spring flowers are also used in church to symbolise nwe life associated with Jesus.

▶ *The resurrection of Jesus from the dead is the cornerstone of the Christian faith.*

TASKS

1. Explain why the paschal candle is an important Catholic symbol.

2. Describe what happens during the Easter Vigil.

3. Describe what links these have with Easter celebrations:
   a. Easter eggs
   b. an Easter garden

✳ DISCUSSION POINT

Why do you think that the **Easter Vigil** links together the death of Jesus, the resurrection of Jesus and the Second Coming of Christ?

78 ASCENSION DAY AND PENTECOST

Ascension Day

In the forty days after his resurrection, Jesus appeared to many of his followers before being taken up from them into heaven. You can find the last words that Jesus spoke to his disciples in extract A. These words are called 'The Great Commission' because they are instructions from Jesus outlining what he expected his followers to do in the days after he left them. They were to be God's witnesses throughout the whole of the known world

> **A** *"...you will receive power when the Holy Spirit comes on you, and then you will be my witnesses not only in Jerusalem but throughout Judea and Samaria, and indeed to the ends of the earth."*
>
> (Acts 1.8)

The ascension of Jesus marked the end of his life on earth so he could return to his Father in heaven and begin his reign with God in heaven. It marked the start of the time when Jesus began to intercede (pray) to God on behalf of all those in his kingdom on earth. Ascension Day always falls forty days after Easter and is a holy day in the Catholic Church. It is always celebrated with a Mass.

Pentecost

Fifty days after Easter, the Christian Church celebrates the festival of Pentecost. The festival of Pentecost was one of three Pilgrimage Festivals for which Jews from all over the Roman Empire tried to be present in the Temple in Jerusalem. On this occasion, the disciples of Jesus were gathered together when they were given the Holy Spirit. You can find Luke's description of this in extract B.

> **B** *"...suddenly there came from heaven a sound as of a violent wind which filled the entire house in which they were sitting; and there appeared to them tongues as of fire; these separated and came to rest on each of them. They were all filled with the Holy Spirit..."*
>
> (Acts 2.1–2)

The disciples began to speak in the different languages of those around them. This marked the birthday of the Christian Church. The disciples went out to preach to the people gathered in Jerusalem and many converts were made.

The Holy Spirit

The Holy Spirit is a very important member of the Christian Trinity and three different activities of him must be noted:

1. *The Holy Spirit is the giver of power.* The disciples were told by Jesus that the Holy Spirit would give them power. When it was given to them, they began to have a great impact on those around them. Christians today believe that they

The ascension of Jesus into heaven marked the end of his earthly ministry and the beginning of his reign with God in heaven.

need the power of God's Spirit. Catholics believe that this comes to them through the sacraments.

2. *The work of the Holy Spirit.* In John's Gospel, this is likened to the wind – everyone knows when it is blowing but cannot see it. Everyone knows when the Holy Spirit is active in the world.

3. *The fruits of the Holy Spirit.* These are the spiritual qualities that every Christian can possess with the help of the Holy Spirit.

The meaning of Pentecost

During the time that Jesus was on earth, people responded to the call of God that came to them through his preaching and teaching. James and John, for example, were fishing in their boat when Jesus called them at the start of his ministry, while Matthew was gathering taxes. All three of them responded to the call of Jesus to become disciples. After the giving of the Holy Spirit, the focus changed from the individual to the community. People needed to repent of their sins and be baptised to become members of the Christian community. This process is continued in the Church today through the sacraments of baptism and confirmation. People are invited to join the Christian Church and become members of God's kingdom – through the Holy Spirit. The same is true today.

TASKS

1. What event is remembered on Ascension Day?
2. What happened on the first day of Pentecost?
3. What are Christians celebrating when they celebrate Pentecost?

✳ DISCUSSION POINT

Do you think that festivals are a very important part of religion? Give some reasons why religious people find it necessary to celebrate festivals.

EXAM HELP

In the examination

Make sure that you know about:

THE SACRAMENTS

- A sacrament is a sign or symbol designed to draw God closer to the worshipper. God is the supreme mystery. It is also a God-given service, which uses material elements, such as bread, water and wine.

- The Catholic Church recognises seven sacraments: baptism, confirmation, penance, the Eucharist, Anointing the Sick, matrimony and ordination to the priesthood. The Anglican Church recognises two sacraments: the Eucharist and the baptism, as do Nonconformist Churches.

- The Catholic service of infant baptism. The Liturgy of the Word. The exorcism of Satan; follwed by anointing with oil of catechisms. The baptism by water and the anointing with chrism. The meaning of infant baptism.

- Preparation and age for confirmation. Catholic service of confirmation – renewal of baptismal vows, laying on of hands by bishop. Anointing with oil and the sign of the cross.

- Background to the Mass – most important Catholic service with roots in the Jewish Passover. What is celebrated at Passover. The Last Supper – a Passover meal. The bread – a symbol of the body of Jesus. The wine – a symbol of sorrow, the blood of Jesus. The Mass as a sacrifice – Jesus, the lamb of God.

- The spiritual preparation for the Mass including: the use of holy water – sign of the cross; the Penitential Rite; the Liturgy of the Word; the Liturgy of the Eucharist – the peoples' offerings; the Eucharistic Prayer; transubstantiation; the Rite of Communion; the final blessing.

- The Mass and Catholics – cleanse from sin, gifts of the Holy Spirit, spiritual energy, insight into heaven, puts people into contact with the death of Jesus. An act of 'holy' communion – unites believers with God and each other.

- Sacraments of healing – penance and reconciliation, and anointing the sick. The importance of confession and contrition.

- Communion and other Christians. The Eucharist (Anglicans) – some share the Roman Catholic view while others hold a Protestant view. The Divine Liturgy (Orthodox Churches), an old liturgy that mainly takes place behind iconostasis. Belief in transubstantiation. Protestant Churches (Lord's Supper and Breaking of Bread), service of remembrance.

Sample exam questions

1. Why do Catholic parents think that it is very important for them to have their children baptised?

2. What happens during the Catholic service of infant baptism?

3. What happens during the Catholic service of Confirmation?

4. What is meant in the Mass by:

   a. the Liturgy of the Word?

b. the Liturgy of the Eucharist?

5. What is the importance of the sacraments of:

   a. penance and reconciliation?

   b. anointing the sick?

FESTIVALS

- The Liturgical Year. The Christmas cycle – Christmas and Epiphany. The Easter cycle – the four celebrations during Holy Week. The climax of Easter Day. The Pentecost cycle – Pentecost and Acsension Day.

- Advent – The three comings – the coming of the Messiah, the coming of John the Baptist and the Second Coming. The three symbols of Advent – Advent wreath, Advent candle and Advent calendar.

- The two Gospel accounts of the birth of Jesus in Matthew's and Luke's Gospels. The Catholic way of celebrating Christmas. The meaning of Christmas. Epiphany –'showing forth' – the Wise Men, the baptism of Jesus and the wedding feast.

- Why Lent is celebrated – the link with the temptations of Jesus, forty days. The way that Catholics use Lent for spiritual preparation for Easter – penance and repentance. Shrove Tuesday – how it was celebrated in the past. Ash Wednesday – the first day of Lent. Sign of the cross on forehead in ash. Sackcloth and ashes.

- Gospel background to Palm Sunday and Maundy Thursday celebrations. Events remembered on Palm Sunday – the entry of Jesus into Jerusalem on a donkey. Reason for the name 'Maundy Thursday'. Link of Maundy Thursday with Holy Communion and the commandment given by Jesus to the disciples.

- Significance of Good Friday. The way in which Catholics celebrate it. Church services. Stations of the Cross and its use on this day.

- Significance of Easter Day. The Easter Vigil (four parts). Easter eggs and Easter gardens as important symbols.

- Ascension Day – Jesus leaving the Earth. Pentecost – the giving of the Holy Spirit. The meaning of Pentecost.

EXAM HELP

Sample exam questions

1. **a.** Explain what Catholics mean by transubstantiation.

   b. Explain how Catholics and Protestants differ in their understanding of Holy Communion.

2. Explain the importance of the sacraments of:

   a. penance and reconciliation

   b. anointing of the sick

3. **a.** How do many Catholics use Advent to prepare themselves for Christmas?

   b. How do Catholics celebrate Christmas?

4. **a.** Why is Lent important?

   b. What is the significance of the different events of Holy Week?

   c. "Easter is more important than Christmas as a Christian festival." Do you agree with this comment? Give your reasons, showing that you have thought about more than one point of view.

5. Explain the significance of:

   a. Maunday Thursday

   b. Good Friday

   c. Easter Sunday

Living the Christian life

In this section you will find out about:

- the Ten Commandments;
- the expression of Christian values;
- two exemplary Christians of the 20th century.

KEY WORDS

Compassion A deep feeling of pity and love for other people.

Concern Christians are expected to show compassion for others and to do everything they can to meet their needs.

Displaying religion The criticism of Jesus against those who followed a religious way of life to impress others.

Golden rule The teaching of Jesus that a person should treat others in the way that they would like to be treated themselves.

Judgement Being critical of and judging the actions and behaviour of others.

Justice A concern that everyone should be treated fairly under the law.

Oppressed Those who are persecuted and not given their rights as human beings.

Sermon on the Mount A collection of the teachings and sayings of Jesus about living the Christian life.

Service Following the example of Jesus by serving others instead of expecting to be served by them.

Ten Commandments The ten laws for the Israelites given to Moses on Mount Sinai during the Exodus.

79 THE TEN COMMANDMENTS (1)

The Catechism devotes a long chapter to the Ten Commandments, showing that these old laws, given by God to Moses on Mount Sinai, have always played an important part in the teaching of the Catholic Church. They describe a person's responsibility to God (see unit 80) and his or her responsibility to others. As extract A shows, this two-fold division went back to Jesus himself.

> **A** **"***Jesus said, 'You must love the Lord your God with all your heart, with all your soul and with all your mind. This is the greatest and the first commandment. The second resembles it: You must love your neighbour as yourself.'***"**
> *(Matthew 22.37–39)*

The Ten Commandments are found in Exodus 20.1–17

Commandment 1: Have no other gods before me

God made himself known to the Israelites through a miracle – He gave them freedom after more than 400 years of Egyptian slavery. One condition for their release was that Israelites would only worship the one God – and not bow down to any false gods. This commandment has enormous implications for every Christian – God is an unchanging Being who is always faithful and merciful. Every Christian is called to love God above everything and everyone else – see extract A.

Commandment 2: Do not make a carved image

The making of any statues of God was strictly forbidden.

> ▶ *There is a reminder of the Ten Commandments on the wall of every Jewish synagogue so that worshippers are aware of their importance.*

Commandment 3: Do not misuse God's name

This commandment calls for great respect to be shown to the name of God. Its use must be reserved for those occasions when a person is blessing, praising or glorifying God. Blasphemy (misusing God's name) is the ultimate betrayal of God. Catholics are also forbidden to blaspheme against the Church of Christ, the Virgin Mary, and all saints and all holy things by the Catechism.

Commandment 4: Keep the Sabbath Day holy

The commandment about keeping the **Sabbath Day** holy recalls two events in Jewish Scriptures:

- the creation of the world, when God worked for six days and then rested on the seventh;
- the release of the Jews from Egyptian slavery – an event known to Jews as the Exodus.

God gave the Sabbath Day, a day of total rest, to the Jews as a sign of the covenant (agreement) that he had made with them. Jesus respected the Sabbath laws but he also commented that:

> **The Sabbath was made for man, not man for the Sabbath; so the Son of Man is master even of the Sabbath.**
> *(Mark 2.27)*

For Christians, the most important event of all was the death and resurrection of Jesus. As Jesus rose from the dead on a Sunday, so, by the 4th century CE, Christians were worshipping on that day instead of the Sabbath. Today, Catholics are expected to either keep the Sunday vigil (Saturday evening) or worship on the Sunday in their parish communities. There they should share in the Eucharist, which declares publicly that Catholics belong to Jesus and to his living community, the Church.

> **B** **Lifting up the mind towards God is an expression of our adoration of God: prayer of praise and thanksgiving, intercession and petition. Prayer is an indispensable condition for being able to obey God's commandments.**
> *(CCC 2098)*

TASKS

1. **a.** What is blasphemy?
    b. What is the link between blasphemy and the second commandment?
2. What do you think Jesus meant when he said, "The Sabbath was made for man, not man for the Sabbath; so the Son of Man is master even of the Sabbath"?

✳ DISCUSSION POINT

The Catechism says that the Ten Commandments are 'grave obligations'. What do you think this means?

80 THE TEN COMMANDMENTS (2)

All Christians are obliged to serve God and to love their neighbour (see extract A in unit 79). According to the Ten Commandments, the love that we are expected to show others begins with our parents and then extends to those around us.

The Ten Commandments are found in Exodus 20.1–17.

Commandment 5: Honour your father and mother

Our duty to love begins with those to whom we owe most – our parents (see extract A). This highlights the sacredness of the family which God has placed at the heart of life. The family is:

- a living symbol of the three persons in the Trinity;
- a community of faith nourished by regular prayer and the reading of the Scriptures.

In the family, children must show respect to their parents and meet their needs in sickness and old age.

> A **"**Respect for parents derives from gratitude towards those who, by the gift of life, their love and their work, have brought their children into the world and enabled them to grow in stature, wisdom and grace.**"**
> (CCC 2215)

Commandment 6: Do not commit murder

This commandment teaches us to respect all life as it is sacred and God-given (extract B). This is true from the moment of conception until the moment of death. The Catholic Church opposes abortion, euthanasia, suicide and Capital Punishment because of this commandment.

Commandments 7 and 10: Do not commit adultery/ do not covet

These two commandments forbidding the coveting (wanting desperately) of a neighbour's wife and adultery are closely linked. Adultery takes place when someone who is married has sexual intercourse with a person who is not their marriage partner, whether the other person is married or not. Our sexuality is a gift from God and, used properly, it helps us to love and cherish each other. To this end, Catholics are called to live chaste lives – inside and outside of marriage. This calling cannot be reconciled with fornication, pornography, prostitution or homosexuality. We can avoid these temptations through the Holy Spirit, the sacraments of the Church and prayer.

Commandment 8: Do not steal

The Catholic Church teaches that all people have a right to their own personal possessions. Jesus recognised this but also taught that people should not become too closely attached to their possessions. A person's treasure in heaven is much more important than his or her possessions on earth (Matthew 6.19–24).

Commandment 9: Do not give false witness

This commandment forbids us to misrepresent the truth. It demands that we live a life that is built on the truth as we know it as Christians.

B *"Human life is sacred because from its beginning it involves the creative action of God and it remains for ever in a special relationship with the Creator, who is its sole end. God alone is the Lord of life from its beginning until its end: no one can under any circumstance claim for himself the right directly to destroy an innocent human being."*
(CCC 2258)

▲ *Looking after one's parents is one of the most solemn obligations laid on each Jew by the Ten Commandments.*

TASKS

1. One of the Ten Commandments is to 'honour our father and mother'.
    a. Describe some ways in which people can honour their parents.
    b. What promise is given in this commandment to those who fulfil its demands?
2. a. What is adultery?
    b. Give one reason why so many people commit adultery today.
    c. How is this commandment linked with the one forbidding covetousness?

✳ DISCUSSION POINT

Jesus said that loving God and loving one's neighbour are the two great commandments. What do you think is the link between them?

81 THE SERMON ON THE MOUNT (1)

The Sermon on the Mount is the name give to a collection of the teachings of Jesus that is brought together in Matthew, chapters 5 to 7. It brings together many of his teachings about how his followers should behave and live.

A re-interpretation of the Law of Moses (Mathew 5.21–42)

The Law of Moses, the Torah, is the most important part of the Jewish Scriptures and believed to be God's greatest gift to the Jewish people. It was sacred and untouchable. As a Jew, the Torah was sacred to Jesus as well but he placed his own emphasis on its teaching. This caused great anguish to many of his Jewish listeners.

Here are six examples of how he re-interpreted the Law of Moses:

1. The Law said do not kill – Jesus said that anyone who is even angry with his brother has broken the Law.

2. The Law said do not commit adultery – Jesus said do not even look lustfully at another woman if you are married.

3. The Law said that a person can divorce by giving his wife a bill of divorcement – Jesus said divorce is against the will of God unless adultery has taken place.

4. The Law said do not break an oath made to God – Jesus said to not take an oath at all.

5. The Law said an eye for an eye and a tooth for a tooth is acceptable – Jesus said that if someone hits you on the right cheek turn the left one to them as well.

6. The Law said love your friends and hate your enemies – Jesus said love your enemies and pray for those who persecute you.

A public display of religion (Matthew 6.1–18)

Here Jesus laid down a general principle for all religious devotion – the right thing must not be done for the wrong reason. Right deeds must stem from the right intention. Jesus explained this by referring to three common religious activities.

Giving Alms

This was money that was given to the Temple in Jerusalem so that it could be used to help those in need. It was considered to be an important spiritual duty. There was an old Jewish saying (extract A):

> **A** **"**One who gives charity in secret is greater than Moses.**"**
> (Jewish saying)

There were even those who blew a trumpet to draw attention to what they were doing. Jesus taught that this was wrong. The only gift that mattered to God was the one that was made to him in secret.

Prayer

There were those who prayed in public places so that they would be seen by others and praised. Many came out with long-winded prayers to impress people with their holiness. To show how worthless their prayers were, Jesus gave his followers the Lord's Prayer – a prayer that is brief and very much to the point.

Fasting

Jews believe that fasting was very valuable as a spiritual discipline. Jesus did not disagree with this. The hypocrites, however, were those who went about looking 'unsightly', drawing attention to their own holiness and hoping to win the praise of others. All that matters is that a person wins God's approval because he will reward them openly.

▲ Jesus taught that prayer is a personal matter between an individual and God and so should be done in private.

TASKS

1. **a.** Why did Jesus say that a public display of holiness and religion was wrong?
   b. Describe one example that Jesus gave of people trying to draw attention to their own personal holiness.
   c. What did Jesus say about them?
2. Which three religious activities did Jesus use as examples of people doing the right thing for the wrong reasons?

82 THE SERMON ON THE MOUNT (2)

The Sermon on the Mount acts as a real guide for those who want to live the Christian life. As the Catechism makes clear, it is the New Law that replaces the Old Law, the Torah, that was given to Moses on Mount Sinai (extract A).

> **A** *"In Jesus, the same Word of God that had resounded on Mount Sinai to give the written Law to Moses, made itself heard anew on the Mount of Beatitudes. Jesus did not abolish the Law but fulfilled it by giving it its ultimate interpretation in a divine way."*
>
> (CCC 581)

Christians and money (Matthew 6.19–34)

Jesus is not just talking about money – he is talking about 'earthly treasure'. This is the treasure that really matters to people and to which they are deeply attached. This attachment stems from the way that they look at their wealth. As Jesus pointed out, it is not possible for a person to love and serve both God and their wealth (extract B).

> **B** *"No one can be the slave of two masters: he will either hate the first and love the second, or be attached to the first and despise the second. You cannot be the slave of both God and of money."*
>
> (Matthew 6.24)

For Jesus the choice was simple. His followers could either serve earthly possessions and wealth – or God. When Jesus was confronted by a rich young man who wanted to know how to inherit eternal life Jesus gave him a stark reply – go and sell all your possessions and give the proceeds to the poor. Only then would he have treasure in heaven (Matthew 19.16–22).

▲ Jesus did not say that wealth was wrong – but that a love of their possessions could hinder people's spiritual progress.

Christians and judgement (Matthew 7.1–5)

Here Jesus lays down a simple rule – do not judge and condemn others and you will not be judged and condemned yourself. The reasoning is simple. No human being is without fault and so no one has the right to judge other people. Jesus makes the point by speaking of being concerned with the speck in someone else's eye and ignoring the plank in your own.

The followers of Jesus are expected to follow God's standards. God alone is perfect and will judge others. The followers of Jesus should judge themselves. They should take the splinter out of their own eye. Only then will they avoid being hypocrites. They can never reach the perfection that God has. Without it, however, they cannot judge others.

The Golden Rule (Matthew 7.7–12)

The Golden Rule (extract C) was already well known in Jewish teaching and so was not original to Jesus. He simply states it as a general rule that all of his followers should follow. Quite simply it states that everyone should treat other people in exactly the same way that they themselves would like to be treated. This not only sums up all of the teaching of Jesus but all of the Jewish Law (the Law and the Prophets) as well.

C *So always treat others as you would like them to treat you; that is the Law and the Prophets.*
(Matthew 7.12)

TASKS

1. Why did Jesus say that a public display of wealth and a love for possessions was wrong – even a hindrance to entering God's kingdom?
2. What did Jesus teach about the good and the bad ways of using judgement?

✻ DISCUSSION POINT

Some people think that Jesus was laying down impossible standards for his followers to live by. What do you think?

83 THE EXPRESSION OF CHRISTIAN VALUES

As we have seen, there are many spiritual values that Jesus came to teach to his followers. In turn, his followers are expected to express those values through a life of service and love for God and for others. There are five such values:

1. *Service to others.* Christians are the followers of Jesus Christ. You can read how Jesus summed up his reason for coming to earth as the Son of God in extract A.

> **A** **"** *For the Son of Man himself came not to be served but to serve, and to give his life as a ransom for many.* **"**
> *(Mark 10.45)*

Just as Jesus came to serve others, so Christians are called to do the same. Some are called to work in the medical profession – as doctors, nurses, orderlies and so on. Some are called to teach. Some are called to run shops. Some are called to do voluntary work running clubs for young children, youth clubs or centres for the elderly. Everyone has a vocation to serve God – and others.

2. Compassion *for those who suffer.* Some people suffer a great deal almost from the time they are born while others suffer far less. Some children are born with considerable physical and mental handicaps, and they need support throughout their lives. Others have a serious illness or accident that changes the course of their life and they suddenly need care and support. At some time or other we are all likely to know a relative or friend who is terminally ill. As Christians we are expected to provide them with the love and support that they need.

▼ *The teaching of Jesus was essentially practical, seeking to help the needy.*

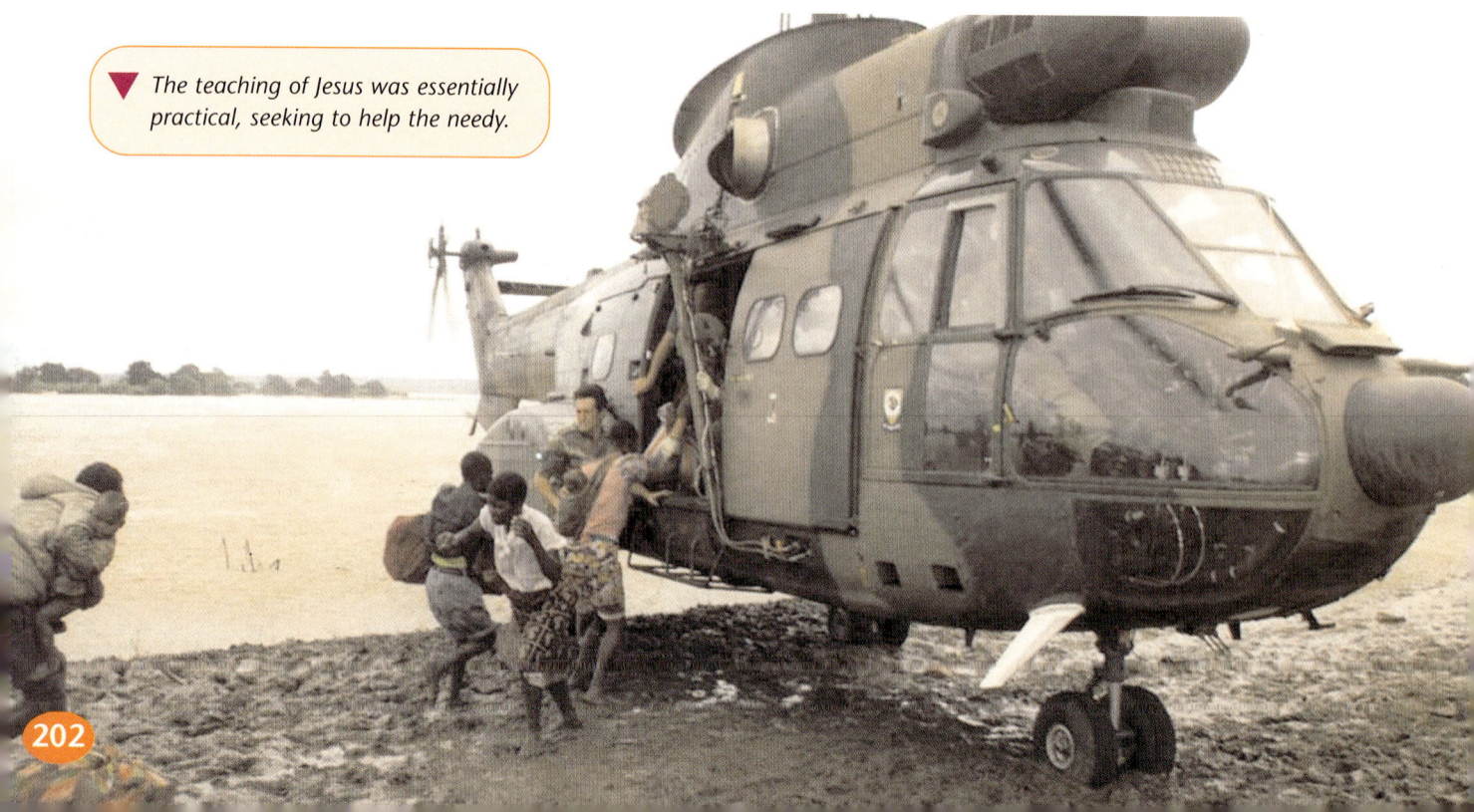

3. Concern *for the causes of suffering.* Many Catholics support charities and organisations that are trying to do something practical to remove the causes of suffering in this country and overseas. It might be to supply fresh drinking water to an isolated village, help improve irrigation or give advice to improve the productivity of the soil. The need might be for improved medical facilities, the provision of a new clinic or the drugs that doctors and nurses need to run it effectively.

> **A** *The duty of making oneself a neighbour to others and actively serving them becomes even more urgent when it involves the disadvantaged, in whatever area this may be. 'As you did to one of the least of these my brethren, you did it to me.'*
>
> *(CCC 1932)*

4. *By helping those in need.* The parable of the sheep and the goats (Matthew 25.31–46) encourages all Christians to see Christ himself in those who are needy – the naked, the prisoner, the hungry, the stranger, the thirsty and the sick. He told his followers that their treatment of these people would determine how they themselves would be treated. In every diocese there are individuals, and groups, who give themselves to support those in need.

5. *To seek* justice *for the* oppressed. All over the world there are people who are treated brutally, or imprisoned, for their beliefs. We become aware of these people through Amnesty International. The Catholic Church seeks to help people who are living under oppressive governments in such places as Latin America.

> **B** *For two thousand years this sentiment has lived and endured in the soul of the Church, impelling souls then and now to the heroic charity of monastic farmers, liberators of slaves, healers of the sick, and messengers of faith, civilization and science to all generations and all peoples for the sake of creating the social conditions capable of offering to everyone possible a life worthy of man and of a Christian.*
>
> *(CCC 1942)*

TASKS

1. What are the main Christian values and how do believers express them in practice?
2. "The most important thing for Jesus and for all Christian believers is that their beliefs should be put into practice." Do you agree with this comment? Give reasons for your answer, showing that you have thought about more than one point of view.

84 TWO EXEMPLARY CHRISTIANS OF THE 20TH CENTURY

Here we look at the lives of two 20th-century Christians who have been an example to many other believers.

Martin Luther King Junior

Martin Luther King Junior was a black American who grew up in the country at a time when blacks were treated as second-class citizens. Many lived in dreadful conditions and were exploited by their white employers. They were also discriminated against in the areas of public transport, education, employment and shopping.

In the 1950s and 1960s black people began to find their voice and protest against these injustices. Things were in danger of getting out of hand when the Reverend Martin Luther King Junior began to teach his fellow blacks that there were other ways of making their voices heard such as:

1. Bus boycotts. Black people refused to use public buses unless they were desegregated (black and white allowed to sit anywhere on the bus, side by side). In 1956 a law was passed making racial segregation on America's buses illegal.

2. Boycotts of cafes, restaurants and schools that followed a policy of segregation.

3. 'Freedom marches' across America. In 1960 he led one such march on Washington DC, where 250,000 demonstrators demanded that black people be given the right to vote. On these marches black and white people walked together.

In April 1968 Martin Luther King Junior was shot dead in Memphis, Tennessee while he was resting in a hotel. To this day no-one really knows why he was killed. He was only 39 years old. The Civil Rights Movement, however, continued after his death and gradually the rights and treatment of black people began to improve.

> **A** 	**"** To resist without bitterness,
> To be cursed and not reply
> To be beaten and not hit back
> Is at the heart of the creed of non-violence. **"**
> (Martin Luther King Junior)

Mother Teresa

Mother Teresa was born Agnes Gonxha Bojaxhiu in Yugoslavia in 1910. She felt, from a young age, that she wanted to devote her life to God and joined the Loreto Nuns when she was 17. After training she became a novice at Darjeeling in India and took the name of Teresa, a favourite saint. From there she went to teach in Calcutta, in a school that was surrounded by the most appalling poverty. She saw both young and old dying in the streets.

Teresa felt that she should leave the convent to work among the poorest people. She trained as a nurse with another Order of nuns and began to help the poorest people by nursing and teaching them. Gradually other nuns joined her and she was offered accommodation to carry out her work, called 'Place of the Pure Heart'. In 1950 she formed a new Order called the Missionaries of Charity, and money and offers of help began to flow in.

The work started to spread beyond India to other parts of the world. Homes for the Dying, Children's Homes and Leprosy Homes were set up in many places of need. Mother Teresa was awarded the Nobel Peace Prize in 1979 and she died in August 1997.

The work of Mother Teresa continues today. The Sisters do not try to convert the people they are helping to Christianity. Daily services are held and the Sisters will speak to people about Christianity if that is requested. Their vocation, however, is to offer help to those who are desperately ill, irrespective of their race or religion. The Homes for the Dying aim to provide the loving and caring environment in which people can end their lives in peace. Extract B sums up the motivation for the work of Mother Teresa and those who follow her.

▲ *The life story of Mother Teresa has inspired millions of Christian believers in the modern world.*

B *"Let no one ever come to you without going away better and happier. Let there be kindness in your face, kindness in your eyes...In each suffering person you see Jesus."*
(Mother Teresa)

TASKS

1. Write a series of bullet points that summarises the lives of Martin Luther King Junior and Mother Teresa.
2. How did Mother Teresa respond to the question of why God allows suffering in the world?

✳ DISCUSSION POINT

What do you think are the main lessons that can be learned from the lives of Martin Luther King Junior and Mother Teresa?

EXAM HELP

In the examination

Make sure that you know about:

- The prominence given to the Ten Commandments in the Catechism. 'Grave obligations'. The supreme claim that God has on the Jews – based on the Exodus. Great respect must be shown to God's name – blasphemy forbidden for all Catholics – including against the Church, all saints and sacred things. The Sabbath Day a reminder of God's creation of the world and delivery of the Jews from slavery. The attitude of Jesus towards Sabbath laws.

- The importance of honouring parents for the gift of life and looking after them. The commandment not to kill covers abortion and euthanasia. Laws against adultery and coveting closely linked. Catholics called to live a 'chaste' life. Sexual activities outlawed include homosexuality, pornography and prostitution. The right of everyone to have personal possessions but must not be too attached to them.

- Jesus re-interpreted the Law of Moses – examples are important. Criticised public display of religion – in giving alms, praying and fasting.

- Christians and money. Christians and judgement. The Golden Rule.

- Service to others. Compassion for those who suffer. Concern for the causes of suffering. Helping those in need. Seeking justice for the oppressed.

- The lives of Martin Luther King Junior and Mother Teresa.

Sample exam questions

1. Why do you think the Catechism insists that the Ten Commandments can help Catholics to live the Christian life?

2. "The Ten Commandments should be followed by all Catholics." Do you agree with this comment? Give your reasons, showing that you have thought about more than one point of view.

3. How did Jesus show that he was re-interpreting the Law of Moses?

4. What did Jesus have to say about the false use of religion in the Sermon on the Mount?

5. How do Christians express the values that really matter in their everyday lives?

6. Explain what Christians can learn from the life of Martin Luther King Junior.

7. Explain what Christians can learn from the life of Mother Teresa.

OPTION 1:
A place of Christian worship

In this section you will find out about:

- the characteristics of the outside of a Catholic church;

- the altar as the focal-point of Catholic churches. The place where the Mass is celebrated. Crucifixes on the altar. Candles – Jesus the Light of the world. **Votive candles** offered with prayer. The Tabernacle which holds the **Reserved Sacrament**. Respect shown to sacrament – genuflecting. Stations of the Cross – fourteen places where Jesus stopped on the way to his execution, places of pilgrimage. Statues of saints, especially the Virgin Mary. Confession boxes;

- the Catholic Church and its parish. Daily celebration of the Mass. Create a sense of family for all Catholics;

- the role of the parish priest. To celebrate the Sacraments. To offer Sacrament of Reconciliation and Penance. To grant absolution of sins. To make Christ real for members of the congregation. To prepare church members for important occasions. To share with those approaching death the viaticum. To establish links with local Catholic schools;

- inside a Nonconformist church. Pulpit the focal-point of building and no altar. Brass bands in Salvation Army citadels. Baptismal pool important in Baptist churches. Two main kinds of church services. Charismatic worship – speaking in tongues.

As this is an optional choice in the specification there are no key words to cover.

85 CATHOLIC CHURCHES (1)

You are required to study the architecture and other main features of a Catholic church or cathedral in this option. In units 86 and 87 we will not be looking at one particular church although you can, if you wish, carry out your own study of a Catholic place of worship in your locality. You will find that each Catholic place of worship has its own style and architectural features, also that all Catholic churches have much in common with each other and it is these features that we will concentrate on.

Outside the church

Traditionally, Catholic churches were built in the shape of a cross or an oblong with the people separated from the altar, often by a screen, called the rood screen, although many of these have now been removed. This stressed the holiness (the otherness) of God and the role of the priest as the mediator, the 'go-between', representing the people in God's presence.

▲ A crucifix on the outside wall of a church is usually a sign that it is Catholic.

Modern Catholic churches are often circular in shape to stress that all people are equal in God's sight. In modern places of worship, for example the Cathedral of Christ the King in Liverpool or Clifton Cathedral in Bristol, the people either surround the altar or sit in a semi-circle in front of it. The symbolism of this is clear: the altar is the place where God meets with his people and so it is appropriate for him to be in the middle of them.

Most Catholic churches either have a crucifix or a statue of the Virgin Mary both outside and inside. Statues are a very important aid to devotion for most Catholics. There will be many reminders of the death of Jesus on the cross. The crucifix is a symbol of the death of Christ for the whole world, whereas it is a symbol of the resurrection of Jesus, the empty cross, that is more important to Protestants.

Inside the church

Just inside the door of every Catholic church there are two symbols of new life – the new life that Jesus offers all worshippers:

1. **The stoup** – a small container holding holy water. This is water that has been blessed by the priest. Each time worshippers enter the building they dip their fingers into the water and make 'the sign of the cross' across their body. This symbolises their new life and their cleansing from sin. The 'sign of the cross' is an indication of the fact that this new life has come to them, as it does to all Christians, by the death of Jesus on the cross and his resurrection from the dead. The water is also a reminder to them of the vows that others made for them when they were baptised – vows that they have renewed for themselves through confirmation.

2. The font – a container that holds the water when a baby is baptised. Traditionally the font was placed just inside the entrance to the church to indicate that it is baptism which brings a person into the warmth and security of the Church. Baptism is still the entrance to the Church but it is now, almost always, carried out as part of the Church's celebration of the Mass. A mobile font is often used so that the baby can be baptised in the middle of the Church family. The Church undertakes to love, cherish and care for the child as it grows up to be a full member of the Christian community.

▲ *People make the sign of the cross on their body with holy water as they enter church to put them in the right mood to worship God.*

TASKS

1. How would you recognise a Catholic place of worship from the outside of the building?
2. The position of the altar in modern churches has changed from the place it occupied in older buildings. What is the symbolic importance of this?

✳ DISCUSSION POINT

Do you feel comfortable going to church? If not, could the building be changed in any way to make you feel more welcome?

86 CATHOLIC CHURCHES (2)

There is a focal point in every church. In Protestant Nonconformist churches, such as Methodist and Baptist churches, it is the pulpit, because the preaching of God's Word, the Bible, is the most important part of each service. In Anglican and Roman Catholic churches the focal point is the altar because it is there that the Mass or the Eucharist is celebrated. Worship in these churches is centred on the celebration of this sacrament. Although these churches do have a pulpit, it is only of secondary importance. They also have a lectern at the front from which Bible readings are given.

The high altar

Crucifixes

In traditional churches the altar stands, together with its crucifix and candles, in the middle of the east wall. The crucifix is, of course, an important reminder to all Catholics of the death of Jesus – a sacrifice offered, and accepted, by God.
At certain times of the year, most notably the end of Lent, the crucifixes in Church are covered or removed as worshippers live through the last few hours in the life of Jesus. Often the letters INRI can be seen above the figure of Jesus as a reminder that the figure on the cross is 'Jesus of Nazareth, King of the Jews'. Many Catholics find it very moving to pray in front of a crucifix.

Candles

There are many candles in a Catholic church reminding everyone that Jesus described himself as being 'the light of the world'. Apart from the candles on the altar there is a side altar in Catholic churches holding small votive candles.
Many worshippers make a small offering and light one of these candles when they want to offer up a prayer.

▶ The high altar is the place where the sacrament of the Eucharist is celebrated and so is the focal point of every Catholic church.

The tabernacle

The tabernacle represents the Tent of Meeting in which Moses kept the Ark of the Covenant that held the tablets on which the Ten Commandments were inscribed. In Catholic churches the tabernacle is given a place of honour next to the altar. It holds the Reserved Sacrament (the consecrated bread that is used every time the Mass is celebrated). Catholics believe that Christ is really present in the consecrated bread and so the Reserved Sacrament is adored. This is why Catholics genuflect (bow the knee) every time they pass in front of the tabernacle.

Stations of the Cross and statues

Around the outside wall of a Catholic church there are carved statues or pictures showing the different **Stations of the Cross**. These Stations are usually in stone, although they can be made out of other materials such as fabric. The fourteen Stations of the Cross illustrate the different places at which, according to the Scriptures and Catholic tradition, Jesus stopped on his way to crucifixion. The Stations of the Cross are 'visited' by worshippers during the service on Good Friday. They were originally installed in Catholic churches during the Middle Ages when it became too dangerous for pilgrims to visit the Holy Land to carry out a real pilgrimage.

Roman Catholics find that statues are often a helpful way of focusing their spiritual devotion. There is a statue of the Virgin Mary in every Catholic church to remind worshippers of the central place that she occupies in Catholic devotion. There may also be statues of saints, especially St Peter, and also one of Jesus.

Confessional box

Most Catholic churches have a confessional box – two cubicles placed side by side with a partition in between. Until recently these were always used when the priest was listening to the confession of a member of the congregation to safeguard their anonymity. In many churches they are still in use. Often, though, the priest and penitent simply sit talking side by side in the church. Either way the person confesses his or her sins to the priest and receives the sacrament of absolution from him.

Describe each of the following and explain their importance in a Catholic church:

    a. the high altar

    b. crucifixes

    c. Stations of the Cross

    d. the tabernacle

TASKS

87 THE CHURCH AND ITS PARISH

The parish is the geographical area for which each Catholic church is responsible. Each Catholic church has a priest who is responsible for organising its worship, although some smaller churches may have to share their priest. The bishop is responsible for the 'spiritual oversight' of all of the churches in a diocese such as Birmingham, or Brentwood in London.

A Catholic church and its parish

The roles expected of each Catholic church in its parish can be listed as follows:

1. The prime responsibility of a Catholic church is to offer the daily celebration of the Mass and the other sacraments to Catholics living in the parish. Most of the sacraments, especially the Mass, can only be offered by a priest.

2. To create a sense of 'family' in which Catholics' spiritual lives and those of the different members of their family can grow and flourish. When children are young, the parish provides Sunday Schools or other groups in which children can find out more about their own Catholic faith. There will also be Catholic schools nearby for the children to attend, whether primary or secondary, and most Catholics believe that it is important for them to support these. The parish priest and the church itself will play some role in school life. The priest will probably be one of the school governors.

3. To offer church members the facilities for baptisms, weddings and funerals. The Church believes that it is important that each of these occasions should take place within the celebration of the Mass.

4. To give children the opportunity of celebrating their first Communion and to later prepare them for their confirmation. These occasions are important milestones in the spiritual journey of every Catholic.

5. To help adult Catholics deepen their spiritual faith and give them opportunities for service in the Catholic community. In many parishes special discussion groups are held at important times of the year, such as Advent and Lent. Occasional weekends away give people the opportunity to discuss their own religious faith in a more relaxed atmosphere.

6. To provide social opportunities, such as camps and weekends away, for young people. Youth clubs and sporting opportunities are a feature of many Catholic churches, especially those working in inner-city areas. In some churches there are uniformed organisations for young people.

7. In every parish there are vulnerable people who need special help. One such group, in particular, is the elderly and almost all parishes have groups to meet its needs.

◄ *It is very important that the Catholic Church manages to hold on to its young people as they grow up because they are the Church of the future.*

1. Describe some of the ways in which the local Catholic church plays a part in the life of its local parish.

2. "What a church does in its local parish is the most important part of the work of a Catholic church." Do you agree with this comment? Give reasons for your answer, showing that you have thought about more than one point of view.

✳ DISCUSSION POINT

Do you think it is true to say that it is the work that a church does in a parish rather than the work of the parish priest that is more important?

88 THE ROLE OF THE PARISH PRIEST

The priest, or presbyter, is a member of one of three orders of ordained ministry in the Catholic Church – the others being the diaconate and the episcopacy. This is what Catholics believe about the priesthood:

1. When priests celebrate the Sacraments they are acting in the place of Christ. They have this authority because they have been ordained by a bishop by the laying on of hands and this gives them a unique authority. This is one of the main reasons given for the Catholic Church's refusal to ordain women – a woman, it is claimed, cannot represent Christ at the altar. You can find out how this works by looking at extract A, a quotation from the Second Vatican Council that is repeated with approval in the Catechism.

A “*(In the Eucharistic Sacrifice a priest acts in the person of Christ and thus joins) the offerings of the faithful to the sacrifice of Christ their Head... and in the sacrifice of the Mass they make present again and apply... the unique sacrifice...of Christ offering himself once and for all a spotless victim to the Father.*”
(Lumen Gentium 28, document of Second Vatican Council)

▲ *The priest acts as a kind of spiritual focus in the parish, encouraging Christian believers to realise their spiritual potential.*

2. One of the most important sacraments is that of reconciliation and penance. Worshippers confess their sins to a priest and he grants them absolution. Only the priest has the power to grant people the absolution (total forgiveness) of their sins. This stems from Matthew 16.19 where Jesus gave Peter the power to bind and loose people from their sins. Catholics are encouraged to go to confession regularly as part of their spiritual discipline and to make sure that they go at least once a year – usually as part of the Lent and Easter festivals.

3. The authority of the priest to conduct the Mass and to absolve sins means that he is not an ordinary Christian believer. In one sense Catholics believe in the 'priesthood of all believers' but the priest exists to make Christ real to members of his congregation. This is why each Catholic church needs to have a priest even though it might have to share him with other churches. Without the priest the people cannot take the Mass or the other sacraments – and so lose the major source of spiritual blessing in their life.

4. It is the priest who prepares members of the congregation for most of the important spiritual occasions. He prepares children for their first communion and confirmation. He prepares couples for their marriage and conducts the Nuptial Mass. He prepares the sick as death approaches and conducts the Requiem Mass. Sharing communion with those who are close to death is called the viaticum – 'food for the journey'. He visits the bereaved as they come to terms with the death of their loved ones and offers them spiritual comfort and help. Visiting the sick is a very important part of the work of the parish priest and this includes taking communion to those who are unable to reach church.

5. It is the priest who usually chairs the Parish Council. This is the group of church members who arrange the life of the Church and keep a close watch on its finances.

6. As we saw in unit 87, the links between the Catholic Church and the local Catholic schools is a very important part of the Church's witness. The parish priest is often the chairman of the governors, meaning that he plays an important part in deciding how the school is run and who is appointed to the staff. He will go into the school, regularly taking assemblies and celebrating the Mass for the pupils. He may also take Religious Education lessons as well.

TASKS

1. What is the most important responsibility of the parish priest?

2. What spiritual tasks does the priest carry out in the Catholic community?

89 OTHER CHRISTIAN CHURCHES

Although some Nonconformist Churches, such as the Baptist Church, date their origins earlier, the great revival in Nonconformist faith took place in the 18th and 19th centuries. It was during this time that the Methodist Church and the Salvation Army were born. They are called 'Nonconformist' because they do not 'conform' to the teachings of the Church of England.

Nonconformist churches

The most important difference between a Roman Catholic church and a Nonconformist church, such as Baptist or Methodist, is the focal point of the building. There is no altar in a Nonconformist building as the bread and wine are not offered up as a sacrifice to God during the Eucharist. Although most Nonconformist churches do celebrate the sacraments of the Eucharist and baptism, the emphasis is very much on the preaching of the Word of God – the Bible. The focal point of a Nonconformist church, therefore, is the pulpit – the raised platform at the front from which this preaching takes place.

Singing has always played a very important part in Nonconformist worship. In many churches this is still led by the traditional organ, although a piano and a choir, or a music group are now more common. Many hymns and choruses have been written in recent years to be used in Nonconformist worship and these have largely replaced the more traditional hymns. In a Salvation Army citadel the singing is likely to be led by a brass band and this band traditionally leads the worshippers through the streets to hold an open-air service of witness beforehand.

In Baptist churches, and some other denominations, there is a baptismal pool at the front of the church that is opened up and filled with water when a service of Believer's baptism is held. This service is a distinguishing mark of Baptist worship and is very different from the infant baptism services held in Catholic and Anglican churches. It is only available for adults who have a personal faith in Jesus Christ as their Saviour.

Different kinds of services

Broadly speaking there are two different kinds of church services:

Liturgical

This kind of worship is typical of services in the Roman Catholic, Orthodox and Anglican traditions. It follows a set pattern or order of service that is laid down in a prayer book. In the Catholic Church, for instance, the prayer book is called the Missal. A typical service out of the Missal would be the Mass with its Penitential Rite, Liturgy of the Word and Liturgy of the Eucharist. Both Catholics and Orthodox Christians believe that the celebration of the Eucharist has to follow the same set pattern to be truly effective – Orthodox Christians believe that their Divine Liturgy follows a pattern that has been unaltered since the 5th century.

Non-liturgical

This kind of worship is typical of the Nonconformist churches where there is no set form of words or liturgy to be followed in services. They do not have a prayer book because they believe that this would restrict the freedom of the Holy Spirit to lead their worship. In a typical non-liturgical service, there are hymns, extempore prayers (prayers that are not written down), Bible readings and a sermon in which the meaning of a passage from the Bible is explained. This places the emphasis in non-liturgical worship on the Bible.

Charismatic worship is a form of non-liturgical worship. This is spontaneous and unplanned worship, with much singing and dancing, in which worshippers are open to the leadings and promptings of the Holy Spirit. Praying in an unknown language, called 'speaking in tongues', is an important characteristic of charismatic worship. Charismatic worship is now found in all the Christian denominations, including Catholic and Anglican, but is mainly associated with the Pentecostal church.

▲ *A Methodist service.*

TASKS

1. **a.** What is meant by a 'Nonconformist church'?
   b. What are the distinguishing marks of a Nonconformist church building?
2. What are the essential differences between a liturgical and a non-liturgical style of worship?

✳ DISCUSSION POINT

Explain what style of worship among those mentioned most appeals to you – and why.

Option 1: A place of Christian worship

EXAM HELP

In the examination

Make sure that you know about:

- The characteristics found inside and outside a Catholic church. The shape of older and more recent Catholic churches. The reason why many modern Catholic churches are round. The crucifix and statue of the Virgin Mary often found outside. The stoup and the font.

- Crucifixes – reminders of the death of Jesus. Candles – Jesus, the Light of the World. The Tabernacle – holding the Reserved Sacrament. Stations of the Cross and other statues. Stations important on Good Friday. The importance of confession.

- Daily celebration of the Mass. Create a Christian 'family'. Facilities of baptisms, confirmations, weddings, funerals and so on. First communion. Deepening of the religious faith. Social opportunities. Look after the vulnerable and needy – especially the elderly.

- The importance of the Sacraments. The hearing of confessions and granting absolution. Important occasions in the lives of members of congregation. Visits to the bereaved by the parish priest, and his Chair of the Parish Council. Establishes links with local schools.

- Nonconformist churches: the focal point is the pulpit – highlighting the importance of the Bible. No altar. Importance of singing in worship. New hymns. Baptismal pool in Baptist church.

- Liturgical and non-liturgical forms of worship and Charismatic worship.

Sample exam questions

1. What are the main features inside a Roman Catholic church?
2. How does a Catholic Church hope to serve its parish?
3. What are the main features inside an Anglican and a Nonconformist place of worship?
4. What is expected from a Roman Catholic priest in his parish?
5. What are two of the differences between liturgical and non-liturgical forms of worship?

OPTION 2: Christian vocation

In this section you will find out about:

- the 'common vocation' that all Catholics share having been initiated through the sacraments of baptism and confirmation. The common priesthood of all believers. The 'holy vocation' that those who have been called to the priesthood and the religious life share;
- the roots of the monastic movement. The Benedictines. The Cistercians. The Franciscans. The Dominicans;
- the Three Vows: the Vow of Poverty; the Vow of Chastity; the Vow of Obedience. The open and the enclosed communities;
- a Benedictine Community – Worth Abbey. The nature of community life and the work of the Abbey. The way that someone is able to join the community.

As this is an optional choice in the specification there are no key words to cover.

90 CHRISTIAN VOCATION

The word 'vocation' comes from the Latin word vocare which means to call. This indicates the meaning of a word that has been used in the Catholic church for centuries in two different ways.

A common vocation

1. The three Sacraments of initiation – baptism, confirmation and Holy Communion – call all Christians to follow a life of holiness. They are called to be servants and witnesses to the Gospel of Christ. This is their vocation or calling. These three sacraments give Christians all the grace that they need to follow the example of Jesus in the service of others.

2. Furthermore, through baptism and confirmation, each Christian is initiated into the 'common priesthood of all believers'. All are members of the Body of Christ, the Church, and have an essential role to play in building up that Body on earth. The idea of all Christian believers being 'priests' is important and needs some explanation at this point. Jesus is the supreme 'Mediator' (go-between) bringing together God and human beings. The ordained priest continues this role as he 'mediates' through the sacraments and especially Holy Communion. Ordinary believers also have a role to play as 'priests' in serving Christ wherever God has placed them.

CHECK IT OUT

Ordinary Christians are involved as 'priests' in God's work of salvation

through prayer.

through the loving service of others.

through works of healing and reconciliation.

through acts of justice and mercy shown to the poor and needy.

through any work that is carried out for God's kingdom.

Through the sacraments, each Catholic has a vocation to be a sign and a symbol of God's kingdom in the world – in their family life, in their business life and in their social life.

A holy vocation

Down the centuries, certain men and women have been 'called' by God to devote themselves to the kingdom of God in a special way. They have taken the three vows first demanded by St Benedict – of poverty, chastity and obedience. They have lived a common life together in a community. These communities have included:

- enclosed, contemplative communities (see unit 92);
- open communities, active in the community (see unit 92).

Most of these communities have dedicated themselves to a particular vocation – teaching, nursing, social work and so on. The vows they take free them from many human responsibilities to devote themselves fully to the service of God.

Priests also have a holy vocation. They have taken up Holy Orders to serve God. In a real way, individual Christians, monks, nuns and priests are all following in the footsteps of the early disciples by leaving everything to follow Christ. Each one of them has a vocation to serve God as he directs in his own way.

A *He called the people and his disciples to him and said, 'If anyone wants to be a follower of mine, let him renounce himself and take up his cross and follow me. Anyone who wants to save his life will lose it; but anyone who loses his life for my sake, and for the sake of the Gospel, will save it.'*

(Mark 8.34–35)

▶ *Monks and nuns give themselves to the spiritual welfare of the Church although many of them also carry out their vocation in the outside world.*

TASKS

1. **a.** What is a vocation?
   b. Give examples of two jobs that you consider to be vocations and explain why.
   c. What makes them different from other occupations?
2. If people look upon their occupation as a vocation what difference do you think it might make to the way they do it?

91 RELIGIOUS COMMUNITIES

Religious communities are communities of Christian men and women who bear witness to the Gospel of Jesus Christ and have pledged themselves to keep the three vows of obedience, poverty and chastity. These vows are known as the Evangelical Counsels. People who enter a religious community are usually called nuns, monks or friars.

The roots of the monastic movement

The roots of the monastic movement are found in the 4th century when groups of men and women moved into the Egyptian desert to dedicate themselves fully to God. Following the example of Jesus, who was tempted in the desert for forty days by the Devil, these people began to work out their baptismal vows in a hostile environment. It was in the desert that traditionally many conflicts between good and evil were fought. To begin with, people lived as hermits (on their own) but, before long, they began to live together in religious communities.

The Benedictines

St Benedict (480–547) is generally regarded as the father of the monastic movement. The first monastery of Benedictines was formed around 529 at Mount Cassino, some 130 km south of Rome. The 'Rule of St Benedict' was used to organise most of the monastic communities that followed and it emphasised:

- the importance of stability in the community. Monks normally remain in the same monastery from the time they take their vows until they die;

- the importance of a balance in the community between communal prayer, work and relaxation;

- the important role of the abbot who is elected by the monks. Within the community he is responsible for running the life of the monastery and organising its worship life;

- the three-fold vow that each monk is expected to take – obedience to the abbot, poverty and chastity. You will find out more about this in unit 92.

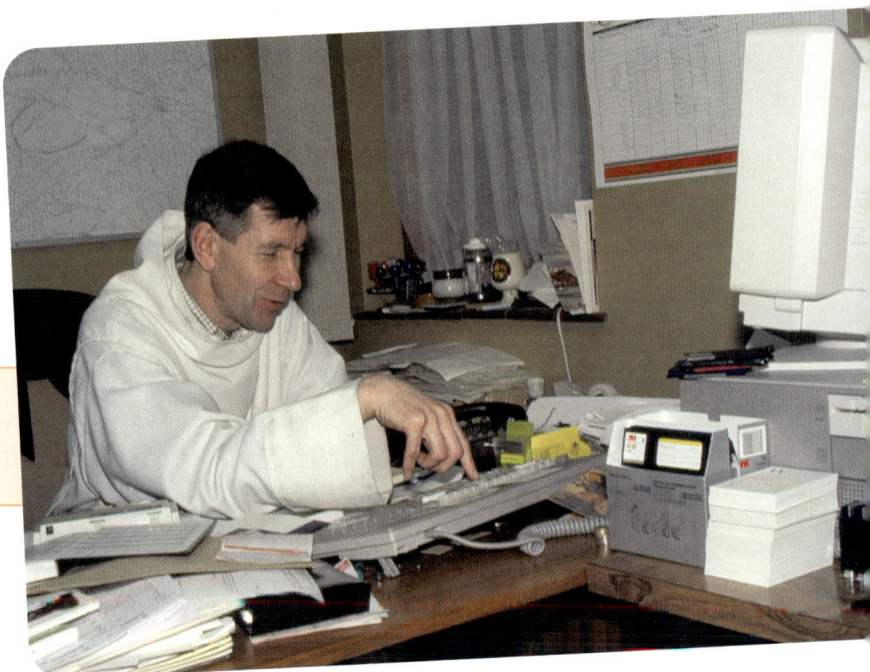

▶ *Monks make use of modern discoveries to deepen their spiritual lives.*

The later monastic movement

By the end of the 13th century three further important religious orders had been established but they were very different from the Benedictines. They were mendicant orders that placed an emphasis on preaching, teaching and living a life of poverty. They were:

- The Cistercians. This order, founded by Bernard of Clairvaux in 1098, called for a spirituality based on personal prayer, devotions and confession. Cistercians have always had a strong allegiance to the Virgin Mary.

- The Franciscans. Based on the teaching of St Francis of Assisi, the Franciscan Order pioneered a life of simplicity and faithfulness to the Gospel of Christ. The life was based on kindness to all creatures – both human and animal. Before long, an order of nuns, the Poor Clares, grew up that was also based on Francis' teaching of repentance, trust and respect for the whole of God's creation.

- The Dominicans. Founded in 1216 the Dominicans dedicated themselves to a teaching ministry in the Church.

In recent years, one modern religious order has had a greater effect on the Catholic church, and society generally, than any other. In 1949 Mother Teresa founded the Missionaries of Charity (an order of sisters, brothers and priests) to work with the sick and dying on the streets of Calcutta, India. It served the poor by providing food, medical help and shelter for those in great need. Within thirty years the Missionaries of Charity had 80 branches working in thirty-two different countries.

TASKS

1. **a.** How did the monastic way of life begin?
   b. Why is St Benedict so important in the history of the monastic movement?
2. Why do you think that Christians in the 4th century made their way out into the desert to give themselves totally to God? Why the desert in particular?

✳ DISCUSSION POINT

Why do you think that fewer people are hearing the call to 'the religious vocation' today than at any time in the history of the monastic movement?

92 THE EVANGELICAL COUNSELS

The three vows that monks and nuns take when entering a religious community are gifts given by God to the Catholic Church. Called 'Evangelical Counsels', these vows are the means by which individual members of religious orders build up the Catholic Church in a special way. The three vows are obedience, chastity and poverty. They are taken by all men and women who devote themselves to the religious life.

The Vow of Poverty

Poverty is the first of the Evangelical Counsels that form the basis of the religious life. By taking up a life of poverty the person is clearly following the example set by Jesus, who taught that anyone who wished to enter the kingdom of God must place God before both possessions and family. The life of complete dependence on God, that Jesus followed, left him completely open to meet the needs of others. It was the life that the apostles and other followers of Jesus sought to imitate in the early years of the Christian Church (extract A).

These nuns are taking their vows prior to committing themselves to their religious community.

A 66 *These remained faithful to the teaching of the apostles, to the brotherhood, to the breaking of bread and prayers... And all who shared the faith owned everything in common.* 99
(Acts 2.42, 44)

When monastic living began, the prime aim of monks and nuns was to live by the same principles and create the same communal life. A life of poverty is fundamental to this because it creates a sense of dependence on God.

The Vow of Chastity

People who enter a religious community take on the Vow of Chastity – a promise not to marry or have any kind of sexual relationship. The purpose is to free people from family responsibilities leaving them free to respond to God and others. Jesus did not have any such responsibilities and so was free to build up the kingdom of God on earth. Roman Catholic priests take the same vow for the same reason. The Second Vatican Council, however, made it clear that those who marry and have a family have the same high vocation as those who join a religious community or the priesthood.

The Vow of Obedience

This draws our attention to the importance of obedience to the will of God in the life of Jesus. For Jesus obedience was demanded all the way through to his death on the cross. Obedience to earthly authority, the authority of the abbot in the community, is obedience to God. By entering a community and accepting its discipline a person is also learning from God.

Two kinds of community

There are two kinds of religious community:

- The open community. Most religious communities are active in the community while still continuing important activities like prayer and worship. The Benedictines, for example, are deeply involved in education. The Missionaries of Charity combine all forms of social and medical work with the spiritual life of the community. Most active communities work outside the community during the day and then return back to the community at night.

- The closed community. Some alternative religious communities are closed with their members being confined to the convent or monastery. Instead of working outside, members give themselves completely to a life of contemplation and prayer. These communities are often silent. Contemplation is a form of prayer that involves a separation from the everyday world leaving the person free to concentrate his or her heart and mind on God. Time is spent reading the Scriptures and other holy books and listening to the voice of God.

B **"** *Contemplative prayer is the prayer of the child of God, of the forgiven sinner who agrees to welcome the love by which he is loved and who wants to respond to it by loving even more… Contemplative prayer is the poor and humble surrender to the loving will of the Father in ever deeper union with his beloved Son.* **"**

(CCC 2712)

TASKS

1. **a.** What are the three Evangelical Counsels?
   b. Why do you think that they are thought necessary for those living in religious communities?
2. What are the main differences between open and closed religious communities?

BENEDICTINE MONASTERY – WORTH ABBEY

Worth Abbey

In May 2005, BBC 2 broadcast a series of three programmes called *The Monastery*. The series followed a small group of men as they spent six weeks living among the monks of Worth Abbey in Sussex: a Benedictine Community with roots going back to the 13th century.

The religious community

At the heart of the religious community, centred on Worth Abbey, is a group of 23 monks following the Rule of St Benedict: a rule written 1500 years ago but which, it is believed, gives an excellent way of organising spiritual life today. The monks at the Abbey have created a sanctuary where the Gospel of Christ is lived out through a community life of prayer and service. The monks take vows of:

* obedience
* stability
* conversatio morum.

The monks at Worth Abbey are very much involved in the lives of people outside. They take on the responsibility of running or helping with:

1. a school
2. a parish
3. the Monastery Guest Wing, which is open to 'enquirers' – those who want to 'test their vocation' to join the community
4. a centre for children who have life-limiting or life-threatening diseases
5. refugees
6. the poor of Peru.

▲ Worth Abbey in Sussex, a Benedictine monastery.

The Abbey Church

The Abbey Church is the most important building at Worth. The monks gather in it six times a day to maintain a spiritual rhythm that is at the heart of monastic life. There are special services in the Abbey and meetings to which Christians of different denominations are invited. The Abbey provides a sanctuary in which people are able to pray quietly on their own.

The foundation stone of the church was laid in 1964 and the church was consecrated in 1974. The structure was completed in 2001 although, like all monastic buildings, there are possibilities for further development. The Abbey Church is able to hold up to 1300 people making it the largest Benedictine church in the country.

Joining the community

To become a monk at Worth Abbey a man must:

- be an active member of the Catholic Church;
- go to stay with the community as a guest for a few days;
- make several more visits over a period of time;
- ask to be admitted as a postulant. He will go to live as a lay person in the guest house, learning to detach himself from his former life;
- spend a year as a novice, dressed in the habit and living a life of intense prayer, spiritual formation and discernment. During this time he decides whether he wants to respond to the call of Christ to take monastic vows;
- if he wishes to proceed, the person takes his vows for three to nine years. He then takes his final vows for his lifetime. He may then go on to be ordained as a priest.

In 2003 the independent national Lay Community of St Benedict was formed from the former 'Worth Abbey Lay Community'. Its members seek to live out the community promise to live in holy communion, create holy space and to offer holy service to those that they meet in the outside world.

> **A** **"**_Do not give newcomers to the monastery an easy entry but test the spirits to see if they be of God. (1 John 4.1)_**"**
> _(St Benedict)_

TASKS

1. Describe the different kinds of work for which the monks at Worth Abbey are responsible.
2. How does a person join the community at Worth Abbey?

❋ DISCUSSION POINT

What do you think might be the attraction of joining the community at Worth Abbey?

EXAM HELP

In the examination

Make sure that you know about:

- The meaning of the word 'vocation'. The 'common vocation' – the three Sacraments of initiation. The 'holy vocation' – the ordained priest who is the 'mediator' between God and human beings. The way in which ordinary Christians are involved in the work of salvation.

- The roots of the monastic movement. The reason for spending time in the desert. The Benedictines – the Rule of St Benedict The later monastic movement – the Cistercians, the Franciscans, the Dominicans.

- The three vows that are required of everyone entering a religious community. Poverty – all possessions and family ties to be left behind. Chastity – free from family responsibilities and to remain unmarried. Obedience – obedience to God through obedience to abbot. Open communities. Closed communities.

- Following the Rule of St Benedict. The work carried on in Worth Abbey. Demands made on those who would join the community.

Sample exam questions

1. **a.** What is a common vocation?

   b. How are ordinary Christians involved as priests in God's work of salvation?

2. "Priests are called to play a special role in the Church." Do you agree? Give reasons for your answer, showing that you have thought about more than one point of view.

3. Write three important facts about:

   a. the Benedictines

   b. the Franciscans

   c. the Dominicans

4. Describe the Evangelical Counsels and why they are important for those entering a religious community.

5. Explain the differences between enclosed and open religious communities.

6. Write an introduction to the work of Worth Abbey.

GLOSSARY

A

ABORTION The removal of a growing foetus from a woman's womb by a surgical procedure.

ABSOLUTION The granting of the forgiveness of sins by a Roman Catholic priest after a person has repented.

ACTIVE EUTHANASIA Euthanasia in which the person seeking death makes the decision for themselves.

ADULTERY Sexual relations between a married person and someone to whom they are not married.

ADVENT 'To come', the start of the Christian Year, a time of preparation for Christmas.

ADVENT WREATH A wreath made from evergreen plants found in many Catholic churches and homes during Advent.

AGNOSTIC A person who is not sure whether God exists.

ALTAR The holiest place in a Catholic, Anglican or Orthodox church, the place where the Mass (the Eucharist) is celebrated.

ANGLICAN CHURCH The Church of England and other worldwide Churches led by the Archbishop of Canterbury.

ANNUNCIATION The announcement to Mary by the Angel Gabriel that she was to be the mother of Jesus.

ANOINTING THE SICK One of the seven sacraments of the Catholic Church, given when a person is near to death and they are anointed with holy oil.

APOCRYPHA Books that were not accepted as part of the Bible, included in Roman Catholic Bibles.

APOSTLE 'Someone who is sent', name given to disciples of Jesus after he left the earth.

APOSTLES' CREED Together with the Nicene Creed, the most important statement of Christian belief in the early centuries of Christianity.

ASCENSION The taking up of Jesus into heaven after he had risen from the dead.

ASCENSION DAY The day on which many Christians celebrate the ascension of Jesus into heaven, follows forty days after Easter Sunday.

ATHEIST A person who believes that God does not exist.

B

BAPTISM A religious practice that involves either pouring water over a baby (Infant baptism – Catholic Church, Anglican Church and Orthodox Church) or immersing adults beneath water (Believer's baptism – Baptist Church and Independent Churches).

BAPTIST CHURCH A Protestant Church that believes in the baptism of believing adults and not children.

BIBLE The collection of sacred writings and books that are holy to the Jews (Old Testament) and the Christians (Old and New Testament).

BISHOP A senior priest in the Catholic, Orthodox and Anglican Churches, given control over many churches in an area called a diocese.

BREAKING OF BREAD The name given to the service of Holy Communion in some Protestant Churches.

C

CAROL A hymn sung at Christmas time, written about the birth of Jesus.

CHRISM Holy oil used on special religious occasions.

CHRISMATION The service in the Orthodox Church that combines infant baptism and confirmation.

CHRISTMAS The festival at which Christians celebrate the birth of Jesus.

CHURCH OF ENGLAND The Protestant Church that broke away from the Catholic church in the 16th century and is now part of the worldwide Anglican Church.

CONFIRMATION The service in the Catholic and Anglican Churches that gives a person the opportunity of renewing his or her baptismal vows.

CONTEMPLATION A way of praying that involves some deep thinking about God.

CONTRACEPTION Anything that seeks to prevent the conception of a baby after sexual intercourse has taken place.

CREED An ancient statement of Christian belief.

CRIB A model showing the birth of Jesus, erected in many Catholic churches and homes during the weeks running up to the Christmas festival.

D

DAY OF PENTECOST A very important day in Church history, the day on which the Holy Spirit was given to the disciples and the Church was born.

DEVELOPED COUNTRY A rich Western country that enjoys a high standard of living.

DISCIPLE 'Pupil', refers to the twelve disciples chosen by Jesus who became apostles after he left the earth and who became leaders of the early Church.

DIVINE LITURGY The name given to the service of Holy Communion in the Orthodox Church.

DIVORCE The legal dissolution of a marriage leaving both partners free to marry again.

E

EASTER The most important Christian festival, stretches from Good Friday to Easter Sunday, celebrates the death and resurrection of Jesus.

EASTER VIGIL Service held in Catholic and Orthodox Churches which celebrates the resurrection of Jesus on Easter morning.

EPIPHANY 'Showing', the festival celebrated shortly after Christmas that celebrates the visit of the Wise Men to the infant Jesus to bring their gifts.

EPISTLE A letter, refers to the letters written by the early leaders of the Christian Church and included in the New Testament.

EUCHARIST 'Thanksgiving', name given to the service of Holy Communion in many Anglican Churches.

EUTHANASIA 'Easy death', the belief of many that someone who is terminally ill should have their death hastened if they request it.

EVANGELICALS Churches that believe the teachings of the Bible should be followed very closely.

EXODUS The journey of the Israelites out of Egyptian slavery towards the Promised Land about 4000 years ago, celebrated each year in the Jewish festival of Passover.

F

FONT The receptacle in which the water used in Infant baptism is held, can be just inside the door of the church or be portable.

FORNICATION Sexual relationships that take place outside marriage.

G

GENTILE Someone who is not a Jew.

GLORIA An important Catholic prayer.

GOOD FRIDAY The day two days before Easter Day on which Christians remember the death of Jesus on the cross.

GOSPEL One of the four accounts in the New Testament – Matthew, Mark, Luke and John – that describe the life, teaching, death and resurrection of Jesus.

H

HAIL MARY Important Catholic prayer which asks that the Virgin Mary will intercede with God on behalf of the worshipper.

HOLY COMMUNION The service that commemorates the death of Jesus by sharing bread and wine to symbolise his body and blood.

HOLY SPIRIT The third person of the Trinity in Christian belief, given to the Christian Church by Jesus after he left the earth.

HOLY WEEK The last week of Lent running from Palm Sunday through to Good Friday.

HOMILY The short talk given by the priest during the Mass.

HOSPICE A place dedicated to the care of the terminally ill.

I

ICON A Christian painting of a saint or the Holy Family that is used as a devotional aid in the Orthodox Church and also by some other Christians.

ICONOSTASIS The screen found in eastern Orthodox churches that separates the altar from the congregation: covered with icons.

IMMACULATE CONCEPTION OF MARY The Catholic belief that Mary was not conceived in the normal way and so did not inherit Original Sin.

INCARNATION The name given to the birth of God as a human being, applied by Christians to the birth of Jesus.

INFANT BAPTISM Service in Catholic, Orthodox and Anglican Churches that admits children into Church membership, a commitment reinforced later by confirmation.

INTERCESSION A prayer that is offered for other people.

J

JERUSALEM A holy city in Israel, the place where Jesus died, now a sacred city to Jews, Christians and Muslims.

JOHN THE BAPTIST The cousin of Jesus, sent to prepare the people for the coming of Jesus the Messiah.

L

LAST SUPPER The last meal that Jesus shared with his disciples before he was arrested.

LECTIONARY A programme of readings from the Bible that is followed in Catholic churches.

LENT The period of forty days leading up to Easter, celebrated in many Christian Churches, based on the time that Jesus spent in the wilderness when he was tempted by Satan.

LESS DEVELOPED COUNTRY (LDC) A poor country with a high level of malnutrition and poor medical services.

LORD'S PRAYER The model prayer that Jesus taught his disciples to use, used in most Catholic services, sometimes called the 'Our Father' by Catholics.

LORD'S SUPPER One of the names used in Protestant Churches for the service of Holy Communion.

M

MAGISTERIUM The teaching ministry of the Church, formed by the Pope and the bishops of the Church.

MASS The name given to the service of Holy Communion in the Catholic Church.

MAUNDY THURSDAY The day before Good Friday when Christians remember Jesus washing the feet of his disciples and also the institution of Holy Communion.

MEDITATION A form of praying that involves deep thinking about important matters.

MESSIAH The spiritual leader that the Jews expected to defeat their enemies, Christians believe that Jesus was the spiritual Messiah.

METHODIST CHURCH A leading Protestant Church, based on the teachings of John Wesley in the 18th century.

MINISTER The person responsible for organising and leading religious worship in a Nonconformist church.

MISSAL The Roman Catholic Prayer Book.

MONK A man who has dedicated himself to God and lives a celibate life in a monastery.

MONOGAMY The marriage arrangement in which one man marries one woman.

MONOTHEIST Someone who believes in one God.

N

NEW TESTAMENT The second part of the Bible, contains twenty-seven books which include Gospels and letters written by leaders of the early Christian Church.

NUN A woman who has dedicated herself to God and lives a celibate life in a convent.

O

OLD TESTAMENT The first part of the Christian Bible; contains the books that are sacred to all Jews.

OMNIPOTENCE Word that describes the Christian belief that God is all-powerful.

OMNISCIENCE Word that describes Christian belief that God knows all things in the past, the present and the future.

ORIGINAL SIN Catholic belief that every human being inherited a tendency to sin from Adam and Eve.

ORTHODOX CHURCH Originally the Church of the eastern region of the Roman Empire, separated from the Western Church (the Roman Catholic Church)] in 1054 over the authority of the Pope.

OUR FATHER Title that Catholics sometimes use for the Lord's Prayer.

P

PALM SUNDAY The first day of Holy Week; celebrates the time when Jesus rode into Jerusalem on a donkey.

PAROUSIA The Second Coming of Jesus.

PASCHAL CANDLE The candle that is lit on Holy Saturday to symbolise the light of Christ's resurrection.

PASSOVER The Jewish festival that celebrates the release of the Jews from Egyptian slavery about 4000 years ago.

PENANCE A penalty that is paid after someone has confessed his/her sins to a priest before God's forgiveness can be given.

PENTECOST The Jewish festival at which the Holy Spirit was given to the early Christians, marked the birthday of the Christian church, celebrated by Christians as a festival.

PERPETUAL VIRGINITY OF MARY The Catholic belief that Mary, the mother of Jesus, remained a virgin for all of her life.

PETER Leading disciple of Jesus, the first Bishop of Rome and Pope.

POPE 'Papa', the chief bishop of the Catholic Church and considered by Catholics to be the Vicar of Christ on earth.

PRIEST Person who has been ordained in the Catholic Church to be the pastor of a church and to dispense the sacraments.

PROPHETS One of three groups of books in the Jewish Scriptures along with the Torah and the Writings.

PROTESTANT A Christian who does not belong to either the Roman Catholic or the Orthodox Churches.

PURGATORY According to the Catholic Church this is the state after death for those who are not yet ready to enter heaven; a place of purification.

Q

QUAKERS A Protestant Church with largely silent meetings and a strong belief in non-violence (pacifism).

R

REQUIEM MASS The Mass that is offered for the dead in a Catholic church.

RESERVED SACRAMENT The Catholic practice of retaining some of the bread used in the celebration of the Mass to use when the sacrament is taken to people who are unwell in their own homes.

RESURRECTION The belief of Christians that their body will be raised from the dead at the Second Coming, a belief based on the resurrection of Jesus.

ROSARY A string of 165 beads that many Catholics use to recite the fifteen mysteries of Christ together with the Ave Maria, Pater Noster and Gloria.

S

SABBATH DAY The Jewish holy day: runs from dusk on Friday to dusk on Saturday.

SACRAMENT An outward, visible sign of an inward, spiritual blessing. The Roman Catholic Church accepts that there are seven sacraments – baptism, confirmation, matrimony, holy orders, the Eucharist, penance and reconciliation.

SALVATION ARMY A Protestant Church, best known for its uniform and the brass bands that lead its worship.

SANCTUARY The area in front of the altar in Catholic and Anglican churches from which the bread and wine are given during Holy Communion.

SATAN 'The Adversary', the evil opposition to God and the source of all sin and temptation in the world.

SAUL The early persecutor of the Christians who was converted to Christ and became Paul.

SECOND COMING The Catholic belief that Jesus will return at some time in the future and set up his kingdom on earth.

STATIONS OF THE CROSS Fourteen statues or carvings around the outside wall of a Catholic church showing events in the last few hours of the life of Jesus.

STOUP Receptacle holding holy water situated just inside the door of the church. Worshippers cross themselves with the water as they enter the church.

SUNDAY The Christian holy day, celebrates the resurrection of Jesus from the dead.

SYNAGOGUE A Jewish place of worship.

T

TEMPLE The beautiful Jewish building in Jerusalem built by King Solomon and rebuilt in the time of Jesus.

TEN COMMANDMENTS The ten laws given to the Jews during the Exodus on their way to the Promised Land of Canaan.

TITHE The Jewish practice of giving 1/10 of wealth to God, continued by some Christians.

TORAH The first, and most important, section of the Jewish Scriptures: contains the laws that God gave to the Jews, including the Ten Commandments.

TRINITY Basic Christian belief in God in three Persons – God, the Father, God, the Son and God, the Holy Spirit.

V

VIATICUM 'Food for the journey', the last celebration on earth of Holy Communion for someone approaching death.

VIRGIN MARY The mother of Jesus Christ, the first among all the saints for Catholics, the one who intercedes with God in heaven on their behalf.

VOCATION The belief that people are called to certain roles in the Church, for example to be a priest.

VOTIVE CANDLES Small candles that Catholics light before they say a prayer in church.

W

WEDDING MASS The special Mass that takes place when two Catholics are being married.

WHITSUN The festival otherwise known as Pentecost, so called because people used to wear white robes if they were baptised on this day.

WRITINGS One of the three divisions of the Jewish Scriptures: contains the book of Psalms among others.

INDEX

INDEX

INDEX